THE MYSTERY OF THE KINGDOM OF GOD

SOCIETY OF BIBLICAL LITERATURE

DISSERTATION SERIES

J. J. M. Roberts, Old Testament Editor
Charles Talbert, New Testament Editor

Number 90

THE MYSTERY OF THE KINGDOM OF GOD

by
Joel Marcus

Joel Marcus

THE MYSTERY OF
THE KINGDOM OF GOD

Scholars Press
Atlanta, Georgia

THE MYSTERY OF THE KINGDOM OF GOD

Joel Marcus

Ph.D., 1985
Columbia University

Advisor:
J. Louis Martyn

© 1986
Society of Biblical Literature

Library of Congress Cataloging-in-Publication Data

Marcus, Joel, 1951–
  The mystery of the kingdom of God.

  (Dissertation series / Society of Biblical
Literature ; no. 90)
    Includes the text of 4:1–34 of the Gospel of Mark.
    Originally presented as the author's thesis
(Ph.D.–Columbia University, 1985).
    Bibliography: p.
    1. Bible. N.T. Mark IV, 1–34–Criticism,
interpretation, etc. 2. Kingdom of God–Biblical
teaching. 3. Sower (Parable) 4. Jesus Christ–
Parables. I. Bible. N.T. Mark IV, 1–34. II. Title.
III. Series: Dissertation series (Society of Biblical
Literature) ; no. 90.
  BS2585.2.M239 1987   226'.306   86-3837
  ISBN 0-89130-983-7 (alk. paper)
  ISBN 0-89130-984-5 (pbk. : alk. paper)

Printed in the United States of America
on acid-free paper

Contents

List of Charts

Preface

This study of the Markan "parable chapter" had its genesis in my first encounter with the Gospel of Mark approximately fifteen years ago, when the "parable theory" that Jesus enunciates in Mark 4:10-12 fascinated me by its strange harshness. Years later, during my second year of doctoral work in the Joint Program between Columbia University's Department of Religion and Union Theological Seminary, I pursued this interest in a seminar on the Gospel of Mark led by Prof. J. Louis Martyn, who later became my dissertation adviser. Prof. Martyn's article on Pauline epistemology gave me a new way of seeing the theme of perception that is so central to the parable theory, and the paper that I wrote for his class was subsequently expanded into my M.A. thesis and revised for publication.

The present study broadens the focus of my earlier work on the parable theory to the entire "parable chapter" of which it forms a part. The idea of making this broadened topic the subject for my dissertation I owe to Prof. Raymond E. Brown, who was the second reader of the dissertation.

The abbreviations, transliterations, and other stylistic particulars in the study conform to the "Instructions for Contributors" published by the Catholic Biblical Association (CBQ 46 [1984] 393-408).

My debt to Professors Martyn and Brown is too great to recount fitly here; acknowledging it is not just an obligation, but a joy. Their devotion to biblical exegesis, critical acumen, encouragement, and friendship have enlightened, inspired, and sustained me in my years of graduate study. I believe that I have been granted an *apokalypsis* of the power of grace through them.

I am also indebted to the other members of my dissertation committee, Professors Thomas L. Robinson of Union Seminary and Robert E. Somerville, Wayne L. Proudfoot, and Eric L. McKitrick of Columbia University, for a careful reading of my work. In addition, I wish to thank Michael Winger, Fleming Rutledge, and Michael Cooper, three friends who

read through the manuscript and offered suggestions from which I bene-
fited a great deal.

Other members of the Columbia/Union community have cheered me on
throughout the dissertation process; I would like to mention particularly
my colleague Marty Soards, now of Louisiana State University, whose
friendship has been precious to me. My parents were generous with aid
and encouragement, and I also derived much appreciated support from the
Columbia University President's Fellowship, the Roothbert Fund Fellowship, the Catholic Biblical Association Memorial Stipend, and Grace
Episcopal Church.

Finally, my wife Gloria has contributed significantly to the dissertation
effort with her good humor, faith in me, and loving encouragement.

1
Introduction

PREVIOUS WORK ON MARK 4:1-34

Mark 4:1-34, the Markan "parable chapter," contains Mark's largest collection of parables (4:3-8, 13-20, 21-25, 26-29, 30-32) as well as the "parable theory" passages (4:10-12, 33-34). In our century, a huge amount of critical attention has been devoted to this chapter, especially to the problematic "parable theory"; recently, too, understanding of the individual parables has reaped the benefits of a resurgence of interest in parables in general.

Despite this scholarly concentration, there is much "land that yet remains" (Josh 13:1-2) in the study of Mark 4:1-34. Stated simply, the problem is that no full-scale study has dealt adequately with the question of how *Mark* intended the parable chapter to be heard by the first readers of his Gospel.

Many of the modern treatments of the chapter have focused rather on the question of what *Jesus meant* by the individual parables and, whenever it is ascribed to him, by the parable theory. The upshot of these studies has often been that Jesus meant something quite different from what Mark meant, and that therefore Mark's understanding of the chapter is of only marginal interest. So, for example, many have viewed the interpretation of the Parable of the Sower (4:13-20) as an ecclesiastical addition which misses the point of Jesus' original parable,[1] and some have

---

[1] See for example C. H. Dodd, *The Parables of the Kingdom* (London: Fontana, 1961; orig. 1935) 135-37; and J. Jeremias, *The Parables of Jesus* (2d rev. ed.; New York: Scribners, 1972; orig. 1954) 77-79. Both Dodd and Jeremias view the interpretation as a layer that must be stripped away in order to arrive at the meaning of Jesus' original parable, which is their main concern. Although Dodd acknowledges the interpretation to be "a

theorized that the Markan parable theory rests on church apologetics[2] or on various kinds of misunderstanding. We note, as examples of the latter position, A. Jülicher's suggestion that the parable theory arose because the parables had become obscure,[3] A. Wendling's attribution of it to misunderstanding of the phrases "those around him" and "those outside" in chapter 3,[4] and the ascription of it to a mistranslation of Aramaic originals by R. Otto, T. W. Manson, and J. Jeremias.[5] This tendency to distance what Jesus meant from what Mark meant, and to concentrate on the former, was especially prevalent prior to the rise of redaction

---

moving sermon," he believes that "in trying to understand the parable we shall do well to leave it aside" (Parables 135). Similarly, for Jeremias, in order to understand the parable "we must reject the interpretation which misses its eschatological point, shifts its emphasis from the eschatological to the psychological and hortatory aspect, and turns it into a warning to the converted against a failure to stand fast in time of persecution and against worldliness" (Parables 149-50).

[2]This is part of A. Jülicher's explanation for the theory (Die Gleichnisreden Jesu [2 vols. in 1; 2d ed.; Tübingen: Mohr, 1910; orig. 1888], 1.147); for the other part, see below. A modern proponent of the apologetic explanation is B. Lindars (New Testament Apologetic: The Doctrinal Significance of the Old Testament Quotations [Philadelphia: Westminster, 1961] 18, 159-67).

[3]According to Jülicher, Mark's unhistorical parable theory had as one of its causes the later church's puzzlement over the dual form of Jesus' speech: sometimes in parables, sometimes without parables (Gleichnisreden 1.147). Cf. A. Loisy (Les Evangiles Synoptiques [Ceffonds, 1907-1908] 737-43), according to whom both the interpretation of the Parable of the Sower and 4:11-12 result from the increasing obscurity of the parables for the church.

[4]Die Entstehung des Markus-Evangelium. Philologische Untersuchungen (Tübingen: Mohr, 1908) 31-41. According to Wendling Mark misunderstood the concrete terms "those outside" and "those around him" in chapter 3 as abstractions.

[5]According to Otto (The Kingdom of God and the Son of Man: A Study in the History of Religion [Boston: Starr King, 1943; orig. 1934] 91-92, 143-44), the "monstrous idea" of the Markan parable theory rests on a mistranslation of the Aramaic mashal; according to Manson (The Teaching of Jesus [2d ed. Cambridge: University Press, 1935] 75-80), Mark's hina is a mistranslation of Aramaic dĕ. J. Jeremias (Parables 14) argues that, because of Mark's misunderstandings of the Aramaic original, 4:11-12 "must . . . be interpreted without reference to its present context."

criticism in the 1950s, and it continues today in some recent "literary" studies of the parables.[6]

Contrary to this concentration on what Jesus meant, redaction-critical studies of the parable chapter reflect an interest in what Mark meant by this section of his Gospel. Often, however, these studies themselves are less than convincing, for a number of them proceed by first identifying what is tradition and what is Markan redaction, then looking only to the *latter* as expressive of Markan theology. Thus, for example, E. Schweizer, J. W. Pryor, and H. Räisänen[7] identify 4:11-12 as a pre-Markan tradition that is in conflict with Mark's own theology, and they therefore effectively dismiss the "parable theory" from consideration as Markan theology. These critics never struggle adequately with the question of why Mark included in his Gospel a tradition that, according to them, he opposed so strenuously.[8]

---

[6]A primary concern with what *Jesus* meant by the parables is stated in a programmatic way by M. A. Tolbert, who concludes that the disadvantages of the Gospel settings of the parables outweigh their advantages because they reduce the "multivalent" parables to a single meaning (*Perspectives on the Parables: An Approach to Multiple Interpretations* [Philadelphia: Fortress, 1979] 51-66).

Partisans of a "literary" approach who have written on Mark 4 include J. D. Crossan, A. Wilder, R. Funk, and B. Scott. Although Crossan ("The Seed Parables of Jesus," *JBL* 92 [1973] 244) attempts to write a history of the tradition of Jesus' seed parables, he does so in order "to isolate the earliest version of the story." Wilder ("The Parable of the Sower: Naivete and Method in Interpretation," *Semeia* 2 [1974] 137) thinks that it was only when the Parable of the Sower was written down "that it would invite the kind of piecemeal scrutiny that led to allegory"; Wilder's aim, contrariwise, is to recapture the "shock of insight" of the original, oral parable. The main concern of Funk's article on the Parable of the Mustard Seed ("The Looking-Glass Tree Is for the Birds," *Int* 27 [1973] 3-9), and of Scott's treatments of the Parable of the Seed Growing Secretly and the Parable of the Mustard Seed (*Jesus, Symbol-Maker for the Kingdom* [Philadelphia: Fortress, 1981] 67-73, 79-88) is what Jesus meant by those parables.

[7]E. Schweizer, "Zur Frage des Messiasgeheimnis bei Markus," *ZNW* 56 (1965) 4-7; H. Räisänen, *Die Parabeltheorie im Markusevangelium* (Schriften der Finnischen Exegetischen Gesellschaft 26; Helsinki, 1976) passim; J. W. Pryor, "Markan Parable Theology: An Inquiry into Mark's Principles of Redaction," *ExpTim* 83 (1971-82) 242-45.

[8]T. J. Weeden (*Mark: Traditions in Conflict* [Philadelphia: Fortress, 1971] 144-49) in some ways agrees with Schweizer, Pryor and Räisänen,

Not all recent studies of Mark 4:1-34, however, have suffered from the defect just described. For example, J. Lambrecht has made an effort to come to grips with how Mark understood the chapter as a whole, and he concludes that it should be read "as a short synthesis of Mark's pronounced and refined theology."[9] Lambrecht's work, however, is not carried out on a scale large enough to support this conclusion, and he fails to relate the theology of Mark 4 sufficiently to that of the rest of the Gospel.[10]

Clearly the most comprehensive study of the parable chapter presently available is that of V. Fusco.[11] This work, which is characterized by common sense and vast erudition, has the stated purpose of viewing the chapter both diachronically and synchronically, although the weight of the work falls mostly on the latter. Indeed, the diachronic aspect of Fusco's work has the appearance of an afterthought.[12] While Fusco thus avoids the danger of an approach that is only interested in Mark's redactional insertions, he makes use only in a very limited way of the illumination that redaction criticism, sensibly applied, can bring to an understanding of the text as it presently stands.[13]

---

but he does seem to realize that it is necessary to ask why Mark left 4:11-12 in his Gospel. Weeden's answer, however, is scarcely satisfactory: in 4:11-12 Mark himself has introduced the proof-text and rationale of the position of his *opponents,* which he then combats by adding the anti-esoteric 4:21-25 and by actualizing 4:11-12 *in reverse* throughout the Gospel.

[9]"Redaction and Theology in *MK.,* IV," *L'Évangile selon Marc. Tradition et redaction* (BETL 34; ed. M. Sabbe; Leuven: Leuven University, 1974) 269-307; *Once More Astonished: The Parables of Jesus* (New York: Crossroad, 1981) 85-109. The citation is from "Redaction and Theology" 307.

[10]A similar criticism applies to the unpublished doctoral dissertation by J. L. Davis, *The Literary History and Theology of the Parabolic Material in Mark 4 in Relation to the Gospel as a Whole* (Union Theological Seminary, Richmond, Virginia, 1966); despite the title, the work does not extensively relate Mark 4 to the rest of the Gospel.

[11]V. Fusco, *Parola e regno: La sezione delle parabole (Mc. 4, 1-34) nella prospettiva marciana* (Aloisiana 13; Brescia: Morcelliana, 1980). See the review by C. Bernas, *CBQ* 44 (1982) 146-47.

[12]In his chapters on the individual passages within Mark 4, Fusco *first* has a section entitled "Exegesis," *then* a section entitled "Tradition and Redaction." This is an unfortunate order, since the main reason for trying to separate redaction from tradition is to inform exegesis of the text in its present form.

[13]Another problem with Fusco's work is that, while he includes a good

Other studies either treat individual parts of Mark 4, but not the chapter as a whole, or deal only with special aspects of the chapter. In the former category belongs W. Wrede's epoch-making book on the messianic secret, which contains an extended discussion of the "parable theory."[14] Also in this category are treatments of the "parable theory" by W. Marxsen, T. A. Burkill, and J. Gnilka; a work by A. Ambrozic that includes excellent discussions of the passages in chapter 4 mentioning the "kingdom of God" (4:10-12, 26-29, 30-32); and a study of Mark 4:1-20 by C. F. D. Moule.[15] In the category of studies of special aspects of Mark 4 are the work by A. Suhl on the OT citations in Mark; that by H.-W. Kuhn on the putative pre-Markan parable collection; that by H. Koester on Mark 4 as a "test case" of synoptic relationships; and that by H.-J. Klauck on parable and allegory in the synoptic parables.[16] All of these studies can

---

chapter on the theme of revelation throughout the Gospel (Chapter 3, "L'economia della rivelazione nel vangelo marciano," 113-150), this chapter is not sufficiently integrated with the work on chapter 4 in the rest of the study.

[14]W. Wrede, *The Messianic Secret* (Cambridge: James Clarke, 1971; orig. 1901) 55-66.

[15]W. Marxsen, "Redaktionsgeschichtliche Erklärung der sogenannten Parabeltheorie des Markus," *ZTK* 52 (1955) 255-71; T. A. Burkill, "The Cryptology of Parables in St. Mark's Gospel," *NovT* 1 (1956) 246-62; cf. *Mysterious Revelation: An Examination of the Philosophy of St. Mark's Gospel* (Ithaca: Cornell University, 1963); J. Gnilka, *Die Verstockung Israels. Isaias 6, 9-10 in der Theologie der Synoptiker* (SANT 3; München: Kösel, 1961); A. M. Ambrozic, *The Hidden Kingdom: A Redaction-Critical Study of the References to the Kingdom of God in Mark's Gospel* (CBQMS 2; Washington, D.C.: Catholic University, 1972); C. F. D. Moule, "Mark 4:1-20 Yet Once More," *Neotestamentica et Semitica: Studies in Honour of Matthew Black* (eds. E. E. Ellis and M. Wilcox; Edinburgh: T. & T. Clark, 1969) 95-113.

[16]A. Suhl, *Die Funktion der alttestamentlichen Zitate und Anspielungen im Markusevangelium* (Gütersloh: Mohn, 1965); H.-W. Kuhn, *Ältere Sammlungen im Markusevangelium* (SUNT 8; Göttingen: Vandenhoeck & Ruprecht, 1971); H. Koester, "A Test Case of Synoptic Source Theory (Mk 4:1-34 and parallels)," SBL Gospels Seminar, SBL Convention, Atlanta, 31 October 1971; H.-J. Klauck, *Allegorie und Allegorese in synoptischen Gleichnistexten* (NTAbh n.s. 13; Münster: Aschendorff, 1978). The recent book on parables by D. Flusser (*Die rabbinischen Gleichnisse und der Gleichniserzähler Jesus* [Judaica et Christiana 4; Bern/Frankfurt/Las Vegas: Lang, 1981]) contains chapters on the parable theory and on the question of allegory in the parables.

be of help in our effort to grasp the meaning of the parable chapter as a whole *for Mark,* but none of them is directed specifically to that task.

METHODS TO BE EMPLOYED IN THE STUDY

Having caught a glimpse of the "land that yet remains," we now turn to a strategy for possessing it.

Our goal is to determine Mark's intention in composing the chapter. Sometimes we will be able to glimpse this intention more or less directly, e.g. by perceiving Mark's redaction of previously-existing tradition and reconstructing the reasons for this redaction. At other times, however, it will be helpful to approach Mark's intention by first asking *how the chapter would have been read by its initial audience.* The answer to this question is often more accessible than the answer to the direct question of Mark's aim, since we can form from the Gospel itself and from general historical knowledge a fuller picture of the Markan community than we can of the shadowy figure of the author. Assuming Mark's familiarity with his audience and his desire and ability to communicate effectively with them, we can proceed with reasonable confidence from discussion of the first hearers' experience to discussion of Mark's intention.

We propose to take as our initial starting place the text as it presently stands.[17] Therefore every chapter will begin with a consideration of the *structure* of the passage under investigation, so that the exegesis may grow out of the text itself. This procedure will help us to identify from the beginning aspects of the passage that are rhetorically highlighted; it will also enable us to begin our work conscious of the relationship to one another of its various parts.

By pointing up syntactical awkwardnesses, this analysis of structure will also lead into an attempt to trace the *composition history* of the passage. An understanding of the phases of growth that the text has undergone, and especially of Mark's own contribution to its shaping, will advance us toward our goal of determining how Mark intended the text as it presently stands to be heard by his audience.[18] This is true both

---

[17]This is also the starting point for V. Fusco, whom we criticized in n. 12. Fusco, however, does not allow a consideration of composition history to illuminate his exegesis; we propose, on the other hand, the order: 1) structure of the text as it presently stands, 2) composition history, 3) exegesis of the text as it presently stands.

[18]In studying Mark 4, we intend to avoid both an extreme "literary" approach, which either does not consider the tradition history of the text

because such an investigation will enable us to reconstruct Mark's intention in reshaping the traditions that came down to him, and because of the
possibility that some of those traditions were already circulating in his
community prior to his composition of the Gospel, so that not only modern
interpreters but also perhaps Mark's first hearers would have perceived his
editorial hand.

After this preliminary literary critical work, several other types of
exegetical discipline will be employed as we move to the exegesis proper.
Of these we will single out three for discussion here. The most important
is *comparison of other passages in the Gospel* to shed light on our passage.
As we have noted above, this factor has been curiously lacking in previous
studies of the parable chapter. Yet if we wish to find out how Mark meant
the chapter to be understood, his treatment elsewhere in the Gospel of
themes similar to those that arise in chapter 4 must be one of our primary
resources. Mark 4 illuminates other Markan passages; but the illumination
also extends the other way.

Exegesis will be furthered by an attempt *to reconstruct the Sitz im
Leben* of the Gospel. One of the weaknesses in some of the recent "literary" study of the Gospel has been a tendency to treat the text as if it
existed in a vacuum, unrelated to concrete communities of people.[19] It is
highly probable that all of the writings in the New Testament were produced for specific Christian communities; thus the more fully we can
reconstruct those communities, the better we shall be able to hear the
writings with the ears of their first hearers.

In this attempt to hear the "parable chapter" as its first hearers did, we
will also be aided by investigation of *background material drawn from the
history of religions,* which will help us to enter the thought-world in which
the author and his hearers lived. To anticipate somewhat our work in the
coming pages, we believe that the most useful parallels to our chapter are
found in Jewish apocalyptic literature.[20] In drawing heavily on such

---

at all, or only uses it to get back to a putative original form; and an
eclectic type of redaction criticism that is *only* interested in the redactor's insertions. Because the latter is identified in the minds of many with
the phrase "redaction criticism," we prefer to use the neutral term "composition history."

[19]This criticism applies particularly to F. Kermode, *The Genesis of
Secrecy* (Cambridge, Mass./London: Harvard University, 1979) and, to a
lesser extent, to D. Rhoads and D. Michie, *Mark as Story: An Introduction
to the Narrative of a Gospel* (Philadelphia: Fortress, 1982).

[20]In a recently published study, V. K. Robbins argues that Greco-

literature for an understanding of the Gospel of Mark, we follow what
H. C. Kee identified in 1978 as an emerging direction in the study of
Mark. This direction flows partly from a recognition that the sociological
backgrounds of Jewish apocalyptic literature and of the Gospel of Mark
coincide in an important way: both emerge from settings where God's
elect community finds itself the victim of fierce persecution from "those
outside." As Kee puts it,[21] Mark's

> aims and structure seem to have been most influenced by
> sectarian Jewish apocalypticism, especially that of Qumran,
> whose sacred writings recounted God's miraculous acts of
> deliverance as signs of his eschatological vindication and
> whose members saw in the teachings and the sufferings of
> their founder models and guide-lines for their own communal
> life and possible martyrdom in the face of the eschatological
> conflicts that lay ahead.

The relevance for interpretation of Mark of parallels from Jewish

---

Roman literature as well as Jewish literature may provide a helpful
background for the study of Mark. At least in the specific case of Mark
4:1-34, however, Robbins has failed to add appreciably to our understanding of the passage by comparing it to Plato's *Theaetetus* (*Jesus the
Teacher: A Socio-Rhetorical Interpretation of Mark* [Philadelphia: Fortress, 1984] 137-39). The parallels to Mark 4 (inquiry by disciples and
secret, enigmatic teaching) are quite general, and closer parallels can be
found in the QL; also, the assumption that Jesus is being ironical when he
speaks of the disciples' privilege in 4:11 is unwarranted.

[21]H. C. Kee, "Mark's Gospel in Recent Research," *Int* 32 (1978) 368; cf.
Kee's *Community of the New Age: Studies in Mark's Gospel* (Philadelphia:
Westminster, 1977); also S. Freyne, "The Disciples in Mark and the Maskilim in Daniel. A Comparison," *JSNT* 16 (1982) 7-23. Cf. N. Perrin and N.
Duling (*The New Testament: An Introduction. Proclamation and Parenesis,
Myth and History* [2d ed.; New York: Harcourt Brace, 1982] 237-39) who
speak of Mark as an "apocalyptic drama," pointing out Mark's apocalyptic
hope for the imminent coming of Jesus as Son of Man, and his seeing of
himself and his community as caught up in the events that mark the end
of history. Perrin and Duling also see Mark's merging of past, present, and
future as reflecting an apocalyptic mode of thought.

On the emergence of apocalyptic from situations of marginalization
and persecution, see especially P. D. Hanson, *The Dawn of Apocalyptic:
The Historical and Sociological Roots of Jewish Apocalyptic Eschatology*
(rev. ed.; Philadelphia: Fortress, 1979).

apocalyptic literature (most of which comes from Palestine) is especially apparent if Kee is right in situating the Markan community in Syria, right next door to Palestine, around the time of the Jewish War (A.D. 66-70).[22] Although no certainty can be claimed for this or any other solution to the problem of where and when Mark's Gospel was written, several pieces of evidence make a Syrian (or Transjordanian) provenance at least as likely as the traditional ascription of Mark to Rome.[23]

Several passages in Mark 13 can be plausibly related to the events of the Jewish War, which culminated in the destruction of the Temple in Jerusalem.[24] If this destruction (or its perpetrator) is the "abomination of desolation" referred to in 13:14,[25] then the Markan aside, "Let the reader understand," assumes that Mark's readers either have heard of the Temple's destruction or believe it to be imminent,[26] and that they are

---

[22]H. C. Kee, Community 100-105.

[23]For a recent sympathetic treatment of the theory of Roman provenance, see R. E. Brown in R. E. Brown and J. P. Meier, Antioch and Rome: New Testament Cradles of Catholic Christianity (New York: Paulist, 1983) 191-97. Brown's argument is partly based on his favorable assessment of the Papias tradition (which according to Brown implies composition in Rome; Antioch 194 n. 406). If the John Mark of Acts 12:12 were the author of our Gospel, however, as Papias claims, his origin in Jerusalem would be difficult to reconcile with the poor knowledge of Palestinian geography displayed in the Gospel. (Brown acknowledges this problem; Antioch 195.) Brown also points to 2 Tim 4:11 and 1 Peter 5:13, both of which, according to him, imply a Mark in Rome (Antioch 192); but the fact that Mark was the commonest name in the Roman Empire makes questionable the conclusion that these two passages refer to the same man who is also the author of our Gospel (see P. Achtemeier, Mark [Proclamation Commentaries; Philadelphia: Fortress, 1975] 113-114). The Latinisms in Mark's Greek, which Brown cites in favor of Rome (Antioch 196), are mostly technical military terminology (W. G. Kümmel, Introduction to the New Testament [Nashville: Abingdon, 1973] 97-98), and "could occur at any place where a Roman garrison was stationed and Roman law was practiced" (H. Koester, Introduction to the New Testament [Philadelphia: Fortress, 1982] 2.167; cf. P. J. Achtemeier, Mark 114-115).

[24]See esp. the reference to the destruction of the Temple in 13:1-2; also the references in 13:7-8 to revolts, earthquakes, and famines, all of which are mentioned by Josephus in connection with the Jewish War (P. J. Achtemeier, Mark 115).

[25]See W. Marxsen, Mark the Evangelist (Nashville: Abingdon, 1969) 178-82.

[26]On these two possibilities, see W. G. Kümmel, Introduction 98.

deeply concerned about the events of the Jewish War. Indeed, Mark presents these events as the prelude to the eschaton,[27] and the eschatological fervor associated with the war may even have been the catalyst for the composition of the Gospel.[28] The urgency Mark feels about the Jewish War is easiest to explain if he and his readers live close to Palestine,[29] although they are probably not from Palestine itself, as is attested by Mark's mistakes about Palestinian geography and customs, and by his need to explain Aramaic terms.[30]

A provenance close to Palestine, but not in it, is thus an attractive possibility. Other arguments for such a provenance include Mark's interest in the non-Jewish cities on the border of Palestine[31] and the intersection of various lines of developed traditions in Antioch and the other cities of the Syrian west coast.[32] We do not believe, however, that our use of Jewish apocalyptic literature to illuminate Mark stands or falls with this theory of Syrian provenance. Jewish apocalyptic literature was popular throughout the larger Hellenistic world;[33] moreover, in each case where we compare Markan passages to apocalyptic texts, the justification for doing so will arise out of peculiarities in the Markan text itself.

Mark's Gospel as a whole, then, and Mark 4:1-34 in particular, will be viewed in an apocalyptic context. Conclusions about the particular *type* of apocalyptic thinking that Mark presents, however, will be determined neither by parallels from the history of religions nor by the presuppositions of twentieth century scholars about what is involved in apocalyptic. Rather, Mark's own appropriation and transmission of apocalyptic motifs will be our primary concern. So, for example, Mark's apocalypticism will

---

[27] In 13:19 the *thlipsis* of Mark's own time seems to be in view ("such affliction as there has not been from the beginning of creation *until now*"); in 13:24-27 this *thlipsis* is immediately followed by universal cataclysm and the return of the Son of Man.

[28] H. Koester, *Introduction* 167.

[29] The war, however, was known throughout the Mediterranean world, and Titus considered it important enough to erect a triumphal arch commemorating it in the heart of Rome, as P. J. Achtemeier notes (*Mark* 116).

[30] P. J. Achtemeier, *Mark* 115.

[31] Cf. N. Perrin and N. Duling, *Introduction* 242-43.

[32] H. Koester, *Introduction* 167.

[33] See D. S. Russell's discussion of the popularity of apocalyptic in *The Method and Message of Jewish Apocalyptic* (Philadelphia: Westminster, 1964) 28-33.

be seen to be reflected not only in passages which speak of a future, cataclysmic end to history, but also in passages which imply the advent of the new age *in the midst of* the old age.

*   *   *   *   *

In order to illustrate the method we propose, and to lay the groundwork for further study of the parable chapter, we now move to a brief consideration of the opening verses of the chapter, Mark 4:1-2, offering first a translation.[34]

TRANSLATION OF MARK 4:1-2

4:1a And again he began to teach beside the sea,
4:1b and there gathers[35] to him a very large crowd,
4:1c so that, getting into a boat, he sits in the sea;
4:1d and the whole crowd was by the sea on the land.
4:2a And he was teaching them many things in parables,
4:2b and he said to them in his teaching:

LITERARY ANALYSIS

Structure

Mark 4:1-2 consists of two sentences, the first of which (4:1) is considerably longer than the second (4:2). These introductory sentences are marked by elaborate repetition of three motifs: teaching ("he began to teach," "he was teaching," "in his teaching"), the sea ("beside the sea," "in the sea," "by the sea"), and the crowd ("a very large crowd," "the whole crowd"). In v 1, the subjects of the clauses alternate between Jesus and the crowd: *Jesus* begins to teach (v 1a), *the crowd* gathers (v 1b), *Jesus* sits in the sea (v 1c), *the crowd* is on the land (v 1d). This juxtaposition of Jesus and the crowd is rhetorically accentuated in 4:1bc by the use of verbs in the historical present tense, which "can replace the aorist

---

[34]This and subsequent translations of the passages in Mark 4 are quite literal, in order to point up syntactical features of the Greek text that are important for exegesis.
[35]Both "gathers" here and "sits" in the next line are examples of the historical present tense, on which see below.

indicative in a vivid narrative at the events of which the narrator imagines himself to be present."[36] In v 2, however, Jesus remains the subject of both clauses, and his teaching emerges as the main theme. That teaching was already mentioned in v 1a; the only new information added by v 2 is that the teaching is parabolic, which consequently receives special emphasis.

Jesus is not mentioned by name in these opening verses, and this circumstance links the "parable chapter" with the previous scene;[37] the chapter is also linked with what precedes it by the word "again" in 4:1, which harks back to 2:13, and by the phrases "those outside" and "those around him" in 4:10-12, which recall 3:31-35. These observations are among the reasons why 4:1 should probably not be considered the beginning of a major section in Mark's Gospel, but rather the continuation of a section that began with the commissioning of the disciples in 3:13-19.[38] It

---

[36] *BDF* 321. The historical present is particularly characteristic of Mark.

[37] J. Gnilka, *Das Evangelium nach Markus* (EKKNT 2/1; Zürich: Benziger/Neukirchener, 1978-79) 156.

[38] The first six chapters of Mark seem to be divided by passages about the commissioning of the disciples (1:16-20; 3:13-19; 6:6b- or 6:7-13; see J. Gnilka, *Evangelium* 1.30-33; E. Schweizer, "The Portrayal of the Life of Faith in the Gospel of Mark," *Int* 32 (1978) 388-89. Thus 3:13 seems to mark the beginning of a major section, and this hypothesis is confirmed by N. Perrin's observation (*Introduction* 239-40) that it follows one of the "transitional Markan summaries" (1:14-15; 3:7-12; 6:6b). There seems to be a consensus among those who have worked on the outline of the Gospel that the section beginning at 3:13 extends into somewhere in chapter 6 (6:6 according to Perrin, Gnilka, and Schweizer; 6:29 according to R. Pesch (*Naherwartungen: Tradition und Redaktion in Mk 13* [Düsseldorf: Patmos, 1968] 58-60).

Two exceptions to this consensus are W. Kelber (*Mark's Story of Jesus* [Philadelphia: Fortress, 1979]) and N. Petersen ("The Composition of Mark 4:1-8:26," *HTR* 73 [1982] 190-95), neither of whom sees a major section as starting at 3:13. (See also the doubts of P. J. Achtemeier, *Mark* 40.) Kelber sees a section, which he entitles "the mystery of the kingdom," stretching from 1:1 to 4:34; this thematic division pays too little attention to *literary* features of the Gospel. Petersen, who sees 4:1-8:26 as a unit, believes that 4:1 marks a break in the narrative: "Prior to 4:1, Jesus had been beside the sea on three occasions (1:16; 2:13; 3:7), but never on it, let alone across it. Yet in 4:1-8:26 he is repeatedly on the sea and crossing it." This observation should be given due weight, but it still does not constitute a valid ground for seeing the beginning of a *major* section at

is worth noting that the privilege of the disciples, which is emphasized in 3:13-19 (see esp. 3:14-15), is also a major theme in chapter 4 (4:11a, 20, 25a, 34b).

Composition History

As H. Koester points out, Mark 4:1-2 is full of Markan redactional vocabulary: *palin* ("again"), *ērxato* ("he began") + infinitive, *thalassa* ("sea"), *synagesthai* ("to gather") used of the crowd, the singular use of *ochlos* ("crowd"), *hōste* ("so that") + infinitive, *pas ho ochlos* ("the whole crowd"), *kai elegen autois* ("and he said to them"), and *didachē* ("teaching").[39] We would also identify *en parabolais* ("in parables") as a characteristically Markan expression.[40]

These observations incline us toward seeing 4:1-2 as basically Markan work, although if, as there is good reason for thinking, there was a pre-Markan parable source,[41] that source must have had a brief introduction such as "and Jesus said" or "Jesus taught them in parables, saying. . . ."[42] H. Koester points out that if the hypothesis of such a brief introduction in Mark's source is accepted, then Matthew, in his redaction of Mark 4:1-2, would have followed a technique similar to Mark's, leaving his source

---

4:1; see Pesch's distinction (*Naherwartungen* 50-53) between caesuras that indicate an *Einschnitt* ("turning point") and those that indicate an *Unterabschnitt* ("minor division").

[39]H. Koester, "Test Case" 28-31.

[40]Cf. the redactional 3:23; 4:11; 12:1. Koester himself ("Test Case" 47-48) seems to consider *en parabolais* a Markan expression, though he does not list it as such on 28-31.

[41]On the pre-Markan parable source, see especially J. Jeremias, *Parables* 13-14; H.-W. Kuhn, *Sammlungen* 99-146; H. Koester, "Test Case" 50-52. Other arguments for the existence of this source will emerge as this study proceeds; but we should mention here especially Koester's succinct reasoning: 1) The formula *kai elegen*, which occurs only in 4:9, 26, and 30, as opposed to Mark's usual *kai elegen autois*, is probably pre-Markan. 2) The three seed parables, which are introduced by *kai elegen*, are form critically very closely related, and have a similar intention: to provide encouragement through which the negative experiences of the present time can be overcome. 3) The existence of other primitive collections (miracle stories, sayings sources) makes plausible an independently-circulating parable collection.

[42]J. Gnilka, *Evangelium* 1.156; H. Koester, "Test Case" 28-31.

intact, but expanding it both in front and behind.[43] Thus, the distinctive
features of 4:1-2, the elaborate setting and the emphasis on Jesus' teaching, are probably attributable to Mark's hand.

EXEGESIS

Mark 4:1-34 is, along with chapter 13, one of the two major teaching
sections in the Gospel. These two teaching sections receive special weight
by their deviation from the short, action-packed scenes of the rest of the
Gospel; they thus slow down the frenetic pace of Mark's narrative and
provide an atmosphere of solemnity.[44]

The importance of Mark 4 in particular as a teaching section is underlined by the repetition of words about teaching in Mark 4:1-2 (see above),
and by Jesus' sitting posture. The latter was the normal position for
teachers in antiquity; in Mark, as V. Fusco notes, Jesus adopts this
"magisterial" position rarely, and only in cases of important and prolonged
teaching (cf. 9:33-50; 13:3-7).[45]

Thus in Mark's eyes the parable chapter is a crucial example of Jesus'
teaching; and Jesus' teaching is of vital concern to Mark. It is "what he
was accustomed to do" in the presence of the crowd (10:1),[46] and, as for
the disciples, being recipients of secret teaching is one of their great
privileges.[47]

---

[43]"Test Case" 33. An objection to the view of 4:1-2 as Markan is voiced
by R. Pesch (Das Markusevangelium [HTKNT 2/1; Freiburg/Basel/Wien:
Herder, 1976] 230), who, in line with his view that Mark is a "conservative
redactor," sees v 1 as coming from a miracle cycle and v 2 as the introduction to the pre-Markan parable chapter. Pesch asserts that the motif
of the boat in 4:1 connects with 3:9-11; 4:35-41, both of which are miracle
sections. It is difficult to see, however, what function 4:1 would perform
in a miracle cycle; by itself it goes nowhere, and it does not lead logically
into the crossing of 4:35-41. Rather, the mention of teaching seems to
identify 4:1 as the introduction to a teaching section. More plausible than
Pesch's view is that of L. E. Keck ("Mark 3:7-12 and Mark's Christology,"
JBL 84 [1965] 349): The boat miracle cycle consisted of 3:7-12; 4:35-5:43;
6:31-52; 6:53-56, and the mention of the boat in 4:1 may be editorial, in
order to reconcile the setting in chapter 4 with 4:36.

[44]Cf. D. Rhoads and D. Michie, Mark as Story 44-45.

[45]V. Fusco, Parola 151-52; cf. C. Schneider, "kathēmai," TDNT 3 (1965)
440-44.

[46]J. D. Kingsbury, The Christology of Mark's Gospel (Philadelphia: Fortress, 1983) 54.

[47]See below, chapter 3, on 4:10-12, 33-34.

The importance of the parable chapter in Mark's scheme of things is also accented by various rhetorical features of the introductory verses. 4:1 releases narrative tension that has been building since the beginning of the Gospel. Previously, as N. Petersen points out, Jesus has been *beside* the sea (1:16; 2:13; 3:7) but never *on* it, as he is in 4:1.[48] In addition, while Mark has introduced the boat in 3:9, the reader's expectation that the boat, which had been readied, would be used, is frustrated until 4:1. When Jesus does finally get into the boat (and therefore onto the sea) in 4:1, the delay of the boarding until this point signals to the reader that something momentous is happening as Jesus begins to teach.[49]

The importance of the parable chapter is also emphasized by the description of the crowd in vv 1-2. Whereas in previous and subsequent sections of the Gospel the crowd is described as "great" (*polys*; 3:7-8; 5:21, 24; 6:34; 8:1; 9:14; 12:37), here it is "very great" (*pleistos*); its size is further emphasized by the phrase "the whole crowd." Indeed, as V. Fusco points out, the previous descriptions of the crowds thronging Jesus (1:33; 2:2, 13; 3:7-10, 20) have appeared in a crescendo that culminates in 4:1.[50] The extraordinary size of the crowd is underlined, in that now for the first time Jesus must avail himself of the boat that had previously been readied, "lest they should crush him" (3:9).

The ability of Jesus' word to attract such a crowd is due to the extraordinary divine power present in it, as is suggested by the juxtaposition of the mention of the boat in 4:1 and the mention of it in 3:7-9, where divine power was manifested in Jesus' healings. The linkage implies that the same overwhelming *dynamis* is present in the parables.[51]

This same linkage between Jesus' proclamation of the word and his other acts of power is made elsewhere in the Gospel. In 1:21-28, the crowd that has just witnessed an *exorcism* exclaims in amazement, "What is this? A new *teaching*! With authority he commands even the unclean spirits, and they obey him."[52] In 6:2 another exclamation of the crowd

---

[48]N. Petersen, "Composition" 194.

[49]At the conclusion of the chapter Jesus immediately departs to the other side of the Sea of Galilee (4:35-5:1). This is the first time that he has been beyond his home region in Mark, and the immediate departure suggests that the parabolic discourse dramatically concluded one phase of his ministry (cf. N. Petersen, "Composition" 194).

[50]V. Fusco, *Parola* 151-52.

[51]J. L. Davis, *Literary History* 368, 397.

[52]On this passage see A. M. Ambrozic, "New Teaching With Power (Mk 1:27)," *Word and Spirit: Essays in Honor of David Michael Stanley, S.J. on his 60th Birthday* (ed. J. Plevnik; Willowdale, Ont.: Regis College, 1975) 113-149.

juxtaposes the *wisdom* displayed in Jesus' teaching with his *mighty acts*.
Furthermore, as P. J. Achtemeier points out, the kind of amazement and
awe that result from Jesus' miracles (2:12; 7:37) also result from his
teaching (9:32; 11:18), and Jesus is identified precisely as "teacher" (or
"rabbi") in several miracle stories (4:38; 5:35; 9:5, 17, 38; 10:51; 11:21). As
Achtemeier correctly concludes: "Whenever Jesus teaches, the same
power is at work that enabled him to do mighty acts," and conversely,
"whenever a mighty act is performed, the power of Jesus' teaching is also
demonstrated."[53]

The linkage between Jesus' teaching and his miracles has a further
ramification. While the motive for Jesus' teaching of the crowd, like the
motive for his miracles, is compassion,[54] yet, as is the case with the
miracles, the teaching sometimes provokes joyful appreciation but sometimes hostility which results in judgment.[55] Why Jesus' teaching has this
double effect upon its hearers is a question that is pondered deeply in
Mark 4:1-34, and it will be a major subject of investigation in the coming
pages.

As noted above, 4:1-2 alternates references to Jesus and to the huge
crowd standing on the shore of the sea. This alternation, together with the
use of historic presents in 4:1bc, focuses attention on the confrontation
between Jesus and the crowd. The setting, not in a synagogue but in an
open place where "the whole crowd" can gather and be face to face with

---

[53]"'He Taught Them Many Things': Reflections on Marcan Christology,"
CBQ 42 (1980) 478-80.

[54]6:34; cf. 1:41; 8:2; 9:22. H. Räisänen (*Parabeltheorie* 33-39) thinks
that the description of Jesus teaching out of compassion in 6:34 is in
tension with the "hardening theory" of 4:11-12. Already J. A. Bengel
(*Gnomon Novi Testamenti* [Edinburgh: T. & T. Clark, 1859; orig. 1742] on
Mark 4:12) noted that 6:34 qualifies the severity of 4:11-12.

[55]The miracles seem to heighten people's appreciation for Jesus in
1:27; 2:12; 5:18-20; 10:52, but they increase their hostility to him in 3:6,
22; 5:17; 6:2-3. Similarly, Jesus' teaching has a salutary effect in 1:21-28;
11:18; 12:35-37, but a negative effect in 6:1-6 and 11:17. On the judgment
that results from opposition to Jesus' revelation, see below, chapter 3. Cf.
the corresponding judgment on those who ascribe his exorcisms to Satan in
3:28-30.

Jesus,[56] suggests the universal scope of this confrontation.[57] Our comments about the double effect of Jesus' teaching imply that the confrontation is of a double nature: Jesus *pro mundo*, Jesus *contra mundum*.

As Jesus opens his mouth to teach in parables, then, a dramatic moment of revelation and of judgment has arrived for the world.[58] A huge crowd has gathered on the shore of the sea to face the bearer of the awesome divine word, drawn by the same extraordinary power that he had demonstrated when he healed the sick and routed demons. He has waited until this precise moment to lay before the crowd matters never previously heard, but which relate intimately to its salvation or ruin. Matthew is certainly in the spirit of Mark's narrative when he applies to the parable chapter the "prophecy" of Psalm 78:2: "I will open my mouth in parables, I will utter things that have been hidden since the foundation of the world" (Matt 13:35).

Reading the first two verses of the parable chapter, then, Mark's hearers would have formed the impression that matters of supreme importance were being broached as Jesus began to teach; and this impression would have been reinforced by the first word in the Parable of the Sower, "Listen!" (4:3a). Of the parables in the chapter, the latter appears to be, in Mark's eyes, the most important (cf. 4:13), and it is to it that we, following Mark's lead, now turn.

---

[56]Cf. V. Fusco (*Parola* 205), who asserts that, after his conflict with the Jewish authorities (2:1-3:6), Jesus no longer teaches in the synagogue, but in the door of a house (2:1-2) or, more often, on the shore of the lake (2:13; 3:7-9; 5:21; 6:30-34). Cf. however 6:1-6, where Jesus again teaches in a synagogue.

[57]In Mark the crowd represents the mass of humanity that is the object of evangelization (see below, chapter 3), and this evangelization, as 13:10 and 14:9 imply, is universal in scope; hence my use of the word "universal" in the text. Chrysostom (*Hom. in Matt.* 44.3, PG 57.467a) picks up this nuance of the picture of Jesus face to face with the people when he says that Jesus "desired so to place the people that he should have none behind him, but all should be before his face." Cf. A. Ambrozic's comment on 8:34a: "The redactionally produced presence of the crowd . . . shows Mark's desire to stress the universal applicability of Jesus' teaching on his own cross and resurrection . . ." ("Teaching" 136).

[58]The reader of Mark's Gospel already knows that Jesus' teaching is revelatory from 1:21-28, where it has been described as "a new teaching with authority," in distinction from the teaching of the scribes. The eschatological newness of the teaching creates astonishment in its hearers; see also 6:2; 11:18.

2

The Parable of the Sower
and Its Interpretation
(Mark 4:3–9, 13–20)

TRANSLATION

4:3	Listen! Behold, a sower went out to sow.
4:4a	And it came to pass in the sowing
4:4b	that one part fell on[1] the path
4:4c	and the birds came and devoured it.
4:5a	And another fell on the rocky ground
4:5b	where it did not have much soil,
4:5c	and immediately it sprang up on account of not having depth of soil;
4:6a	and when the sun came up it was scorched,
4:6b	and on account of not having root it withered.
4:7a	And another fell among the thorns,
4:7b	and the thorns came up and choked it,
4:7c	and it did not yield fruit.
4:8a	And others fell into the good soil
4:8b	and were yielding fruit, coming up and growing,
4:8c	and were bearing, thirtyfold and sixtyfold and a hundredfold.[2]
4:9	And he said, He who has ears to hear, let him hear!

---

[1]On this translation of *para*, see BAG (2d ed., 1979) 611 (IIIld). Unless otherwise noted, all citations of BAG are to this edition.

[2]On the translation of *hen* as "-fold," see BAG 232 (4).

* * * * *

4:13a	And he says to them, Do you not know this parable?
4:13b	How then will you know all the parables?
4:14	The sower sows the word.
4:15a	And these are those on the path where the word is sown,
4:15b	and when they hear
4:15c	immediately Satan comes and takes away the word sown in them.
4:16a	And these are those sown on the rocky ground
4:16b	who when they hear the word immediately receive it with joy
4:17a	and do not have root in themselves but are temporary;
4:17b	then when tribulation or persecution on account of the word arises, immediately they are offended.
4:18a	And others are those sown among thorns;
4:18b	these are those who have heard the word,
4:19a	and the cares of the age and the deceitfulness of wealth
4:19b	and the desire for other things, entering in, choke the word,
4:19c	and it becomes unfruitful.
4:20a	And these others are those sown on good soil—
4:20b	who hear the word and accept (it) and bear fruit
4:20c	thirtyfold and sixtyfold and a hundredfold.

LITERARY ANALYSIS

Structure

The structure of the parable itself (Mark 4:3-8). The parable is framed by an *inclusio* consisting of the word "listen" (*akouete*) in 4:3 and the exhortation to listen in 4:9.[3] After a double introduction ("Listen! Behold!"), it unfolds in two main steps: the presentation of the sower, and the history of the seeds.[4] Although the sower is not at the center of the narrative,[5] he is not incidental to it, since the whole of the subsequent

---

[3]X. Leon-Dufour, "La Parabole du semeur," *Études d'Evangile* (Paris: Editions du Seuil, 1965) 269-70.

[4]Ibid., 272-73.

[5]See E. Linnemann, *Parables of Jesus: Introduction and Exposition* (London: S.P.C.K., 1966; orig. 1961) 180 n. 2: After 4:3 he is not mentioned, and the real action of the parable begins with *kai egeneto* in 4:4.

history is set in motion by his act of sowing.[6] The experience of the sower and the fate of the seed are inextricable themes.[7]

Our parable tells not one story but four, stopping after each seed has been described to go back to the beginning of the next seed.[8] Yet the basic structure of the parable is binary. Biblical parables often use a number of images for a single condition, which is then contrasted with a second condition.[9] Here the history of the seeds (vv 4-8) contrasts the unsuccessful seed of vv 4-7 with the successful seed of v 8; the threefold yield of the latter balances the threefold loss of the former.[10] A binary structure is also indicated by the contrast between the singular pronouns referring to seed in vv 3-7 (ho men . . . allo . . . allo), and the plural pronoun referring to seed in v 8 (alla).[11] In addition, "good soil" in v 8 implies a contrast to the bad soil of vv 4-7.[12]

Furthermore, v 8 departs from the previous verses in speaking of continuous action as opposed to simple action. Whereas all the finite verbs in vv 3-7 are aorists, implying simple action in the past, v 8 begins with an aorist (epesen, "fell") but then has two imperfects (edidiou, "were yielding," and epheren, "were bearing"), implying continuous action in the past.[13] The implication of continuous action in v 8 is furthered by the two

---

[6]X. Leon-Dufour, "Parabole" 277.

[7]See R. Bultmann, "Die Interpretation von Mk. 4, 3-9 seit Jülicher," *Jesus und Paulus. Festschrift für Werner Georg Kümmel zum 70. Geburtstag* (eds. E. E. Ellis and E. Grässer; Göttingen: Vandenhoeck & Ruprecht, 1975) 31; cf. A. Wilder, "Parable" 136-37.

[8]X. Leon-Dufour, "Parabole" 272-73.

[9]J. Dupont ("Le Parabole du semeur," *Foi et Vie* 66 [1967] 5-7) points out that in Judges 9:9-15 the first three trees are mentioned only to place the fourth in sharper relief, and asserts that similar comments apply to the figures in the Parable of the Talents (Matt 25:14-30) and in the Parable of the Workers in the Vineyard (Matt 20:1-16).

[10]See X. Leon-Dufour, "Parabole" 274; this point was already made by Jerome (*In Matt.* 2; CChrSL 77. 105-106) and Theophylact (PG 123.532).

[11]J. D. Crossan, "Seed Parables" 246; cf. F. Hahn, "Das Gleichnis von der ausgestreuten Saat und seine Deutung (Mk iv. 3-8, 14-20)," *Text and Interpretation: Studies in the New Testament Presented to Matthew Black* (eds. E. Best and R. McL. Wilson; New York/London: Cambridge University, 1979) 135.

[12]V. Fusco, *Parola* 312-313.

[13]E. Schweizer, *The Good News According to Mark* (Atlanta: John Knox, 1970; orig. 1967) 90.

present participles (*anabainonta kai auxanomena,* "coming up and growing").

J. D. Crossan[14] states that the phrase at the end of v 7, "and it did not
yield fruit," is also evidence for the binary structure of our parable. While
Crossan exaggerates when he asserts that this phrase refers not just to
the seed in v 7 but to *all* the lost seed in the parable,[15] his basic insight is
correct.[16] The phrase "and it did not yield fruit" marks a transition point
from negative to positive in the parable.[17] The statement that the third
seed did not yield fruit raises a question in the hearer's mind as to
whether *any* of the seed was fruitful; this question is immediately
answered in the affirmative in v 8.

The binary structure of our parable, however, does not exclude a progression within the bad soils and in the parable as a whole. The seed sown
in the first three soils is lost at increasingly late stages of its growth, so
that the third soil is better than the second soil, which is better than the
first soil; also, within the fourth soil an increasingly good yield is
described.[18] The parable gains an optimistic tinge from this progression.[19] Because of the progression within the first three soils, the parable
is not simply reducible to a contrast between bad soil and good soil; a
fourfold superstructure (the four soils) lies over the twofold structure (bad
soil vs. good soil).

Within the first three soils, the descriptions of the first and third soils
(v 4bc and v 7ab) have what H.-J. Klauck correctly describes as a parallel,
almost rhythmic structure:[20]

epesen + PLACE + *ēl then* + NEW SUBJECT + *katephagen* + auto
"fell"   "came"   "devoured"   "it"

epesen + PLACE + *anebēsan* + NEW SUBJECT + *synepnixan* + auto
"fell"   "came up"   "choked"   "it"

---

[14]"Seed Parables" 249.

[15]H.-J. Klauck (*Allegorie* 187) correctly points to the singular verb
edōken as refuting Crossan; the referent is the singular seed (*auto*) just
mentioned.

[16]See V. Fusco (*Parola* 312 n. 19), who asserts that *indirectly* the
phrase *kai karpon ouk edōken* refers to all three bad soils.

[17]J. Gnilka, *Evangelium* 1.159.

[18]X. Leon-Dufour, "Parabole" 277; C. E. Carlston, *The Parables of the
Triple Tradition* (Philadelphia: Fortress, 1975) 144.

[19]J. Dupont, "Parabole" 5-7.

[20]*Allegorie* 187.

This parallelism is broken by the description of the second, rocky soil (vv 5-6), which is considerably longer than the descriptions of the first and third soils and contains several repetitions: 1) Three phrases having to do with lack of ground or rootlessness, two of which begin with *dia to*, "on account of." 2) Two forms of the verb *anatellein*, "to spring up," one compounded, the other simple. 3) "Scorched" and "withered."[21] Another anomaly in the parable is the phrase *anabainonta kai auxanomena*, "coming up and growing," in v 8. This "strange and somewhat belated way of specifying the already noted *edidou karpon* [were yielding fruit]"[22] is omitted by Matthew and Luke.

Gos. Thom. logion 9[23] records a version of our parable:

> Jesus said, Now the sower went out, took a handful (of seeds), and scattered them. Some fell on the road; the birds came and gathered them up. Others fell on rock, did not take root in the soil, and did not produce ears. And others fell on thorns; they choked the seed(s) and worms ate them. And others fell on the good soil and produced good fruit: it[24] bore sixty per measure and a hundred and twenty per measure.

Later in this study the tradition-historical relationship between Mark 4:3-8 and *Gos. Thom.* logion 9 (and *1 Clem* 24:5) will be investigated. For the present we will content ourselves with a few comments about the similarities and differences in structure of these passages.

As Chart 1 shows, the *Gospel of Thomas* version is shorter and simpler than Mark's parable. The repetitions in Mark's description of the rocky soil are absent in *Thomas*, and there is no mention of the sun. Similarly, *Thomas* lacks the "belated" description of the good seed "coming up and growing" of Mark 4:8.[25] Other differences from the Markan parable are

---

[21]J. D. Crossan, "Seed Parables" 245-46; H.-J. Klauck, *Allegorie* 187. Both Matthew and Luke shorten the description of the seed falling on rocky soil, so that the repetitions do not occur.

[22]J. D. Crossan, "Seed Parables" 246.

[23]Unless otherwise noted, all translations of Nag Hammadi documents are from J. M. Robinson, *The Nag Hammadi Library in English* (San Francisco: Harper & Row, 1977).

[24]The antecedent of the pronoun is the good soil; see H.-J. Klauck, *Allegorie* 199-200.

[25]J. D. Crossan, "Seed Parables" 248-50.

CHART 1

Mark 4:3-8	*Gos. Thom.* logion 9
1. listen	
2. behold	
3. sower went out	3. sower went out
	and took handful
4. to sow	
5. and came to pass	
6. in the sowing	6. and scattered them
7. some fell along road	7. some fell on road
8. and came birds	8. birds came
9. and devoured it	9. and gathered them up
10. and other fell on rocky	10. others fell on rock
	16. did not take root
11. where did not have	
much soil	11. in the soil
	21. and did not produce ears
12. and immediately sprang up	
13. on account of not having	
depth of soil	
14. and when sun came up	
15. was burned	
16. and on account of not having	
root	
17. was dried up	
18. and other fell into	18. and others fell on
thorns	thorns
19. and came up the thorns	
20. and choked it	20. they choked the
	seed(s)
	and worms ate them
21. and fruit it did not give	
22. and others fell into	22. and others fell on the
good soil	good soil
23. and gave fruit	23. and produced good fruit
24. coming up	
25. and growing	
26. and it bore	26. it bore
27. thirtyfold	
28. and sixtyfold	28. sixty per measure
29. and a hundredfold	
	and one hundred and
	twenty per measure

the worm as a cause of destruction; the good soil, rather than the seed, producing fruit; and the yield of sixty and 120.[26]

H. Koester[27] complains that the occurrence of the parable in *1 Clem* 24:5 has been disregarded. The only real points of comparison with the other forms of the parable, however, are the first part of the first sentence and, in a loose way, the ending:

> The sower went forth and cast each of the seeds into the earth. . . . And from one (grain) many grow and bring forth fruit. (Koester's trans.)

1 Clem 24:5 agrees with *Gos. Thom.* logion 9 in speaking of the sower casting (scattering) seed, but this minor agreement is probably due to a coincidence.

The bearing of these observations concerning comparative structure on the question of the tradition history of the Parable of the Sower will be discussed below.

The structure of the interpretation (Mark 4:14-20). Jesus' explanation of the Parable of the Sower is introduced by the reproof of 4:13. This reproof, like the word *akouete* ("Listen!") in 4:3, calls attention to the importance of understanding what is to follow.

In the interpretation itself, all emphasis is on the seed and the soils; even less attention is paid to the sower than in 4:3. The interpretation begins by identifying the seed with the word (4:14), though without *saying* "the seed is the word." In the rest of the interpretation, several other elements of the parable are similarly allegorized by implication. The birds (4:4) represent Satan (4:15); the plant's lack of root (4:6) refers to people who "have no root in themselves" (4:17); the sun (4:6) represents tribulation or persecution (4:17); the thorns (4:7, 18) represent the cares of the age, the deceitfulness of wealth, and the desire for other things (4:19).

Besides these indirect linkages between the parable and the interpretation, the latter makes a series of direct equations of the form $x = y$,[28] "these are those sown . . ." (4:15a, 16a, 18a, 18b, 20a). These equations are

---

[26] J. Gnilka, *Evangelium* 1.158.

[27] "Three Thomas Parables," *The New Testament and Gnosis: Essays in honour of Robert McLachlan Wilson* (eds. A. H. B. Logan and A. J. M. Wedderburn; Edinburgh: Clark, 1983) 195-96.

[28] R. Pesch, *Markusevangelium* 242. Pesch compares the identifications to the deciphering formula of 1QpHab, "its interpretation is . . ."

confused, however, by the identification of the seed both with "the word" and with human beings who hear the word.[29]

Finally, several elements in the parable are *not* allegorized in the interpretation. These include the devouring of the seed by the birds in the case of the first soil; the scorching and withering of the plant, and the lack of deep ground, in the case of the second soil; the "coming up and growing" of the plant, and the various yields, in the case of the fourth soil; and above all the sower.[30]

In contrast to the parable itself, in which the predominant tense is the past,[31] in the interpretation the predominant mood is the present.[32] "The world is not narrated, but discussed."[33]

As in the parable itself, a statement about the sower (v 14) is followed by statements about the seed and the soil (vv 15-20). The latter set of statements follows a fairly consistent pattern, which is summarized in Chart 2. Each sentence begins with a masculine plural pronoun ("these," "others," "those") followed by the words "are those," a preposition, and the place sown; a form of the verb *speirein*, "to sow"; a form of the verb *akouein*, "to hear," either preceded or followed by the noun *logos*, "word"; and then the result of the sowing, preceded in the first two cases by the

[29]In 4:14, the seed is identified with the word, and 4:15ac speak of the word being sown. In the references to "the word" in 4:16b, 18b, 19b, 20b, also, it is clear that the seed in the parable is being allegorized. On the other hand, 4:15a, 16a, 18a, 20a speak of human beings as "those sown." J. Dupont ("Parabole" 12) asserts that *hoi . . . speiromenoi* in vv 16, 18, 20 are the sown *places*. This explanation, however, founders on the full wording of the expressions to which Dupont appeals: *hoi epi ta petrōdē speiromenoi* (v 16), *hoi eis tas akanthas speiromenoi* (v 18), and *hoi epi tēn gēn tēn kalēn sparentes* (v 20). In each case, the place sown is designated by the object of *epi* (*eis*), not by the phrase *hoi speiromenoi* (*sparentes*).

[30]F. Hahn, "Gleichnis" 139.

[31]All indicative mood verbs are either aorist or imperfect.

[32]All indicative mood verbs are in the present.

[33]J. Gnilka, *Evangelium* 1.175. Unless otherwise noted, all translations from modern languages are mine.

CHART 2
Mark 4:1-20

(1)

	MASC. PLURAL PRONOUN	+	EISIN HOI +	PREP. +	PLACE SOWN +	
v 15	houtoi de "and these"	+	eisin hoi "are those"	para "beside"	tēn hodon "the path"	· · · ·
vv 16-17	kai houtoi "and these"		"	epi "on"	ta petrōdē "the rocky"	
vv 18-19	kai alloi "and others"		"	eis "in"	tas akanthas "the thorns"	· · · ·
v 20	kai ekeinoi "and those"		"	eis "in"	tēn gēn tēn kalēn "the good soil"	

(2)

	FORM OF SPEIRŌ +	LOGOS + 1st time	FORM OF AKOUŌ AND LOGOS +	EUTHYS + RESULT	
v 15	hopou speiretai "where is sown"	ho logos "the word"	kai hotan akousōsin "and when they hear"		· · · ·
vv 16-17	speiromenoi "sown"		hoi hotan akousōsin ton logon "who when they hear the word"	euthys "at once"	
vv 18-19	speiromenoi "sown"		houtoi eisi hoi ton logon akousantes "these are they who hear the word"		· · · ·
v 20	sparentes "sown"		hoittines akouousin ton logon "whoever hear the word"	euthys "at once"	
			Last 3 x	1st 2 x	

adverb *euthys*, "immediately."[34] In the first three sentences, "to sow" is in the present tense (v 15 indicative, vv 16, 18 participle), while in the fourth it is in an aorist participle; conversely, in the first three sentences "to hear" is in the aorist (vv 15, 16 subjunctive, v 18 participle), while in the fourth it is in a present indicative.

When we move to the *results* of the sowing, we see that in the first and third soils the word miscarries as a result of external factors,[35] whereas in the second soil the miscarriage is due to a combination of internal factors (not having root, being "temporary") and external ones (affliction or persecution; cf. passive voice of the verb *skandalizontai*, "are offended").[36] The perfection of the fourth, good soil is brought out by the presence of two "threesomes" in v 20, the threefold yield and the threefold paratactic construction of the verbs "hear," "accept," and "bear fruit."

The structure of vv 15-20, then, is remarkably homogeneous with regard to each soil. For this reason, the overall structure of the interpretation is fourfold, as opposed to the binary structure of the parable itself. In the parable, the similarity among the soils ends after the description of the seed falling and of the place where it fell, whereas in the interpretation it extends until the yield of each soil is described.

---

[34]The switch in v 20 from present to aorist of *speirein* and from aorist to present of *akouein* strikes E. Schweizer as significant: "In contrast to vv 15-19, the form of the verbs in this verse describes the sowing as a completed action that has fulfilled its purpose. The hearing, on the contrary, is pictured as an action which goes on and on" (*Good News* 97). H. Koester ("Test Case" 63) concurs, asserting that the aorists of *akouein* in vv 15-19 imply that "they hear only once," and H.-W. Kuhn (*Sammlungen* 119-20) thinks that the switch in v 20 suggests that those described there *cannot* fall away. These interpretations probably read too much into the tense changes; the aorist signifies, not a completed action that has fulfilled its purpose, nor a one-time action, but merely an action that "is viewed without reference to duration, interruption, completion, or anything else," an action that is viewed simply as occurring (F. Stagg, "The Abused Aorist," *JBL* 92 [1972] 223). Also, under Schweizer's theory, what are we to make of the perfect participle *esparmenon* in v 15?

[35]This is unambiguous in the case of the first soil, where the cause is Satan. In the case of the third soil, the miscarriage is attributed to "the cares of the age, the deceitfulness of wealth, and the desire for other things entering in." These are psychological realities, but the description of them as "entering in" makes them demonological.

[36]Cf. V. Fusco, *Parola* 334.

Superimposed on this fourfold structure, however, is a twofold super-structure. The demonstrative pronoun *ekeinoi,* which introduces the fourth soil, sets this soil off from the first three soils, which are introduced by less dramatic pronouns (*houtoi . . . houtoi . . . alloi*).[37] There is a distinction between the first three soils and the fourth in terms of the tenses of *speirein* and *akouein.* The perfection of the fourth soil, which is emphasized by the two "threesomes" in v 20, contrasts with the miscarriage of the first three soils, which is summed up by the phrase *kai akarpos ginetai,* "and it becomes unfruitful," in v 19.[38]

Thus, when we consider the respective structures of the Parable of the Sower and of its interpretation, we see that, while the parable is basically binary and the interpretation basically four-part, a four-part overlay is discernible in the parable and a binary overlay is discernible in the interpretation. The parable and the interpretation can be compared to the same picture being examined under two different magnifications. Each magnification reveals a particular pattern as predominant, while the other pattern is visible, but secondary.

Composition History

Already before Mark wrote his Gospel, the Parable of the Sower and its interpretation were handed down as a unit, as emerges from evidence that 4:11-12 has been introduced by Mark into a previous context of 4:10, 13-20.[39] The disciples' question in 4:10 is strange, since in the immediate context they have heard only one parable, but they ask about the meaning of *parables,* plural. This question receives two answers, the general statement about the purpose of parables in 4:11-12, which is introduced by the Markan formula *kai elegen autois,*[40] and the specific deciphering of

---

[37]One of the usages of *ekeinos* is to denote well-known persons; see LSJ 505 (2); BAG 239 (1c). On the way in which this word sets off the last group from the first three, see H. Koester, "Test Case" 62.

[38]As was the case with the corresponding phrase in the parable itself, this phrase refers *directly* only to the third soil, but *indirectly* to all of the first three soils.

[39]The argument here essentially follows the classic treatment by J. Jeremias, *Parables* 13-14.

[40]On *kai elegen autois* as a Markan formula, see H. Koester ("Test Case," 30-31), who identifies two ways in which Mark uses the formula: 1) Most often, to connect materials which were not connected in his sources (e.g. 3:23; 7:9; 8:21; 9:1). 2) Occasionally, however, "to give

the Sower parable in 4:13-20. Jesus' reproof in 4:13 seems to assume that
the disciples have asked only about the Parable of the Sower. The best
way to explain these data is to hypothesize that, before Mark's redactional work, the disciples asked Jesus about the *parable*, singular, and
received essentially the reply now found in 4:13-20.

Interpretation not an original part of parable. Was the interpretation,
however, an original part of the parable, or did it come in at some point
prior to Mark? Because of the well-documented tendency of the early
church to adapt Jesus' parables to its own situation,[41] the assertion of the
interpretation's originality has significant hurdles to overcome in bearing
the burden of proof; and several considerations point in the contrary
direction.

One strong argument for the secondary character of the interpretation
is evidence for an Aramaic substratum in the parable, whereas the interpretation contains many features that are possible only in Greek.[42]
Furthermore, J. Jeremias has identified the absolute use of *logos*, in a
technical sense, as an early Christian coinage.[43] Much of the vocabulary
in the interpretation is not found elsewhere in the Synoptics, including
Mark,[44] but is common in the rest of the New Testament, especially in

---

special emphasis to a saying of Jesus which was already part of a traditional context in his sources or traditions (2:27; 6:4; 11:17)."

[41] On the necessity of working backward from the Gospels to Jesus, see
N. Perrin, *Rediscovering the Teaching of Jesus* (New York/Hagerstown/
San Francisco/London: Harper & Row, 1976) 15-49, esp. 21.

[42] On the Semitisms in the parable, see H.-J. Klauck, *Allegorie* 186-87.
The interpretation, on the other hand, lacks Semitisms, and the words
proskairos, "temporary" (v 17a) and *karpophorein*, "bear fruit" (v 20b), as
well as the changes in tense of *akouein* and *speirein*, are only possible in
Greek (Klauck, *Allegorie* 200). Cf. H. Koester, "Test Case" 53.

[43] R. E. Brown ("Parable and Allegory Reconsidered," *New Testament
Essays* [New York: Paulist, 1982; orig. 1962] 261) counters that the absolute use of *logos* could have a background in "the prophets' use of *dabar*
(*logos*) for the divine message entrusted to them." The usage to which
Brown refers, however, speaks of "the word of Yahweh," not of "the word"
used absolutely; see BDB 182 (I2a). The OT concept of the word of God is
certainly in the *background*, as Brown asserts, but it is also significant
that Mark's exact wording has no OT parallel.

[44] There are several Markan hapaxes; see H.-J. Klauck, *Allegorie* 200.

the letters of Paul.[45] This suggests that the interpretation is substantially the work, not of Jesus, but of the early church.

Beyond these stylistic criteria, the *emphasis* of the interpretation is subtly different from that in the parable. The parable has a binary structure, whereas the interpretation has a fourfold structure. The parable is basically optimistic, whereas the interpretation devotes proportionally more space to failure.[46] Moreover, the description of persecution in the interpretation goes beyond anything that can be attributed to Jesus' ministry.[47] Although R. E. Brown[48] has established the *possibility* that the interpretation *in an earlier form* may go back to Jesus himself, his argument does not progress beyond possibility to probability, nor does it tell us much about the shape of this putative original explanation. Methodologically, it is sounder to assign the explanation to a second, distinct phase in the development of the parable chapter, while leaving open the possibility that Jesus himself may have given some sort of interpretation to his parable.

Expansions in the parable. Evidence that the interpretation is secondary to the parable itself is helpful in identifying secondary elements within the parable.

In the parable, the double introduction ("Listen! Behold!") suggests that

---

[45]J. Jeremias, *Parables* 78.

[46]R. E. Brown ("Parable and Allegory" 259-60) asserts that, "Proportionally, if we place the explanation side by side with the parable, the explanation gives no more attention to the fate of the lost seed than does the parable itself." H.-W. Kuhn (*Sammlungen* 114), however, notes that there are almost twice as many words dealing with failure in the interpretation (about one hundred) as in the parable (about sixty), whereas there are about the same number of words dealing with the good growth.

[47]R. E. Brown ("Parable and Allegory" 262-63) points out that Jesus, like Jewish apocalypticists, could well have warned his followers about the eschatological woes which were soon to come upon them. V. Fusco (*Parola* 333-34), however, rightly observes that the elaborateness of the description of persecution points toward a Christian *Sitz im Leben*. Fusco adduces an additional argument for the secondariness of the interpretation: the differences between parable and interpretation as to the culpability for the failure of the seed. In the parable, the fault is always with the soil, and external causes like the birds are only incidental. In the interpretation, the fault is sometimes with the soil, sometimes with external forces (see above).

[48]R. E. Brown, "Parable and Allegory" 259-64.

one of the first two words may be secondary. The secondary word is probably *akouete*, "listen," since the theme of "hearing" assumed major importance when the interpretation was added to the Parable of the Sower; this happened before Mark,[49] but, as we have argued above, after Jesus. The exhortation to hear in 4:9 was probably placed in its present position at the same time.[50]

In the description of the second, rocky soil (vv 5-6), the length of the description, the breaking of the pattern set by the descriptions of the first and third soils, and numerous repetitions have been noted above. By themselves, such features do not necessarily indicate editorial expansion, since they are characteristic not only of redacted texts but also of oral narrative.[51] However, since vv 5-6 contain several elements that lend themselves extraordinarily well to the theme of apostasy developed in the interpretation (immediate, shallow reaction, lack of deep soil, lack of root), the possibility must at least be entertained that some of these features came in when the interpretation was added to the parable.[52]

We suggest that the original parable contained vv 5ab, 6a. The expansions of the parable, then, would be the reference in v 5c to the seed springing up immediately on account of (*dia to*) not having depth of soil (elements 12-13 in Chart 1), and the reference in v 6b to it withering on

---

[49]An emphasis on hearing is found in 4:3a, 4:9, 4:11-12, and 4:14-20. Of these verses, 4:11-12, which was probably introduced by Mark, is least compatible with the exhortation to hear in 4:3a, since 4:11-12 states forthrightly that some listeners are intended *not* to hear.

[50]On 4:3a, 9 as pre-Markan additions to the parable, see J. Gnilka, *Evangelium* 1.156. That 4:9 is pre-Markan is supported by the formula *kai elegen*, "and he was saying," which introduces it; on this formula see J. Jeremias, *Parables* 14 n. 8.

We would suggest that 4:9 was the original ending of a collection of the three seed parables, the second and third of which were also introduced by *kai elegen* (4:26, 30). When the interpretation of the Parable of the Sower was added to this collection, 4:9 was moved to its present position, both to provide a transition to the theme of "hearing" which the interpretation emphasizes, and to mark the last element in Jesus' public discourse until it is resumed in 4:26. On *kai elegen* as a formula for Jesus' public discourse, see V. Fusco, *Parola* 96-97.

[51]See J. Gnilka, *Evangelium* 1.157.

[52]The construction *dia to* + infinitive being rare in Mark (the only other example is 5:4), it is questionable whether these expansions can be attributed to him.

account of (*dia to*) not having root (elements 16-17).[53] These expansions represent precisely those points that are accentuated by the interpretation of the rocky soil: the immediate positive response (cf. v 16b, "immediately receive it with joy") and the shallowness and rootlessness that lead to catastrophe (cf. v 17).[54] This hypothesis also eliminates from the original parable the repetitions noted above and in Chart 1.

The other expansion within the parable itself is *anabainonta kai auxanomena*, "coming up and growing," in v 8 (elements 24-25), the belatedness of which has been noted above. Since this expansion shows the same concern for perseverance that the additions to vv 5-6 show, it probably came in at the same time as they did, when the interpretation was added to the parable at some pre-Markan stage.

Relationship to Gos. Thom. logion 9. H. Koester[55] is of the opinion that *Gos. Thom.* logion 9 represents a more primitive version of our parable than the Synoptic versions, since it lacks their redactional traits. The parable is narrated simply, and gives no sign of having suppressed the allegorical interpretation found in the Synoptics. Similarly, G. Eicholz[56] believes that it is not easy to see gnostic elements in the *Gos. Thom.* parable.

Taking up the last point first, Eichholz notwithstanding, two features of the *Thomas* parable are probably gnostic in character. The seed sown on rocky soil, which neither sent root deep into the earth (*epesēt epkah*), nor ear high up to heaven (*ehrai etpe*), "appears to be a reference to the

---

[53]See J. D. Crossan ("Seed Parables" 246) and H.-J. Klauck (*Allegorie* 187) for slightly different reconstructions. Klauck thinks that the references to shallow earth, seed springing up, and rootlessness are all secondary, but one of these factors must have been in the original parable, so that the rockiness of the soil would be a cause of the miscarriage of the seed. Crossan opines that the "lack of soil" imagery conflicts with the "sun" imagery, but Calvin has a surer exegetical instinct when he says that "the heat of the sun discovers the barrenness of the soil" (*Commentary on a Harmony of the Evangelists, Matthew, Mark, and Luke* [3 vols.; Grand Rapids: Eerdmans, 1949; orig. 1555] 2.115).

[54]Thus we are in general agreement with J. D. Crossan's conclusion ("Seed Parables" 247) that "the changes in 4:5-6 were effected to bring the parable into closer alignment with the interpretation in 4:16-17."

[55]"Thomas" 195-97.

[56]G. Eicholz, *Gleichnisse der Evangelien. Form, Uberlieferung, Auslegung* (Neukirchen, 1971) 67-68.

heavenward ascent of the soul of the true gnostic."[57] The fact that in *Gos. Thom.* it is the ground rather than the seed which brings forth fruit is also significant. The ground is probably the kingdom within the gnostic, while the seed is the spark of divine light.[58]

Koester's points, too, can be questioned. The gnostic elements identified above are probably redactional, as is the yield of sixty and 120 in the case of the good soil.[59] Neither is Koester's argument from silence about the absence of the allegorical interpretation in the *Thomas* version compelling. It is entirely possible that the tradents of the Thomas tradition, like many modern interpreters of the Sower parable, found Mark's allegory too "prosaic," and omitted it in their search for a deeper meaning in the parable. For such tradents, the Markan interpretation would have represented a premature attempt to decipher the parable's secret, which in actuality could only be grasped through a flash of insight: "The images are manifest to man, but the light in them remains concealed in the image of the light of the Father" (logion 83).[60]

In summation, then, *both* the Markan parable *and* its *Gos. Thom.* counterpart have redactional features. The possibility that the *Gos. Thomas* parable represents a reworking of the Markan version cannot be excluded, but the reverse is quite unlikely.

Expansions in the interpretation. Mark 4:13a probably is part of the

---

[57] J. D. Crossan ("Seed Parables" 248 n. 18), citing H. E. W. Turner and H. Montefiore.

[58] H.-J. Klauck, *Allegorie* 199-200. H. Koester ("Thomas" 196) asserts that, also in Mark 4:8, it could be argued that the ground rather than the seeds bears the good fruit. In the Markan verse, however, the seeds are definitely the bearers of the fruit, since they are the referents both of the neuter plural participles *anabainonta kai auxanomena*, "coming up and growing," and of the neuter singular numbers *hen . . . hen . . . hen*, "one . . . one . . . one."

[59] See J. D. Crossan, "Seed Parables" 249-50: Mark's triple yield is probably more nearly original than the double yield in *Gos. Thom.*, since it continues the "threesome" format of the preceding elements. We would add that the lack of proportion in a yield of thirty, sixty, and one hundred may have bothered *Gos. Thom.* circles, and that therefore the "more perfect" proportion of sixty and 120 is a sign of redaction.

[60] See D. Flusser, *Gleichnisse* 1.128. This gnostic emphasis is strikingly similar to that of A. Wilder ("Parable" 137), whose aim is to recapture the "shock of insight" of Jesus' original parable, and who therefore has a negative view of the explanation; see above, chapter 1, n. 6.

tradition inherited by Mark. It responds to the question asked by the disciples in v 10 and not directly answered in vv 11-12; also, it is introduced by *kai legei autois* ("and he says to them") rather than Mark's characteristic *kai elegen autois*.[61] 4:13b, however, is probably Markan, since it expresses the characteristic Markan reproach of the disciples,[62] and implies that, in explaining the Parable of the Sower, Jesus explained "all the parables"; cf. the Markan v 34b.[63]

In the interpretation itself (vv 14-20), J. Dupont[64] has identified the phrase *alla proskairoi eisin* ("but are temporary") in v 17 as Markan, but his arguments are weak. *Alla* here is not a Markan, explanatory *alla*, but has its normal, adversative meaning; and indeed explanatory *alla* is not characteristic of Mark.[65] Dupont is right that *proskairos* is impossible in Aramaic, but this does not necessarily mean it is *Markan*; it could have come from a pre-Markan Greek-speaking layer of tradition.[66] Similarly

---

[61]See A. Ambrozic, *Hidden Kingdom* 50. Ambrozic is of the opinion, which has a great deal in its favor, that the units introduced by *kai elegen* are the earliest segments of chapter 4, that the units introduced by *kai elegen autois* are Markan, and that 4:13-20, which is introduced by *kai legei autois*, represents an intermediate stage.

[62]E. Schweizer, "Frage" 1-8.

[63]On 4:34, at least 4:34b, as Markan redaction, see the discussion of the composition history of 4:33-34 in chapter 3 below.

[64]"Parabole" 15-18.

[65]Of the examples listed by Dupont (3:26-39; 4:22; 6:52), only 6:52 contais an *alla* which could be characterized as explanatory. Explanatory *alla* is not listed as a Markan feature in any of the major works on Markan style: M. M. Zerwick, *Untersuchungen zum Markus-stil* (Scripta pontificii instituti biblici; Rome: Biblical Institute, 1937); J. C. Doudna, *The Greek of the Gospel of Mark* (JBLMS 12; Philadelphia: Society of Biblical Literature and Exegesis, 1961); V. Taylor, *The Gospel According to St. Mark* (2d ed.; Grand Rapids: Baker, 1966), 44-54; F. Neirynck, *Duality in Mark: Contributions to the Study of the Markan Redaction* (BETL 31; Leuven University, 1972); E. J. Pryke, *Redactional Style in the Marcan Gospel: A Study of Syntax and Vocabulary as Guides to Redaction in Mark* (Cambridge/London/New York/Melbourne: Cambridge University, 1978).

[66]V. Fusco (*Parola* 336-337) finds the phrase "but are temporary" somewhat redundant after "do not have root in themselves." Actually, however, the two statements are complementary, representing a positive and negative expression of the same reality. Fusco himself also points out that persecution on account of the word, a typical situation for the early church, is in line with the other causes of apostasy already mentioned in the pre-Markan explanation.

questionable is Dupont's identification of the phrase *ē diōgmou dia ton logon* as Markan on the basis of the parallels in 8:35; 10:29-30.[67] These parallels speak not of "persecution on account of the word" but of losing life, house, and family "for the sake of the gospel."[68] Persecution *dia ton logon* is not a Markan proprium; cf. the use of the phrase, in contexts having to do with persecution, in Rev 1:9; 6:9; 20:4. Furthermore, the combination of *diōgmos* and *thlipsis,* "persecution" and "tribulation," found in 4:17, is an early Christian cliche (Rom 8:35, 2 Thess 1:4), so Dupont's separation of the two words is premature.

Neither, *contra* Dupont, is Mark's hand visible in v 19;[69] the elaborate description of dangers facing the church could just as well have come from the church prior to Mark as from Mark himself, and *eisporeuesthai* is not a particularly Markan verb; Mark's preferred verb for "to enter," especially in demonological contexts, is not *eisporeuesthai* but *eiserchesthai*.[70]

*   *   *   *   *

On the redaction of the Parable of the Sower, then, our conclusions are as follows. The parable that now appears in Mark 4:3-8 has undergone a few expansions, which emphasize temptations and the necessity of

---

[67] "Parabole" 16-17.

[68] V. Fusco (*Parola* 337 n. 109) cites H. Räisänen's objection that, if the phrase in 4:17 were Markan, it would be "for the sake of the gospel" (*heneken tou euangeliou*). Fusco retorts that 4:17 speaks of "the word" because of the larger context of 4:14-20. We would ask Fusco, in turn, why Mark says *dia ton logon,* "on account of the word," rather than *heneken tou logou,* "for the sake of the word," which would retain the construction of 10:29 but substitute "word" for "gospel."

J. Jeremias views *logos* used absolutely in a technical way, as in 4:17, as a coinage of the primitive church, but in some Markan cases (1:45; 2:2) he ascribes the term to the evangelist (*Parables* 77 n. 8) and in other cases (4:17, 33) to a pre-Markan stage (*Parables* 14 n. 11).

[69] "Parabole" 17-18.

[70] *Eiserchesthai* is somewhat more frequent in Mark than *eisporeuesthai* (ten usages as opposed to seven). Of the ten usages of *eiserchesthai,* five are clearly redactional (1:21, 45; 2:1; 3:1; 11:11) and two possibly so (7:17; 9:28). *Eiserchesthai* seems to be Mark's verb of preference in demonological contexts (5:12, 13; 9:25), so that the use of *eisporeuesthai* in the demonologically colored 4:19 may actually suggest that the word is pre-Markan.

perseverance. These expansions were made when the interpretation, which displays tendencies similar to those of the expansions, was added to the original parable. Mark took over the parable and its interpretation virtually unchanged from his source, altering their meaning only by the context in which he placed them and the insertion he put between them.

EXEGESIS

The Parable of the Sower and its allegorical interpretation were already joined when Mark received them, and for Mark the meaning of the parable is inseparable from the meaning of the interpretation. Nevertheless, the parable and its interpretation represent two discrete stages within the unfolding of chapter 4, and this discreteness has been underlined by the Markan redaction, which has interposed between parable and interpretation the statement in 4:11-12. Our method of investigating the meaning of the two interrelated parts, therefore, will be first to examine the parable itself, asking how Mark's readers would have heard it *before* they heard the interpretation. Then we will look at the interpretation, asking in what way, if any, an exposure to it might have modified the hearers' initial experience of the parable.

The Parable Itself

With characteristic clarity and brevity, J. Dupont[71] summarizes the basic exegetical questions in regard to the Parable of the Sower:

1.   Is the central point in the parable the action of the sower, and if so, with whom is the sower to be identified?
2.   Or is the central point the fate of the seed, and if so does the accent fall on the obstacles which the seed encounters or on its final success?
3.   Or is the accent on the various kinds of ground where the seed falls?

The identity of the sower. We have already noted above that, although the sower is not at center stage in our parable, he is not incidental to it. While the tradition that came down to Mark did not specifically allegorize the sower, the Markan understanding of this figure is indicated by the

---

[71]"Parabole" 5.

placement of our passage within chapter 4 and the Gospel as a whole, which reveals that Mark probably intended his readers to understand the sower as Jesus.[72] The "going out" (*exelthein*) of the sower would remind Mark's readers of the redactional verses 1:38; 2:13,[73] in both of which *Jesus* "goes out." Mark 1:38 is particularly significant for the meaning of 4:3, for in 1:38 *exelthein* connotes not just a physical exit from a house, but Jesus' moving out into the world to accomplish his mission; cf. the "full" sense of *ēlthon*, "I came," in 2:17.[74]

The context within chapter 4, also, would have suggested to Mark's hearers that the sower in 4:3 is Jesus. In the redactional verses 4:1-2,[75] an elaborate picture has been given of Jesus beginning to teach from the seashore, then getting into a boat and going out into the sea, from which he teaches the crowd that is *epi tēs gēs*, "on the land." Although the verb *exelthein* is not used in 4:1-2, the picture is of Jesus going out into the sea in order to teach the crowd. Therefore, when Mark's readers, immediately after 4:1-2, heard of a sower "going out to sow," it is likely that they would identify this figure with Jesus "sowing the word" in the crowd.[76] Furthermore, the solemn description of the crowd *epi tēs gēs*, "on the land," facing Jesus, would remain in their minds as they heard about the sower casting his seed "on the land" (4:8, 20; cf. a further use of *gē* in 4:5). Another passage in chapter 4 which supports the same conclusion is the exhortation to listen in 4:3a, which relates "the action of the parable to the public occasion and therefore to [Jesus'] own work and mission."[77]

In addition, the sower's experience in the parable corresponds to that of Jesus throughout the Gospel. As the sower scatters the seed everywhere, even where it will not bear fruit, so Mark's Jesus teaches everyone (4:1-2,

---

[72]J. Dupont ("Parabole" 10-11) argues that the sower is God, since God is usually the principal actor in parables of the kingdom of God; but in the Parable of the Mustard Seed, which is a parable of the kingdom, there is no actor who can be identified with God.

[73]An impressive consensus of Markan exegetes views these verses as redactional; see E. J. Pryke, *Style* 11.

[74]H.-J. Klauck, *Allegorie* 198. Cf. the assertion by A. Wilder ("Parable" 141) that the parable "relates to man's ultimate *conatus* or striving or going out from himself in search of fulfillment." This statement, however, is too general; the man in question is not Everyman, but Jesus.

[75]On 4:1-2 as redactional, see above, chapter 1.

[76]Cf. R. Pesch (*Markusevangelium* 1.230), who, however, rejects such allegorizing.

[77]A. Wilder, "Parable" 144; cf. R. Pesch, *Markusevangelium* 1.234.

33), even those who are vehemently opposed to him (6:6; 11:17; 14:49).[78] The parable chapter occurs in a section of the Gospel in which some people accept Jesus' word, while others reject it, just as in the parable one soil brings the seed to fruition, while others kill it.[79] As in the parable the badness of the bad soils is accentuated by external factors (birds, sun, thorns), which attack the seed; so, in this section of the Gospel, Jesus struggles not merely with the hardness of human hearts, but also with Satan (3:23-30; cf. 4:15).[80]

Finally, a secondary argument for the identification of the sower in Mark 4:3 with Jesus is that both Matthew[81] and Luke[82] seem to make this equation.

If Mark expected and wished his readers to think of Jesus when they heard about the sower in 4:3, however, why did he not allegorize the sower specifically in 4:14? It is insufficient to reply that the sower was not allegorized in the tradition which came down to Mark, although we believe this to be the case. Mark was perfectly capable of expanding traditions that were passed down to him, as we have seen above.

Two other lines of reasoning are more fruitful. First, it corresponds to Jesus' usual style of preaching in Mark that he refers to himself only indirectly.[83] Second, as we will demonstrate below, Jesus as sower continues to sow the word through the missionaries of the Markan community.

What sort of contrast? The first readers of Mark's Gospel, then, building on clues within the Gospel, would have identified the sower of 4:3 with

---

[78]Cf. 12:13-17, although the verb *didaskein* is not used.

[79]V. Fusco, *Parola* 337-38.

[80]Cf. also the struggle between Jesus and Satan in 1:12-13. A comparison of 3:23-26 with 4:15 reveals that Satan is not the one who casts out demons, as Jesus' opponents claim, but the one who casts out the word.

[81]X. Leon-Dufour ("Parabole" 298-99), pointing to *exelthōn* in 13:1 and *exēlthen* in 13:3.

[82]A. Jülicher (*Gleichnisreden* 2.534), pointing out that in Luke the sower sows *his* word (*ton sporon autou*).

[83]R. Pesch, *Markusevangelium* 1.235 n. 24. A good example of an indirect self-reference in another parable is provided by 12:1-12, in which, although Jesus does not identify himself with the "beloved son," the reader, and even his enemies in the narrative, get the point (12:12). Cf. also Jesus' reference to himself throughout the Gospel in the third person as "the Son of Man."

Jesus. The sower, however, quickly drops from sight, and the remainder of the parable (vv 4-8) is a history of the seed in various kinds of soils. The fate of the seed is given more prominence in terms of the number of words devoted to it than is the variety of soils.

As we noted above, vv 4-8 are binary in structure and the parable is thus a parable of contrast. What *sort* of contrast, however, is involved, and what purpose does the contrast serve?

It is easier to say what sort of contrast is *not* involved. As V. Fusco points out,[84] although the images of fruitbearing and sterility often are used in a parenetic way in the New Testament, there are good reasons for denying any but a secondary resonance of parenesis to the Parable of the Sower. The image of different kinds of soils is ill-suited to parenesis; a soil cannot change its nature.[85] Furthermore, parenetic metaphors and parables usually place the negative element at the end, as a stern warning, whereas the Parable of the Sower saves the good element for last.[86]

J. Jeremias, in his influential study,[87] sees the primary contrast not as parenetic but as temporal, between the time of sowing and the time of eschatological harvest. As X. Leon-Dufour points out, however,[88] such a contrast would require a juxtaposition of the smallness of the beginnings with the magnificence of the end. In our parable (contrast 4:30-32) it is not said that the beginnings are small, and there is no definitive *end* in the form of a harvest. V. Fusco[89] supports the last argument by recalling that the predominant tense in v 8 is not the aorist, as Jeremias's interpretation would require, but the imperfect, which emphasizes not the end result but the *process* of maturation. Furthermore, Fusco adds, the interval between beginning and end is different for each soil, and there is no sense of waiting in the parable; success and failure do not follow each other, but happen at the same time.

The primary contrast in the parable is thus not temporal but spatial, between the different areas of the field. As we will suggest below, this

---

[84] *Parola* 309-312.

[85] *Contra* X. Leon-Dufour ("Parabole" 280, 284), who sees the main point of the parable as the duty to be good soil.

[86] E.g. Matt 7:24-27 par.; Matt 7:16-20; Matt 24:45-51 par.; Matt 25:14-30 par.; Matt 25:1-12; Matt 25:31-46; Matt 13:47-50; Heb 6:7-8 (V. Fusco, *Parola* 310).

[87] *Parables* 149-51.

[88] "Parabole" 274-75.

[89] *Parola* 315-25.

contrast is *apocalyptic* without being "eschatological" in the sense that J. Jeremias understands that term.

Parable proper or similitude? First, however, it is necessary to consider the question of whether the Parable of the Sower is a parable proper (*Parabel*) or a similitude (*Gleichnis*), since Jeremias's "eschatological" interpretation would be supported if it were the former.[90] If the story of the sower were a parable proper, it would have as its subject an extraordinary occurrence, and thus might easily be interpreted as speaking of a miraculous yield in spite of small beginnings. One point in favor of calling our text a parable proper is that, like most such parables, its predominant tense is the aorist.

Our parable, however, ultimately belongs in the category of *Gleichnis* because it presents a basically realistic picture, at least according to first-century methods and conceptions of agriculture. The method of sowing is normal; Jeremias himself has been influential in publicizing G. Dalman's results,[91] according to which the seemingly extraordinary features of the sowing (sowing on the path, on rocky soil, and among thorns) actually correspond to the usual agricultural methods practiced in first century Palestine, where ground was often sown *before* being plowed.[92] Although some of the details may be exaggerated in the interest of the narrative, the main points are realistic.[93] It follows that, since a normal method of sowing is being described, the amount of seed lost is normal also. It is not implied that three-quarters of the seed is lost,[94] as the alternation between singular pronouns for the bad seed and the plural pronoun for the good seed proves.

------

[90]I follow here the classic definitions of A. Jülicher (as reported by J. Gnilka, *Evangelium* 1.157): a *Parabel* tells of a specific case which only occurs once, is usually narrated in the past, and often has extraordinary features; a *Gleichnis* tells of an everyday happening and is usually narrated in the present. According to Gnilka, *Gleichnisse* usually deal with the kingdom of God.

[91]*Parables* 11-12.

[92]P. B. Payne ("The Order of Sowing and Ploughing in the Parable of the Sower," *NTS* 25 [1978] 123-29) finds that plowing before sowing and after sowing were both done in Jesus' time, although the latter was more usual. Payne adds that it makes little difference to the realism of our parable when the field was sown.

[93]H.-J. Klauck, *Allegorie* 190-91.

[94]J. Gnilka, *Evangelium* 1.158-59.

The crucial question, however, is the nature of the seed's yield. J. Jeremias and others maintain that yields of thirty, sixty, and a hundred-fold are abnormal, and symbolize "the eschatological overflowing of the divine fullness, surpassing all human measure." A normal yield, as Dalman's studies of agriculture in Palestine in the 1920's and 1930's showed, would be seven and a half.[95] Others have objected to this line of reasoning, citing ancient authors who speak of yields of 100 or even 400,[96] giving contradictory data about normal yields in Palestine,[97] or hypothesizing that "seed" in our parable refers, not to individual kernels, but to portions of seed.[98] The scholarly battle, fought along these lines, appears to be a stalemate.

A way forward would be to ask, not whether yields of thirty, sixty, and a hundredfold actually *were* extraordinary in ancient Palestine, but whether they were *perceived to be* extraordinary. J. Jeremias,[99] answering affirmatively, cites Gen 26:12, where Isaac reaps a hundredfold, *because Yahweh blesses him.* As V. Fusco[100] points out, however, the Genesis text actually works against Jeremias's point, since it speaks, not of a fantastic, eschatological yield, but of the "normal" blessing that the righteous can expect within history, along the lines of Deut 28:1-4. From

---

[95]J. Jeremias, *Parables* 150, citing G. Dalman ("Viererlei Acker," *Palästinajahrbuch* 22 [1926] 129-130); cf. H.-J. Klauck, *Allegorie* 191; M. Zohary, "Flora," *IDB* 2.285-86.

[96]X. Leon-Dufour ("Parabole" 275), citing Pliny. H.-J. Klauck (*Allegorie* 191) retorts that such reports are either hyperbolic or simply false; cf. J. Jeremias, "Palästinakundliches zum Gleichnis vom Sämann (Mark IV:38)," *NTS* 13 (1966) 53.

[97]E. Linnemann, *Parables* 117.

[98]V. Fusco (*Parola* 316-319) asserts that the sown "seed" must be collective, since the *birds,* plural, come and eat it. Fusco adds that the interpretation of the parable (Mark 4:14-20) assumes that the seed is collective, since it consistently uses plural pronouns to refer to it (vv 15, 16, 18, 20); similarly, Matthew's and Luke's versions presuppose the collectivity of the seed. The arguments against the collective interpretation advanced by F. Hahn ("Gleichnis," 135) are not convincing; the variation between singular and plural pronouns in the parable does not exclude a reference to portions of seed.

[99]"Palästinakundliches" 53.

[100]*Parola* 318 n. 42.

a time closer to that of Jesus,[101] Fusco cites *Sib. Or.* 3:261-264 to prove the same point:

> [For the Heavenly One gave the earth in common to all
> and fidelity, and excellent reason in their breasts.]
> For these alone the fertile soil yields fruit
> from one- to a hundredfold, and the measures of God are
>   produced.

Here again the context is not eschatological; the preceding verses treat the Exodus, and the succeeding verses the Babylonian exile. As did Gen 26:12, *Sib. Or.* 3:261-264 rather speaks of a divine promise of material abundance *in this age* to the righteous in Israel.

Yields of thirty, sixty, and a hundredfold, then, are not "eschatological" in the sense that Jeremias uses the term. They are in line with what ancient writers, including biblical writers, expected to receive from fertile fields, and they are nowhere near the fantastic yields expected in the Age to Come in some apocalyptic and rabbinic traditions.[102] Our text is thus a similitude, rather than a parable proper, in spite of its use of the aorist.[103] The yields described in Mark 4:8 would be excellent, but not unheard-of. For those with eyes to see (4:9), the fruitfulness of which Jesus speaks in 4:8 would be a sign of the arrival of the kingdom, but the very "realism" of the numbers would also leave room for a reaction of skepticism about the arrival of the kingdom. The Parable of the Sower, therefore, *is* "eschatological," but in a different way than that suggested by Jeremias.

The mystery of the kingdom. In order to determine more precisely the sense in which Mark understands the parable's contrast, we consider it

---

[101]Book 3 of the Sibylline Oracles dates from the middle of the second century B.C.; see J. H. Charlesworth, *The Pseudepigrapha and Modern Research with a Supplement* (SBLSCS 7; Chico, Calif.: Scholars, 1981; orig. 1976) 18485; J. J. Collins, "Sibylline Oracles," *The Old Testament Pseudepigrapha* (ed. J. H. Charlesworth; 2 vols.; Garden City: Doubleday, 1983) 1.354-55. Unless otherwise noted, all translations of OT pseudepigrapha are from the Charlesworth volume.

[102]J. Dupont ("Parabole" 8) cites the yield of 1000 in *1 Enoch* 10:19 and the yield of 10,000 in *2 Apoc. Bar.* 29:5. V. Fusco (*Parola* 319 n. 45) refers to a rabbinic text which implies a yield of 150,000 times.

[103]As J. Gnilka (*Evangelium* 1.157) concludes; *contra* H.-J. Klauck, *Allegorie* 191.

necessary to analyze the parable within its larger Markan context, and particularly to pay attention to the way in which Mark's insertion of 4:11-12 affects the meaning of the parable.

As R. Schnackenburg has observed, the close connection between the Parable of the Sower and the two other seed parables in chapter 4 suggests that it deals with the *basileia*.[104] J. Gnilka, on the other hand,[105] claims that the Parable of the Sower is not a parable of the kingdom of God, because it is not controlled by a contrast between beginning and end. Gnilka, however, is operating with a restricted definition of parables of the kingdom of God, which seems to be different from that used by Mark.

In 4:11 Jesus says that the mystery of the kingdom of God *has been given* (*dedotai*) to the disciples. The perfect tense of *dedotai* should limit the mystery of the kingdom to something which has already put in an appearance in the Gospel, and J. L. Martyn has suggested that the disciples' question in 4:10 provides a key to what that "something" is. They ask Jesus about *the parables*, and his answer in 4:11a is related to their query.[106] The mystery of the kingdom of God has been given *in the parables*, particularly in the Parable of the Sower.[107] The continuation of

---

[104] *God's Rule and Kingdom* (Freiburg/Montreal: Herder/Palm, 1963) 147.

[105] *Evangelium* 1.161.

[106] Martyn's oral suggestion on this point is developed in my "Mark 4:10-12 and Marcan Epistemology," *JBL* 103 (1984) 563-67, esp. nn. 32, 33. Cf. S. Pedersen, "Is Mark 4, 1-34 a Parable Chapter?" *SE* VI (= TU 112; 1973) 411.

[107] To the plural "parables" in 4:10 cf. the plural in 12:1; in each case only one parable has been narrated.

I no longer think, as I did when I wrote the article cited in the preceding note, that the plural "parables" refers to the parables in 3:23-27 along with that of 4:3-8. The caesura between chapter 3 and chapter 4 is too radical for the reference in 4:11 to reach back to the parables in 3:23-27. It is more likely that Mark thinks of each individual comparison in 4:3-8 as a parable (see P. Lampe, "Die markinische Deutung des Gleichnisses von Sämann Markus 4:10-12," *ZNW* 65 [1974] 148; cf. R. Pesch, *Markusevangelium* 1.237). This hypothesis is supported when it is remembered that our parable tells not one story but four. V. Fusco (*Parola* 80-81), however, solves the problem differently, by suggesting that 4:2a be translated, "and among the parables he taught them was the following," i.e. the Parable of the Sower. This explanation seems unlikely because the rest of the parables Jesus spoke publicly on this occasion are given in 4:26-32, *after* 4:11.

Jesus' reply in 4:11b-12, like the interpretation of the Parable of the Sower, implies that God's word in the parables is a two-edged sword: to the disciples it reveals "the mystery of the kingdom of God," but to "those outside" it is a weapon of blinding.

That for Mark the Parable of the Sower pictures "the mystery of the kingdom of God" is also suggested by a consideration of 4:9, 13, together with some of the nuances of *mystērion*. The exhortation to hear in 4:9 implies that there are depths to be plumbed in the Parable of the Sower,[108] and the reproof in 4:13 identifies that parable as the key to *all* parables; both verses are compatible with the view that the Parable of the Sower imparts a mystery to those with ears to hear.

Already A. Jülicher[109] argued against the suggestion that the "mystery of the kingdom of God" in 4:11 had a special relationship to the Parable of the Sower, citing the perfect tense of *dedotai*, "has been given," in 4:11, whereas the disciples do not understand that parable until its interpretation (4:14-20) has been appended. Investigation of the Semitic background of the term *mystērion*, however, reveals the possibility that the mystery may have been *given* already in the parable, even though it is not *understood* until later. The most important passage for comparison is Daniel 2, especially 2:27-30, Daniel's reply to Nebuchadnezzar's question of whether he can make known Nebuchadnezzar's dream along with its interpretation:

> No wise men, enchanters, magicians, or astrologers can show to the king *the mystery which the king has asked,* but there is a God in heaven *who reveals mysteries,* and he *has made known* to King Nebuchadnezzar what will be in the latter days. . . . To you, O king, as you lay in bed came thoughts of what would be hereafter, and *he who reveals mysteries made known to you what is to be.* But as for me, not because of any wisdom that I have more than all the living has *this mystery* been revealed to me, but in order that *the interpretation* may be made known to the king, and that you may *know* the thoughts of your mind.

The "mystery" that has stumped the king's wise men and magicians is the dream itself; in 2:9-11 they declare that the interpretation is no problem,

---

[108]Cf. Bede (*In Marcum,* CChrSL 120.481-82) on Mark 4:9: "As often as this is inserted in the Gospel or in the Apocalypse of John, that which is spoken is mystical."

[109]*Gleichnisreden* 1.123-26.

as long as the dream is told to them. The king has seen the mystery;[110] the "God . . . who reveals mysteries" *has made it known* to him (2:28, 29) even though he does not yet *understand* the meaning of his vision (cf. 2:30, "that you may *know* the thoughts of your mind").[111] This language of the mystery's having been given can be used because the meaning of the dream is already present with God, even though its contents have not yet been decoded for the king, and the events that it pictures have not yet occurred.[112]

Indeed, the very presence of the interpretation is an argument for the mystery having been given in the parable, since the root idea in the Semitic concept of "mystery" is not intrinsic obscurity, but that which can only be known by divine communication.[113] The interpretation of the Parable of the Sower, like the explanations given to dreams and visions in the OT and Pseudepigrapha, is a second revelatory step which unlocks the "mystery" of the parable.[114]

---

[110]This is explicit in the LXX 88 text of 2:27, which reads *to mystērion ho heōraken ho basileus*, "the mystery which the king has seen." Theodotion, however, reads *eperōta*, "asks," instead of *heōraken*, following the MT.

[111]In 2:30 Daniel may be making a distinction between the mystery that has been revealed to him (i.e. the dream) and the interpretation. However, the referent of "mystery" in Daniel 2 is fluid; in 2:47 it clearly includes both the dream and the interpretation. 2:19 is ambiguous. On the one hand, the mystery is revealed in a *vision,* implying perhaps that the mystery is the dream itself; cf. 2:28, in which "dream" is parallel to "the visions of your head." On the other hand, comparison with 2:24-25 seems to suggest that the interpretation is included. See the conclusion of R. E. Brown (*The Semitic Background of the Term "Mystery" in the New Testament* [FBBS 21; Philadelphia: Fortress, 1968; orig. 1958-59] 7-8): In chapter 2 "*mystērion* is used eight times, always translating the Aramaic *rāz*, to refer both to the dream and to its contents; for the dream itself is a series of complicated symbols which envelop a further mystery: the future of the kingdom."

[112]Cf. H. Giesen, "Mk 9,1—ein Wort Jesu über die nahe Parusie?" *TTZ* 92 (1983) 141.

[113]B. W. Bacon, *The Beginnings of the Gospel Story* (New Haven: Yale University, 1909) 46-49. On the Semitic concept of mystery in general, see R. E. Brown, *Semitic Background.*

[114]Cf. S. Freyne, "Disciples" 13-14; also H.-J. Klauck, *Allegorie* 201. The Markan mystery, like apocalyptic secrets generally, does not lose its mysterious character from its decipherment, since it can be transmitted only in signs and is restricted to an esoteric circle; cf. H. Giesen, "Mk 9,1" 141.

In the Markan redaction, then, the Parable of the Sower imparts the "mystery of the kingdom of God."[115] In what does this mystery consist? In the Judaism of Jesus' time, the main nuance of the concept "kingdom of God" was eschatological; the term designated "that final and decisive act of God wherein he manifests himself as king as he visits and redeems his people."[116] This expectation of a dramatic divine intervention confronts, in Mark's Gospel, a king whose kingship is manifest in a hidden manner, not visible to all, and *sub specie contraria*. For Mark, the Parable of the Sower itself proclaims the paradoxical nature of this kingship. We will substantiate this point by looking at 1) the parable's modification of traditional imagery for the coming of the eschaton, and 2) the way in which this modification accords with references to the kingdom of God in other Markan passages.

4 Ezra 4:27-29 and the Parable of the Sower. C. E. Carlston, in his interpretation of the Parable of the Sower, writes that N. A. Dahl's emphasis on a future eschatological harvest has the disadvantage of "minimizing the complex shift in imagery involved when the 'eschatological harvest' has in some sense begun." In arguing against J. Jeremias's version of the eschatology of the Parable of the Sower, we have already pointed to the absence of a harvest in our passage. Carlston agrees with X. Leon-Dufour that Jesus' parable deliberately omits any mention of harvest "because the Kingdom is present in Jesus' ministry but the day of harvest is not."[117]

Comparison with 4 Ezra 4:27-29 buttresses the point made by Carlston and Leon-Dufour about the shift in imagery embodied in our parable. 4 Ezra is especially rich in background material for understanding the

---

[115]The connection between the parable and the kingdom is explicit in the Matthean version, where the seed is allegorized as *ton logon tēs basileias*, "the word of the kingdom" (13:19). B. Gerhardsson ("The Parable of the Sower and its Interpretation," *NTS* 14 [1967-68] 167 n. 1) also points out that there is a traditional connection between the Shema, which he sees as the background for the Parable of the Sower, and the kingdom of God.

[116]N. Perrin, *Rediscovering* 54-60, esp. 56.

[117]C. E. Carlston, *Parables* 142 n. 18. In the context of the Markan chapter 4, however, the harvest that is missing in the Parable of the Sower is supplied in the Parable of the Seed Growing Secretly (4:29; see below, chapter 5).

seed parables in Mark 4, particularly the Parable of the Sower.[118] The book contains much use of seed imagery, and it is remarkably close to Parable of the Sower in its shift between identifying seed with the word and with the human beings who hear the word. In 4 Ezra 9:31 the divine word of the Law is compared to God's seed, but in 8:41 the seed that God sows is the human beings he has planted in the world.[119] This similarity between the seed imagery in 4 Ezra and that in Mark 4:3-8, 14-20 suggests that it is legitimate to use the configuration of ideas found in the former as background for the latter. Although 4 Ezra itself is from the end of the first century A.D.,[120] its seed parables could have been ancient and well known, and these or similar traditions probably have influenced the final shaping of the Markan parable and its interpretation.[121]

In the passage that particularly concerns us, 4 Ezra 4:27-29, we read that the present age

> will not be able to bring the things that have been promised to the righteous, because this age is full of sadness and infirmities. For the evil about which you ask me has been sown, but the harvest of it has not yet come. If therefore that which has been sown is not reaped, and if the place where the evil has been sown does not pass away, the field where the good has been sown will not come.

Like the Parable of the Sower as understood by Mark, 4 Ezra 4:27-29 speaks of two sorts of sowing, one with a good result and one with an evil result. The 4 Ezra passage presupposes a contrast, common in Jewish apocalyptic, between the old age as a time of fruitlessness and

---

[118]Cf. U. Luck, "Das Gleichnis von Säemann und die Verkündigung Jesu," *Wort und Dienst* 11 (1971) 82.

[119]J. Jeremias, *Parables* 79. According to H.-J. Klauck (*Allegorie* 203; cf. 192) the confusion in the interpretation of the Parable of the Sower comes from the combination of the OT image of God sowing or planting human beings, with the Greek concept of *logos* as *sperma*. Klauck is probably right, but the Greek concept is mediated through its effect on the Jewish concept of Torah as God's seed, which is found in 4 Ezra 9:31.

[120]J. H. Charlesworth, *Pseudepigrapha and Modern Research* 111-113.

[121]Cf. R. E. Brown ("Parable and Allegory" 261-62) who makes this point specifically about the parable in 4 Ezra 8.

sterility[122] and the new age as a time of fruitfulness and fertility.[123] The 4 Ezra parable describes the present time as containing not four soils but one, the *bad* soil; only *after* that soil has passed away can the good soil be sown.[124]

In the Parable of the Sower, on the other hand, the good soil and the bad soil exist simultaneously. Assuming as a background the conception found in 4 Ezra 4:27-29, the coexistence of the good and bad soils in the Parable of the Sower would be a sign that the kingdom of God is making its dramatic but hidden advent without totally abolishing the kingdom of Satan. The coexistence of the two kingdoms is part of the "mystery of the kingdom of God." The new age has indeed arrived; the excellent yields pictured in 4:8, which *almost* strain credulity, bear witness to its advent for those who have eyes to see.[125] Yet, contrary to what was commonly expected of the eschaton, evil has not evaporated from the universe. The bad soil, with its accompanying sterility and death, the signs of the old age, still exists.

As V. Fusco puts it, then, our parable speaks of the kingdom of God "not as a sudden overturning which puts an end to the old age, substituting for it the future one, but as the irruption of the new age *within* the old."[126] Such a vision of the kingdom of God, although it goes beyond anything found in the OT or Judaism, is consonant with the Semitic concept of "mystery," which can denote the strange reality that God's action in the world meets with opposition.[127]

---

[122]Cf. H.-J. Klauck (*Allegorie* 194-95), who cites 4 Ezra 6:22; Hag 1:6; 2 *Apoc. Bar.* 10:9; *1 Enoch* 80:2-3.

[123]See for example 1QS 4:6-7, where the visitation of those who walk in the Spirit includes "fruitfulness of seed"; cf. also the passages referred to in n. 102.

[124]U. Luck, "Gleichnis" 81.

[125]G. Eichholz (*Gleichnisse* 73) suggests that the sterility of the bad soils recalls the curse of Gen 3:17-18 (cf. particularly the mention of *thorns* in 4:7); the fruitfulness of the good soil, therefore, may suggest the repeal of the curse.

[126]V. Fusco, *Parola* 388-389.

[127]See e.g. 1QM 14:9-10, which speaks of what happens "in the *dominion* of Belial and in all the *mysteries* of his hostility" (trans. A. Dupont-Sommer, *The Essene Writings from Qumran* [Glouchester, Mass.: Peter Smith, 1973; orig. 1961]; throughout this study I have checked Dupont-

The hiddenness of the irruption of the kingdom of God would have been especially meaningful to the Markan community, which, as we can see from numerous texts, was experiencing intense suffering. The community, rent apart by internal divisions (13:6, 21-22) and buffeted by attack from outside, was suffering "tribulation and persecution" (13:8-13; 10:30), indeed such tribulation as had never been before (13:19). Its members were being called upon to take up their crosses and follow Jesus (8:35-38), to drink the cup he had drunk and to be baptized with the baptism in which he had been baptized (10:39), to follow him on an unexpectedly terrible journey (10:32-34). In such a situation, the advent of the kingdom of God in Jesus' ministry was anything but obvious, and it is this clash between belief in God's kingdom and experience of evil that our parable, with its emphasis on hiddenness, addresses.

The use of seed as a metaphor for the word in 4 Ezra, as well as the juxtaposition of 4:1-2 with 4:3 means that Mark's readers, even before they reached 4:14, would have interpreted the seed as the word. With this identification in mind, the "mystery of the kingdom" would emerge for them also from the differing effects of the word in our parable. Although in the case of the good soil the dynamic and effective word of God, in fulfillment of conceptions such as those found in Isa 55:10-11, does indeed accomplish that for which God sends it, yet in the case of the three bad soils it seems to "return to him void." This frustration, too, is part of the mystery of the kingdom, since the Semitic concept of "mystery" includes the paradox that, in spite of God's sovereignty, some human beings continue to be under the dominion of sin and the devil.[128] Indeed, it is part of

---

Sommer's translations against the Hebrew texts in E. Lohse, *Die Texte aus Qumran. Hebräisch und Deutsch* [München: Kösel, 1964], altering the translations in some cases, which I have noted). Here the "mystery" is that God's dominion meets with opposition from the dominion of Belial. It is helpful to recall Wellhausen's dictum that the kingdom of God is always conceived antithetically to another kingdom (cited by J. Weiss, *Jesus' Proclamation of the Kingdom of God* [Philadelphia: Fortress, 1971; orig. 1892] 101).

[128]See 1QH 5:36; 1QS 3:22-23, cited in my "Mark 4:10-12" section VI. Cf. K. Barth's reference to the mystery of the frustration of God's word in his exegesis of the Parable of the Sower: "Contrary to every rule, intention, and hope, . . . the true and living and effective word of the kingdom does not accomplish in the world that which it should accomplish in accordance with its nature and the world situation created by its proclamation" (*Church Dogmatics* [Edinburgh: T. & T. Clark, 1961] 4.3.1.188-91).

the "mystery" that this hardening occurs *according to the will of God*.[129]

The mysteriousness of the kingdom in Mark. The same tension between "already" and "not yet" that we discern when we compare the Parable of the Sower with 4 Ezra 4:27-29 is apparent when we investigate the references to the kingdom of God in Mark. In the very first such reference, Jesus announces, "The time has been fulfilled, and the kingdom of God has drawn near" (1:15a). While the first part of this announcement emphasizes what has already been accomplished, the second part points to a reality which is near, but has not yet fully manifested itself.[130] The imperatives in 1:15b correspond to the respective indicatives in 1:15a; the call to repentance is an exhortation to turn away from the old age which is now passing away, while the call to faith is an exhortation to turn toward the new age which, though not yet fully arrived, is already making its effect felt in the present.[131]

Outside of 4:11, "kingdom of God" occurs twice in chapter 4, in the

---

[129] In 1QS 3:22-23, for example, it is "according to the mysteries of God" that some people fall under the dominion of the Angel of Darkness.

[130] A. Ambrozic (*Hidden Kingdom* 21) and H. Giesen ("Mk 9,1" 136-137) both argue that *engizein* should be translated "has come" rather than "has drawn near," Ambrozic (*Hidden Kingdom* 15) acknowledging the influence of C. H. Dodd on this translation. Ambrozic and Giesen argue partly on the basis of the parallelism between the two statements in 1:15a. As J. L. Kugel has recently shown, however (*The Idea of Biblical Poetry: Parallelism and its History* [New Haven/London: Yale University, 1981] 51), the essence of biblical parallelism is not identity of the two parallel parts but the sharpening of the first by the second in a way that can only be determined by the context. Mark 1:15a might thus be paraphrased, following Kugel's suggestion, "The time has been fulfilled, and *what is more*, the kingdom of God has drawn near."

Giesen also cites 14:42 to show that *engizein* implies a nearness which is just about to become arrival; Judas is so near that he arrives without delay. Still, an interval, however small, is presupposed here, as also in the other Markan occurrence of *engizein*, 11:1. J. Schlosser (*La règne de Dieu dans les dits de Jésus* [2 vols.; EBib; Paris: Gabalda, 1980] 1. 106-108) shows that *engizein* in 1:15 means "to draw near," its usual meaning in the OT and NT. On the few occasions in the NT when the verb *does* mean "arrive," the context is always spatial, never temporal. Similarly, the Hebrew verbs that are translated by *engizein* in the LXX (the two most common are *qrb* and *ngš*) almost always mean to "draw near"; and the ones that can mean "arrive" can only do so in spatial contexts.

[131] Cf. A. Ambrozic, *Hidden Kingdom* 7.

introductions of 4:26-29 and 4:30-32. These passages will be treated in detail later; for the present it is sufficient to notice that the introductory formulas link the kingdom both with the present moment of hiddenness and inchoate growth, and with the eschaton.[132]

In 9:1, which probably has been placed in its present position by Mark himself, "the kingdom of God come in power" is related by its placement both to 8:31-38 and to 9:2-13.[133] The kingdom's coming in power is thus linked both with the transfiguration, which points forward to the resurrection,[134] and with the parousia.[135] As E. Nardoni puts it, the transfiguration shows "in advance the glory with which the Son of Man will be invested in the resurrection; this is the glory he will display publicly and universally in the parousia."[136] Yet the glory of the kingdom is qualified by references to Jesus' sufferings (8:31; 9:12), as well as those of his OT

---

[132]Cf. A. Ambrozic (Hidden Kingdom 23): These are parables of contrast, but "the very contrast suggests that the final result is not confined entirely to the future."

[133]See E. Nardoni, "A Redactional Interpretation of Mark 9:1," CBQ 43 (1981) 365-84. According to Nardoni, the introduction of 9:1 into its present context by Mark is indicated by its introduction by the Markan link-phrase kai elegen autois. The link with 8:38 is by means of the binomial "glory and power," while the link with the Transfiguration narrative is by means of a) the time indication in 9:2; b) the verb "to see" in 9:9; and c) the OT background (Malachi) linking Elijah (cf. 9:11-13) with the coming of the kingdom in power.

[134]The strongest reason for seeing the transfiguration as proleptic of Jesus' resurrection is 9:9, upon which R. Pesch (Markusevangelium 2.67) comments: "Already in the transfiguration account the three disciples are made witnesses of Easter." In the NT generally, as J. Schlosser (Règne, 1.338) points out, dynamis is often used to describe the condition of the resurrected Jesus; H. Giesen ("Mk 9,1" 146, citing C. H. Dodd) points particularly to Rom 1:4 to prove this point. We might add that in the transfiguration account Jesus is portrayed in post-resurrection glory (9:2-3), speaking with two dead people (9:4).

[135]The linkage of 9:1 with the parousia is strengthened by 13:26, 30. In 13:26, an obvious parousia reference, the words meta dynameōs pollēs, "with great power," are inserted into the citation of Dan 7:13-14; cf. the words en dynamei, "in power," in Mark 9:1. (According to A. Ambrozic [Hidden Kingdom 205-206], it is "at least possible" that en dynamei in 9:1 is a Markan addition.) Mark 13:30, which is also a parousia reference, has a striking structural similarity to 9:1; see J. Schlosser, Règne 1.324-27.

[136]"Interpretation" 377.

antitype (9:13) and his followers (8:34-35).[137] The "mystery of the kingdom of God," as it emerges from Mark 9:1, then, is the mystery of a kingdom whose glory is already visible to those who have faith in the risen Christ, but a kingdom which is still subject, and will be subject until its final manifestation at the parousia, to outrage at the hands of "those outside."

The references to "entering the kingdom of God" in chapters 9 and 10 (9:47; 10:14-15; 10:23-25) also demonstrate a tension between "already" and "not yet." In 9:47, the kingdom is clearly future, as the contrast to being thrown into Gehenna shows.[138] In 10:14-15 the situation is less clear. In form, the saying in 10:15 seems to be one of the "sentences of holy law" identified by E. Käsemann,[139] linking present acceptance of the kingdom with future entry into it. In 10:14, however, the kingdom already belongs to the children, and even the mention of entry into the kingdom in 10:15 may gain a secondary present reference from its association with 10:14.[140]

Similarly, the references to entering the kingdom in 10:23-25 have both a future and a present nuance. A comparison of the former passage with 10:17 reveals that entering the kingdom is equivalent to inheriting eternal life, which according to 10:30 happens in the age to come. A future reference also emerges from 10:26, where the disciples, reacting to Jesus' statement that it is difficult for a rich man to enter the kingdom, exclaim: "Who then can be saved?" Salvation, as a theological concept, is exclusively future in Mark.[141]

On the other hand, Jesus' statement in 10:23-25 that the rich will enter the kingdom with difficulty is also a commentary on what has just happened, the rich man's refusal to follow him (10:21-22), and thus entry into the kingdom has a present nuance. Furthermore, the conclusion to the pericope in 10:28-30 contrasts to the rich man's reaction that of the disciples who have left everything to follow Jesus. These disciples are *already* receiving a reward in houses, lands, and family, albeit with perse-

---

[137]Cf. E. Nardoni, "Interpretation" 381-84.

[138]A. Ambrozic, *Hidden Kingdom* 176-77.

[139]"Sentences of Holy Law in the New Testament," *New Testament Questions of Today* (Philadelphia: Fortress, 1969) 66-81.

[140]Cf. A. Ambrozic, *Hidden Kingdom* 158.

[141]8:35 (2x); cf. 13:13, 20. See esp. 8:35 in its context: he who *loses* his life in this evil age will *save* it at the eschaton.

cutions; and 10:28-30 thus seems to speak of the foretaste of the kingdom in the life of the community.[142]

The statements in Mark about entering the kingdom, therefore, point on the one hand to a paradisiacal reality, for the sake of which everything in this age should be sacrificed, if need be, in order to enter it at the eschaton. On the other hand, they also affirm that people are *now* entering the kingdom, although to "those outside" this entry looks like poverty, failure, suffering, and death.

Mark 11:10, although it does not use the phrase "kingdom of God," speaks of a *basileia* which is linked to one who comes "in the name of the Lord." Irony is built into 11:9-10, since the crowd probably understands the "coming kingdom" as future, but Mark takes it as already arriving in the person of the "one who comes," Jesus.[143] A relation is thus established between the kingdom and Christology. Such a relation was already implicit in the proximity between redactional references to the kingdom and two of the three proclamations of Jesus' divine sonship (1:11; 9:7),[144] as well as in the link between Jesus' exorcisms and the kingdom.[145]

It is significant, however, that the "king" title is missing from 11:10; it is not until the Passion Narrative that Jesus reveals his kingship.[146] There, for the first time in Mark, Jesus is called a king,[147] but this acclamation occurs in a context of hiddenness and contradiction such as we have come to associate with God's strange and mysterious kingdom. Jesus' kingship is acclaimed by the soldiers, but in mockery, and his crown is made of thorns (15:16-19); later, his enemies in derision challenge the "King of Israel" to come down from the cross (15:32).[148] Their gibe that

---

[142]A. Ambrozic, *Hidden Kingdom* 158, 170, 181.

[143]Cf. A. Ambrozic, *Hidden Kingdom* 39-40.

[144]Ibid., 23. Ambrozic does not note that the third proclamation of Jesus' divine sonship, 15:39, is also close to a reference to the kingdom of God, 15:43, on which see below.

[145]Jesus' reply to the scribes' charge in 3:22-27 implies that it is not the kingdom of Satan that is responsible for his exorcisms, but the kingdom of God. Cf. A. Ambrozic (*Hidden Kingdom* 45), who speaks of the manifestation of the kingdom in Jesus' miracles and powerful preaching.

[146]J. Gnilka, *Evangelium* 2.118-19.

[147]Prior to chapter 15, only Herod (6:14, 22, 25, 26, 27) and other earthly kings (13:9) have been designated by the term *basileus*. Then, in the Passion Narrative, Jesus is five times called "the king of the Jews" (15:2, 9, 12, 18, 26) and once "the king of Israel" (15:32).

[148]Cf. F. J. Matera, *The Kingship of Jesus: Composition and Theology in Mark 15* (SBLDS 66; Chico, Calif.: Scholars, 1982) 147-49.

he saved others, but cannot save himself (15:31), goes to the heart of the paradoxical kingship that is revealed in his crucifixion. God's kingdom suffers the violence of humanity, indeed appears powerless before that violence; yet in this very powerlessness and frustration, the "ransom for many" is being given (10:45).

Returning to direct references to the kingdom of God, we see that 12:34 probably contains the same tension between "already" and "not yet" that we have observed in most previous citations of the phrase. The scribe is *not yet* in the kingdom, although he is close to it; but the power of the kingdom is already manifesting itself, in that *from this time forward* no one dares to ask Jesus a question.[149]

On the other hand, in 14:25 the main emphasis is on the kingdom of God which lies in the future, as the plain wording of the verse shows.[150] There are two possible hints of a present kingdom, however. One comes from the reference to the "blood of the covenant" in 14:24, since, as recent work on Ancient Near Eastern suzerainty treaties in relation to biblical covenants has shown, the idea of covenant itself is undergirded by the conception of God's kingship. The pouring out of Jesus' blood in his death, and the prolepsis of that event at the Last Supper, would then have associations with God's kingship as it was manifested by the covenant sacrifice of Exod 24:8.[151] Furthermore, Jesus' reference to the "new wine" of the kingdom might remind Mark's readers of 2:22, in which new wine is a metaphor for the present freedom of Jesus and his disciples from contemporary religious practices. Neither of these allusions, however, is certain, and they are secondary if present.

Finally, in 15:43 Joseph of Arimathea is described as one who was "awaiting the kingdom of God." One possible interpretation of this statement is that the respected member of the Sanhedrin, because he focuses

---

[149]The tension between "already" and "not yet" is developed by means of a remarkable accumulation of negatives: *ou makran . . . oudeis ouketi*, "not far . . . no one, no longer." On the silencing of Jesus' enemies as a sign of the presence of the kingdom, see A. Ambrozic, *Hidden Kingdom* 179-81.

[150]See A. Ambrozic (*Hidden Kingdom* 189-90), who adduces the primary eschatological sense of "kingdom of God" itself, and the banquet image and the adjective "new" with their OT associations.

[151]The reminiscence of Exod 24 is stronger in Mark than in any of the parallel Last Supper accounts. Jesus does not speak of a "new covenant," but directly echoes Exod 24:8: "Behold the blood of the covenant." See J. Gnilka, *Evangelium* 2.246.

on the dead body of Jesus and therefore still awaits the coming of the kingdom, does not realize that God's kingship has *already* been revealed in Jesus' crucifixion. On the other hand, Mark's implication may be that Joseph *has* begun to find the kingdom he was awaiting, as is indicated by his courage in asking for the body of Jesus.[152] In either case, Mark suggests (either by contrast with Joseph's obtuseness or by identification with his perspicacity) that in Jesus' death there is an inciplent manifestation of God's kingship.

Taken as a whole, then, the references to the kingdom of God in Mark are in accord with our interpretation of the Parable of the Sower as revealing "the mystery of the kingdom." In the ministry of Jesus, in his proclamation of the word and his miracles, as later in his death and resurrection, God reveals his world-transforming, kingly power. Strangely, however, this revelation does not convince everyone, but only those who are enabled to look toward Jesus, and ultimately toward his cross, as the epiphany of God's kingship. The rest, "those outside,"[153] who look away from Jesus and his cross or confront them with derision, see only the same old unredeemed world. Redemption has come, but in the unbelief of the outsiders the shadow of the old age falls mysteriously on the dawning kingdom.

Our interpretation of the mystery of the kingdom of God as presented in the Parable of the Sower is supported by other Markan passages which, although they do not explicitly mention the kingdom, paint a similar picture of its hidden, mysterious presence. Mark 9:12-13 implies that the "restoration of all things" has already occurred in John the Baptist's ministry, although this restoration is invisible to most.[154] Jesus' reply to the request of the sons of Zebedee (10:35-40), and his further instruction to the disciples on true greatness (10:41-45), point to a kingdom which, according to God's will, exists *sub specie contraria*; in which rule is exercised, not by lording it over others, but by service; so that the kingdom is visible only to those who have been given eyes to see. Indeed, as A. Ambrozic points out,[155] the hiddenness of the kingdom is attested by the very fact that proclamation is necessary.

---

[152] A. Ambrozic, *Hidden Kingdom* 240-43.

[153] On this term, see below, chapter 3.

[154] Cf. C. H. Dodd (*Parables* 135-37), who cites the passage in his discussion of the Parable of the Sower.

[155] *Hidden Kingdom* 245-47.

The opposition which Jesus experiences in the Gospel, then, an opposition that is pictured in the Parable of the Sower, is not a sign that God's kingship still awaits its earthly manifestation. Indeed, if the genitives in the phrase "mystery of the kingdom of God" are taken seriously, then God is at work in the outbreak of opposition, and the violence of the opposition is actually a *sign* of his inbreaking.[156] A similar idea is expressed later in the Gospel by the juxtaposition of two clauses in Jesus' announcement: "The hour has come; behold, the Son of Man is delivered into the hands of sinners" (14:41).

The strange fact of opposition, which causes even the Sower himself to marvel (6:6a), does not prevent him from continuing his sowing (6:6b), even though he knows that not all the seed will bear fruit. Neither, by implication, should the Christian preachers who carry on the sowing of Jesus' word give up when the word seems not to strike fertile ground.[157] They must continue in their sowing, and thereby enter into the same mystery of contradiction that confronted their master. The optimistic tinge of the parable assures them that all will come out right in the end. Our parable is thus a word of empowerment for those who are amazed at the only partial success of the word.[158]

The exhortation to hear in 4:9. After Jesus has concluded the parable proper, and before he retires with his disciples, he adds the exhortation, "He who has ears to hear, let him hear!" This call to alertness, coming right after the mention of good soil in 4:8, links that soil with those who hear rightly.[159] It thus provides a bridge between the parable proper and 4:10-12, 13-20, passages in which the opposition that is part of the kingdom's mystery is explicated in terms of the division between the differing sorts of *hearers* of the word.

Already, 4:9 implies what 4:10-12, 13-20 make explicit, that not all can hear Jesus in the profound way that his message requires. Only "he who has ears to hear" is addressed by Jesus' exhortation. This designation of

---

[156]E. Schweizer, *Good News* 91. Cf. J. Gnilka, *Evangelium* 1.160, citing C. Dietzfelbinger.

[157]Cf. Justin, *Dial.* 125; *Clem. Rec.* 3.14; and Chrysostom *Hom. Matt.* 44.5, in all of which the Parable of the Sower is cited as warrant for continuing to preach the word in situations where one knows that one will be contradicted.

[158]See V. Fusco, *Parola* 325-29.

[159]G. Lindeskog ("Logia-Studien," *ST* 4 [1952] 157) terms 4:9 a *Deutewort* to the Parable of the Sower.

the true hearers is reminiscent of passages in the QL which speak of the
sectaries as those "whose ear is uncovered."[160] One of these passages, CD
2:2-3, is worthy of particular notice: "Therefore *hear* now, all you who
have entered the covenant, and *I will uncover your ear* (w'glh 'znkm)
concerning the ways of the wicked." As in Mark 4:9, an exhortation to
hear is combined with a recognition that such hearing only arises through
an act of God.[161]

If such passages provide significant background for Mark 4:9, then B.
Gerhardsson's hypothesis that the exhortation to hear, paradigmatically
expressed in the Shema, is vital for understanding the Parable of the
Sower,[162] must be qualified in an important way. Gerhardsson is right
about the relevance of the Shema for understanding Mark 4; Mark's audience could not have heard the repeated references to hearing in that
passage without being reminded of the Shema. The Parable of the Sower,
however, is not addressed to all of Israel in an undifferentiated manner, as
the Shema was in its original Deuteronomic setting and in rabbinic Judaism. Rather, at least in Mark's understanding, the parable is addressed
only to "him who has ears to hear,—let *him* hear." The Shema has thus
been modified in the direction of apocalyptic restriction and dualism.[163]

Such a modification is in accord with the Markan Jesus' one explicit
citation of the Shema, in Mark 12:29-30. In the context of this citation,
we read of some, like the scribe, who have ears to hear, and are not far
from the kingdom of God (12:34); and of others whose hearing is warped
by hypocrisy (12:15, 40) and error (12:24). Jesus' quotation of the Shema

---

[160]See P. Parente ("Un contibuto alla riconstruzione dell'apocalittica
cristiana originaria al lume degli scritti esseni rinvenuti nel deserto di
Giuda. Isaia 6.9-10 in Marco 4.12," *Rivista Storica Italiana* 74 [1962] 686-
87), who cites 1QM 10:11: Those "whose ears are uncovered and who hear
profound things."

[161]E. Schweizer, *Good News* 100.

[162]"Parable" 165-193. P. Parente ("Contributo" 686) asserts that 4:9,
23 also constitutes a paraphrase of the words "that hearing they may
hear" in Isa 6:9-10 as quoted in Mark 4:12. Isa 6:9-10 itself is an
apocalyptic-like modification of the theme of hearing expressed paradigmatically in the Shema.

[163]The movement toward such a modification had already begun in
some circles in OT times; see Deut 29:4: "But to this day the Lord has not
given you a mind to understand, or eyes to see, or ears to hear." This
passage is probably part of a second framework attached to Deuteronomy
in the exilic period; see E. Sellin and G. Fohrer, *Introduction to the Old
Testament* (Nashville: Abingdon, 1968) 176.

thus comes in the context of an apocalyptically divided Israel. Such a picture of a divided Israel, and more largely of a divided world, is of central importance in Mark. As P. Parente points out,[164] an image of a world divided into two mutually exclusive battle formations is implicit in Mark 9:40, "He that is not against us is for us."

Mark 4:9, then, both implicitly continues the theme of opposition found in the Parable of the Sower, and provides a bridge to 4:10-12, 13-20, in which this opposition is linked with the differing "responses"[165] of Jesus' hearers to his message.

The Interpretation

Points of continuity with the parable. We note first a basic continuity in theme and structure with the parable.[166] For Mark, the interpretation makes explicit what was implicit in the parable itself: the "mystery of the kingdom of God," the way in which, contrary to all expectation, the coming of God's kingdom is accompanied by opposition and failure, as human beings who have heard the word afterwards fall away from it.[167]

In terms of structure, as we have remarked, the interpretation, like the parable, moves from an introduction (v 13) to the figure of the sower (v 14) to the history of the seeds, which occupies its major focus (vv 15-20). The four-part structure of the interpretation is implicit in the binary parable, as we saw above.

Neither is the allegory of the interpretation a departure in principle from the mode of parable. As recent research has shown, A. Jülicher's

---

[164]"Contributo" 695.

[165]I have placed this word in quotation marks because of the complexity discussed below. Those who respond positively to Jesus do not do so autonomously.

[166]Consideration of the introduction to this interpretation, Jesus' question to the disciples (4:13), we will reserve for chapter 3.

[167]H. Koester remarks that, if the singular *mystērion* in Mark 4:11 corresponds to apocalyptic usage, then "'the mystery of the Kingdom' must be understood as the specific secret of the Kingdom of God and of its coming: its varied success as it is being established on earth." Koester ("Test Case" 40-41) also thinks it possible, however, that the singular *mystērion* corresponds not to apocalyptic usage but to that in the Deutero-Paulines, in which case the mystery of the kingdom would be equivalent to the Christian proclamation about Jesus Christ, i.e. the "mystery of the gospel" (Eph 6:19).

sharp distinction between parable and allegory is inaccurate, particularly where Semitic forms are concerned.[168] With regard to the Parable of the Sower specifically, we have already noted that seed is a fixed metaphor for God's word, and we have speculated that Mark's readers would have linked the seed in the parable with the word even before they arrived at the specific identification of 4:14. R. Pesch points to other elements in the parable that represent stock metaphors: the birds in v 4; the swift sprouting of the seed, and its scorching by the sun and withering because of rootlessness, in vv 5-6; and the thorns in v 7.[169]

Is the interpretation parenetic in character? Some scholars have seen a discontinuity between the parable and the interpretation in that the interpretation, unlike the parable, is thought to be parenetic. The arguments for this assertion, however, are weak, and the arguments against it are strong.

E. Schweizer,[170] for example, supports the parenetic interpretation by asserting that, if the thrust of this passage were consolation, the good seed would be highlighted more, and that in other passages Mark shows a tendency to convert proclamations of salvation into exhortations. Schweizer does not document the latter assertion, however, and as for the first, it can be consolatory to recognize that, although one's situation is indeed bad, the world is in God's hand, as Mark 4:14-20 strongly suggests.

J. Gnilka[171] asserts that the interpretation has a "*paranätische Ton*," and that its thrust is, "*Prove* that you are a believer!" He is never specific, however, about how the interpretation reveals this "note." His most concrete observation is that Mark has followed the interpretation with the parenetic 4:24-25. He ignores, however, the intervening 4:21-22, which implies that, at least for a time, God's truth *must* be hidden; this is consonant with an apologetic, rather than a parenetic, interpretation of 4:14-20.

Finally, while admitting that 4 Ezra uses the seed metaphor to describe

---

[168]See our discussion of allegorical exegesis below in chapter 5.

[169]*Markusevangelium* 1.232-33. On the portrait of the birds, cf. Job 11:11; on vv 5-6, cf. the similar picture in Jonah 4. Root is a common Palestinian metaphor, and in the post-exilic period the rooted = the just and the unrooted = the godless. Thorns are also a common OT image.

[170]*Good News* 98.

[171]*Markusevangelium* 1.176.

an unchangeable fate, H.-J. Klauck[172] distances 4 Ezra from Mark's parable by asserting that 4 Ezra is apocalyptic, whereas Mark's parable is not apocalyptic, since it suppresses the eschatological harvest. In the total Markan context of chapter 4, however, the harvest that is missing from 4:3-8 is supplied by 4:29. Furthermore, Klauck's is a restricted definition of apocalyptic; we have shown above that the Markan Parable of the Sower *is* apocalyptic, but in a peculiar and paradoxical way.[173] Klauck further asserts that Mark 4:14-20, like the visions in Shepherd of Hermas, is addressed to a group that has settled down for a long stay in the world. In terms of the *Markan* understanding of the interpretation, however, this exegesis is clearly false, since especially chapter 13 evidences a lively expectation of the parousia.[174]

Moreover, H.-W. Kuhn[175] and V. Fusco[176] have argued convincingly against the view that parenesis is the primary intent of the interpretation. Kuhn notes that the picture in vv 14-20 is unsuited to parenesis. The confusion about whether human beings are seed or soil already suggests that anthropology is not the central concern of the interpretation, and neither metaphor is consistent with parenesis. A soil cannot change the sort of soil it is, and, according to the logic of both the parable and the interpretation, part of the seed *must* be lost. The interpretation contains no specific warning, nor, as Fusco adds, does it use imperatives.

The first and third soils offer further evidence against a parenetic

---

[172] *Allegorie* 205.

[173] Klauck's comments assume that "apocalyptic" is synonymous with "eschatological." For a good criticism of this common identification, see C. Rowland, *The Open Heaven: A Study of Apocalyptic in Judaism and Early Christianity* (New York: Crossroad, 1982) 23-48. Rowland's own definition of apocalyptic emphasizes revelation of divine mysteries (ibid., 70-72), but such a definition provides no method for distinguishing apocalyptic from prophecy on the one hand or Gnosticism on the other. In order to produce a useful definition, the theme of revelation must be combined with the elements noted by P. Vielhauer (*New Testament Apocrypha* [E. Hennecke and W. Schneemelcher, eds.; Philadelphia: Westminster, 1964] 2.582-600): the doctrine of the two ages, pessimism about this world, a hope for the future that bursts national boundaries, and determinism. All of these motifs are present in the Markan Parable of the Sower, as is the motif of divine mysteries, since for Mark the parable reveals the mystery of the kingdom.

[174] See especially 13:14, 28-31.

[175] *Sammlungen* 116-119.

[176] *Parola* 329-31.

interpretation. In the first soil (v 15), as Kuhn points out, the word *euthys*, "immediately," excludes any notion of testing. In the third soil (vv 18-19), as Fusco notes, people are presented as the helpless victims of attack from outside. Furthermore, Fusco adds, the *good soil* is not allegorized in a parenetic manner, although the different yields would have provided a perfect opportunity for parenesis.

Finally, considering the Parable of the Sower and its interpretation in their context within chapter 4, Kuhn notes that the phrase *kathōs ēdynanto akouein*, "as they were able to hear," in 4:33, excludes parenesis. Here ability to hear is divinely given, not something that can be improved. We might add that 4:9, 11-12 point in the same direction.

The apocalyptic character of the interpretation. Kuhn's last point is related to his analysis of the apocalyptic nature of the interpretation, in support of which he cites specific vocabulary: *Satanas*, "Satan," *thlipsis*, "tribulation," and *aiōn*, which here means "this age." More important than vocabulary, however, is the apocalyptic determinism that, as we have seen, underlies the picture of human beings as seed or soil, and subject to outside powers. As P. Bonnard puts it, the allegory is "dramatic, satanological, rather than psychological and pietist."[177]

Indeed, Satan is a major actor in the interpretation. He is specifically mentioned in v 15, but it is difficult to believe that his presence is restricted to that verse. Verse 19 describes a host of evils "entering in" and choking the word; what we would call psychological factors are here personified and endued with malicious intent. Even the more anthropological description in vv 16-17 presents human existence in a way that would be unrecognizable to the humans described, and thus represents an "apocalypse" of their existence.[178]

The spectrum in vv 15-20 between a thoroughly demonological description of why people fall away (v 15), a moderately demonological description (vv 18-19), and a mainly anthropological description (vv 16-17), is

---

[177]Cited by C. E. Carlston, *Parables* 144 n. 27. Cf. B. Gerhardsson ("Parable" 179-82), who notes that Mark's version of the interpretation is more apocalyptic than Matthew's, in that it places more emphasis on external causes.

[178]The people described would not ascribe their lack of endurance to a lack of "root in themselves"; they would probably say that what Mark calls apostasy was actually a new-found realism.

G. Eicholz (*Gleichnisse* 81) speaks of the interpretation as "an apocalypse of man as hearer of the word."

itself significant, as it indicates what J. L. Martyn has described as the "bi-focal" epistemology of apocalyptic writings.[179] In apocalyptic, only one who, like the attentive reader of Mark 4:14-20, sees *both* earthly realities *and* the heavenly realities that stand behind them (thus "bifo-cally") has true insight into them. The alternation in vv 15-20 between more anthropological and more demonological explanations of human sin is also found in other apocalyptic texts.[180]

Although we have spoken above of an "alternation" between anthropo-logical and demonological explanations of sin, it is clear that these two ways of describing reality are not of equal weight in Mark. The interpre-tation of the bad soils in Parable of the Sower *first* mentions Satan (v 15), then moves on to a more or less anthropological description (vv 16-17), then concludes with a personification that approaches demonology (vv 18-19), so that the demonological descriptions "frame" the more anthropolog-ical one. For Mark, earthly realities cannot be truly perceived without perception of the heavenly realities that stand behind them; otherwise one is in touch only with an appearance.[181]

Thus, as S. Freyne puts it, "The understanding of the parables becomes

---

[179] See "From Paul to Flannery O'Connor with the Power of Grace," *Katallagete* 6 (1981) 12.

[180] See for example 1QH 4:12-14. In 4:12-13, we hear a demonological explanation for the sin of the hypocrites, the "thought of Belial." In 4:14 we hear a more anthropological explanation: "A root is in their thoughts bearing fruits that are poisoned and bitter." Cf. CD 20:1-13, where the apostate is described both as one "who has melted in the midst of the furnace," an anthropological description, and one whose "lot has not fallen among the disciples of God." CD 4:15-18 combines the two types of expla-nations in a manner that is significant for understanding Mark 4:15-20: the three nets of Belial are lust, riches, and defilement of the sanctuary (cf. the reference to lust and wealth in Mark 4:19). Preoccupations such as those depicted in Mark 4:19, then, are tools of Satan for the destruction of human beings.

In the QL generally, sin is sometimes ascribed to the Angel of Dark-ness, sometimes to the Evil Impulse. On the whole subject of the human will and supernatural powers in the QL, see G. Maier, *Mensch und freier Wille. Nach dem jüdischen Religionspartien zwischen Ben Sira und Paulus* (WUNT 12; Tübingen: Mohr/Siebeck, 1971) 165-205.

[181] J. M. Robinson, *The Problem of History in Mark and other Marcan Studies* (Philadelphia: Fortress, 1982; orig. 1957) 125, and J. Marcus, "Mark 4:10-12" 557-58.

one aspect of the cosmic conflict between Jesus and Satan."[182] Indeed, as
we have noted above in our discussion of the parable itself, Jesus' proclamation of the word actually *provokes* the opposition, as the interpretation
makes even more clear. When the word is sown, *immediately* Satan comes
and removes it (4:15); persecution arises *on account of the word* (4:17);
the cares of the age, the deceitfulness of riches, and other desires, as if
stirred to hatred, come in and *choke the word* (4:19).

In the rest of the Gospel, as in 4:14-20, Jesus' work and word are presented as a battle against Satan.[183] Of particular relevance for 4:14-20 is
comparison with 8:32-33. Here concern with *ta tōn anthrōpōn*, "the things
of human beings," as opposed to *ta tou theou*, "the things of God," is
attributed to Satan, just as in 4:14-20 the "cares of this age" belong to the
same field of force as Satan.

By unmasking the cosmic forces behind acceptance or rejection of the
word, Mark speaks to his community a word of empowerment. Defections
from God's word are not a sign that the word is impotent, but rather
testimony to its power, in that it can provoke such a strong counter-
reaction. Moreover, as J. L. Martyn has suggested, after his description of
the "bad soil" in 4:15-19, Mark turns to his own congregation in 4:20,
perhaps even expecting that, when the passage is read in the Markan
community, the reader will indicate his audience with a gesture: "But
these are those sown on good soil, who hear the word and accept it and
bear fruit!"[184]

---

[182]"Disciples" 16. Cf. the Freer Logion. When Jesus reproaches the
disciples for their incredulity and obstinance, they excuse themselves by
saying that this age is "under Satan," who "does not allow those under the
yoke of unclean spirits to understand God's truth and power."

[183]J. Schniewind (*Das Evangelium nach Markus* [8th ed.; NTD 1;
Göttingen: Vandenhoeck & Ruprecht, 1958; orig. 1933] 45), citing 1:23-28;
3:22-27; cf. J. Kallas, *Jesus and the Power of Satan* (Philadelphia: Westminster, 1968) 20-28. This battle is apparent, not only in the specific
references to Satan himself, but also in the frequent stories of Jesus'
exorcisms in the first part of the Gospel.

An interesting difference between 3:23-27 and 4:15 is that, in the
former, *Jesus* seems to be the usurper of a cosmos under the control of
Satan, whereas in the latter *Satan* is the usurper who casts out Jesus'
word. Both passages, however, speak of the mutual enmity between the
kingdom of God and that of Satan.

[184]Oral suggestion; cf. above n. 37 on *ekeinoi* as referring to "well-
known persons."

Points of development beyond the parable. In terms of structure, metaphor, and apologetic intent, the interpretation of the Parable of the Sower is in basic continuity with the parable itself. On the other hand, since the interpretation is probably from a later stratum of tradition than the parable itself, it is not surprising that it reflects a certain development beyond the parable.

Several points of discontinuity between parable and interpretation have been alluded to in the course of this study. We have mentioned, for example, that the interpretation devotes proportionally more space to failure than does the basically optimistic parable. Morever, the four-part structure of the interpretation focuses attention on specific groups of people, whereas the binary structure of the parable focuses attention more on the simple fact of the clash between the kingdom of God and that of Satan.

The groups of people described in 4:15-20. The groups pictured in 4:15-20 conform in general outline to groups encountered in the Gospel's narrative.[185] For example, those "along the way," from whom Satan immediately removes the word (4:15), are Jesus' determined enemies, the scribes and Pharisees, who from the start of the Gospel oppose him with blind fury.[186]

The rocky soil consists of those who immediately receive the word with gladness, but fail to persevere when persecution "on account of the word" arises. On the one hand, we might think of the crowd in 12:37, which *hears* Jesus *gladly,* but in the Passion Narrative turns against him (15:11-14); cf. 6:20, where Herod's initial response to the preaching of John the Baptist is described in nearly identical words.

However, the reference in 4:16 to *persecution on account of the word* makes it more likely that Mark's readers would have understood the people described in 4:16-17 as unfaithful disciples. The word *proskairoi* in 4:17 points in the same direction, since this rare word has martyrological connotations, referring to those who, when confronted with a choice

---

[185]Cf. R. E. Brown, "Parable and Allegory" 264 and X. Leon-Dufour, "Parabole" 283-84. For a comparison with the groups in the book of Daniel, see S. Freyne, "Disciples" 10.

[186]In 2:1-12 Jesus "preaches the word" and for the first time encounters the scribes, who accuse him of blasphemy, and later make plans to destroy him (3:6), because they ascribe his exorcisms to Satan (3:22). Thus from the beginning of Mark they respond negatively to Jesus' "sowing" of the word.

between martyrdom for the kingdom of God and apostasy for the sake of the things of this age, choose the latter.[187]

Can the identity of these unfaithful disciples be determined any more closely? Should they be linked, for example, with the Twelve, as some American scholars assert?[188] Certain clues might at first seem to point in this direction, e.g. the picture in 14:50-52 of the Twelve forsaking Jesus when the "tribulation" of his arrest arises. D. Rhoads and D. Michie even suggest that there is a link between Peter's nickname "the Rock" (3:16) and the rocky soil of the Parable of Sower.[189]

In the broader context of the Gospel, however, such conjectures fail to convince. Jesus' promise in 14:27-28, which is reiterated by the angel in 16:7, is not annulled by the disciples' temporary abandonment of him in the Passion Narrative; indeed, as 14:27 indicates, that abandonment has been forseen, but the promise of 14:28 still holds good.[190] The bad soil in our parable is not to be identified with those who turn away from Jesus and refuse to hear him *once*, but with those who continually resist his word and call.

There are numerous indications in the Gospel that the Twelve (minus Judas) belong in the end not to the group represented by the bad soils but to that represented by the good soil. In 10:28-31 they are *contrasted* to the rich man (who, like the thorny soil in 4:18-19, has been led astray by the "deceitfulness of riches"), in that they have given up everything "for the sake of the gospel," and will therefore receive the hundredfold reward of the kingdom (cf. 4:20)—with persecutions.[191] Although in 10:40 a promise of places on Jesus' right and left hand is withheld from James and

---

[187]See B. Gerhardsson ("Parable" 176), who cites 4 Macc 15:2, 8, 23; 2 Cor 4:17-18; Heb 11:25; Diog. 10:8; cf. H.-J. Klauck, *Allegorie* 203. In the 4 Maccabees text, the mother of the seven martyrs rejects the temptation of being swayed by a desire for her sons' *proskairos sōtēria*, "temporal safety," and is enabled to overcome her *proskairon philoteknian*, "temporal love of children." Gerhardsson suggests that *proskairos* be translated, "having the inconsistency of time itself." Given some of the usages of *kairos* in Mark, however (1:15; 10:30), a better translation of *proskairos* in his Gospel might be, "marked by the inconstancy of this age."

[188]See especially T. J. Weeden, *Traditions* and W. H. Kelber, *The Kingdom in Mark* (Philadelphia: Fortress, 1974), and more recently *The Oral and the Written Gospel* (Philadelphia: Fortress, 1983).

[189]D. Rhoads and D. Michie, *Mark as Story* 128.

[190]See E. Best, "The Role of the Disciples in Mark," *NTS* 23 (1977) 377-401, esp. 388-389.

[191]See E. Nardoni, "Interpretation" 372.

John, 10:39 makes evident that they *will* be baptized with the same baptism and drink from the same cup as Jesus will, i.e. they will die martyrs' deaths.[192] Again, in 13:9-13 Jesus predicts that they will suffer great hatred and persecution for his sake, but that in the midst of this persecution they will preach the word with the power of the Spirit. Those who endure to the end, Jesus adds, will be saved.[193]

Thus the Twelve should be linked, not with those who "fall away immediately" when persecution arises (4:17),[194] but with those who persevere in persecution, who "hear the word and accept it and bear fruit, thirtyfold and sixtyfold and a hundredfold" (4:20).[195] If, in the Gospel, they are portrayed as unperceptive, even blind, if Jesus can address Peter as "Satan" (8:33), if, at Gethsemane, they forsake Jesus, this portrait of them serves two main purposes.

First, it underlines the power of the kingdom that is arrayed against that of God, a dominion so mighty that it can reach even into the elect community, "to lead astray, if it were possible, the very elect" (13:22). In so doing, the portrait of the disciples implicitly points to Jesus as the only ray in the darkness;[196] the disciples' hope of renewed fellowship with him rests, not on their protestations of faithfulness to him (14:29-31), nor on any other human capability, but solely on his promise to reveal himself to them (14:28; 16:7). Second, this portrait points up the difference between the pre-Easter and post-Easter periods, since the cowardice of the pre-Easter disciples contrasts sharply with the boldness that Jesus prophesies of them e.g. in 13:9-13.

The thorny soil (4:18-19), then, stands for those like the rich young man

---

[192]J. Gnilka, *Evangelium,* 2.102.

[193]13:13 has a conditional note to it, and 13:22 says that things will get so bad "as to lead astray, if possible, the elect." The purpose of both statements, however, is hortatory, and the qualifier "if possible" in 13:22 suggests that Mark finds it difficult to conceive such an eventuality, but is rather stating that the endurance of the faithful will be tested to the limit. 13:22 presents the apostasy of the elect in a purpose clause (*pros to*), not in a future indicative; the purpose is probably that of Satan.

[194]Cf. Jerome's pastoral comment (*In Matt.,* CChrSL 77.105, ad Matt 13:21): In speaking of those who *immediately* fall away when persecution arises, Jesus is distinguishing them from those who, because of *many* tribulations and tortures, eventually deny their faith.

[195]Cf. the hundredfold "yield" that the disciples receive in 10:30.

[196]Cf. E. Best ("Role" 388, 399), who describes the disciples as a "foil" for Jesus.

in 10:17-22, whose riches seduce them into making the wrong choice concerning the kingdom,[197] and the good soil of 4:20 stands for faithful disciples of Jesus. In the Gospel as a whole, models of faith are presented not only by the Twelve and other disciples who are associated with them (cf. 4:10), but also by faithful individuals who are healed by Jesus or who request healing for others (2:1-5; 5:25-34; 7:24-30; 9:14-29; 10:46-52),[198] and by the centurion (15:33-39). It is the disciples, however, who will persevere faithfully and bear fruit in the midst of persecution, so that they are the primary referent of 4:20.[199]

The Gospel also presents examples of the *division* between good and bad soil which the Parable of the Sower depicts. In 10:17-31, one party is choked by the "deceitfulness of wealth" (10:22-25), while others are good soil and receive a miraculous bounty (10:28-31).[200] In 11:18-19, the high priests and scribes, when they *hear* Jesus' teaching, seek to destroy him; cf. the soil on the path in the parable. The crowd, on the other hand, is "astonished" at his teaching, but this astonishment does not amount to deeply rooted faith, as later events will show (15:11-15); cf. the rocky soil. Immediately afterward, in 11:20-25, Jesus calls his disciples to have faith, so that the good soil also is in view.

---

[197]Already *Herm. Sim.* 9.20.2 links Mark 4:18-19 with Mark 10:23. Other examples of people in the Gospel whose "worldly" concerns similarly stand in the way of their entry into the kingdom might include the Gerasenes, whose plea to Jesus to leave their borders may be based at least partly on an economic consideration, the loss of their swine (5:14-17); Herod, whose anxiety not to lose face is greater than his anxiety to spare John the Baptist's life (6:26); and Judas, who receives money for betraying Jesus (14:11).

[198]In the cases of both the woman with the hemorhhage (5:25-34) and the Syro-Phoenician woman (7:24-30) the chain of events leading up to the healing starts with the woman *hearing* about Jesus. Hearing itself, however, is not enough; the woman with the hemorhhage moves forward to *touch* Jesus, and the Syro-Phoenician woman must persevere in the face of the temptation to despair, seeing the promise hidden in the apparent rejection of Jesus' first reply. Cf. 4:20; the people described there "hear *and* accept" the word.

[199]Cf. E. Best ("Role" 390-396, esp. 392), who contrasts the role of the disciples (including the Twelve and other groups) with that of the crowd. One of the points of difference is that the latter "are not given a position in the post-resurrection period."

[200]Jesus looks upon (*emblepsas*) both the rich young man (10:21) and the disciples (10:27), thus emphasizing the division.

The Kerygma of the Parable of the Sower for the Markan Community: Mark 4:3-9, 13-20 as a Two-Level Narrative

In spite of links between Jesus' disciples and the "good soil," in the time-frame pictured by the Gospel itself there are no consistent examples of good soil. Individuals who are healed by Jesus, and even the centurion, do not have their faith tested by "persecution on account of the word." The disciples, whose faith *is* tested, abandon Jesus, and flee. Their restoration, their endurance of persecution for Jesus' sake, lies beyond the end of the Gospel. It is true that the persecution which will cause others to fall away (4:17) is a trial the disciples will endure, and in the midst of which they will bear fruit (4:20). We have already pointed out, however, that this persecution points toward a *Sitz im Leben* in post-Easter Christian communities. The use of the word *ekeinoi* in 4:20 would have directed the attention of Mark's hearers to well-known persons: the members of his own community.

Furthermore, we have noted that, while the predominant tense in the Parable of the Sower is the aorist, the predominant tense in its intepretation is the present; in the former, the world is narrated, while in the latter, it is discussed. In addition, we have seen that, while from the immediate context of the parable, Mark leads his readers to connect the sower with Jesus, yet he transmits an interpretation which conspicuously fails to allegorize the sower.

All of these data add up to the conclusion that, in the parable itself, the primary horizon is the time of Jesus' ministry, while in the interpretation, the primary horizon is the time of the church.[201] The parable is narrated in the past, because it deals with the past; the interpretation is narrated in the present, because it deals with the present. The sower is not specifically allegorized in the interpretation because, in the present, Jesus continues to sow his word through Christian missionaries. To adopt

---

[201] For Mark, writing perhaps in the late sixties or early seventies, the "time of the church" has already existed for about forty years, and Mark draws on traditions that come to him from the earliest post-resurrectional preaching (e.g. the parables themselves) and from an intermediate stage of church history (e.g. the interpretation of the Parable of the Sower). For the purposes of this study, however, the earliest post-resurrectional stage and the intermediate stage can be amalgamated with Mark's own time in the "time of the church"; all three belong to the epoch after the Son of Man has risen from the dead (9:9) but before his coming in the clouds with power and glory (13:26).

the terminology of J. L. Martyn's study of the Fourth Gospel,[202] Jesus is "doubled" with evangelists who are members of the Markan community, and Mark 4:3-9, 13-20 represents a "two-level" narrative. The continuity between these two "levels" is provided by Jesus' word, which endures forever (13:31), and which, through the Spirit, becomes the word of the church (13:11).[203]

For Mark's hearers, then, our passage alludes both to the present and to the past, in order to link them. The present to which it calls attention, as we have seen, is not a pleasant one. The Markan community is experiencing "tribulation." The interpretation puts more emphasis on failure than does the parable itself, because the community knows that Jesus' story had a joyful ending, while in its own situation there seems to be a real possibility that frustration of its mission, apostasy, and extermination will speak the last word.

To such a suffering community, our text addresses a word of empowerment. In the sufferings of the present, the community is recapitulating Jesus' own way, experiencing, as he did, the "mystery of the kingdom of God," not least *in the form of the opposition* that is provoked by the preaching of the word. Thus the situation of Jesus' ministry, which is pictured in the Parable of the Sower, illuminates the true situation of the Markan community, pictured in the interpretation.

The illumination, however, also extends the other way, from the fate of the Markan community backward to the fate of Jesus. In our exegesis of the Parable of the Sower and its interpretation, we have emphasized that, although the "mystery of the kingdom of God" *has been given* in the parable, *comprehension* of that mystery does not take place without the allegorical explanation. If we take seriously the link between the explanation and the post-Easter period, then the conclusion follows: As the

---

[202] *History and Theology in the Fourth Gospel* (2d ed.; Nashville: Abingdon, 1979; orig. 1968), esp. 27-30.

[203] A. Ambrozic (*Hidden Kingdom* 13) points out the continuity between Jesus' proclamation of the gospel (1:14-15) and that of the community (13:9-11). Cf. V. Fusco (*Parola* 338): The "word" in the Parable of the Sower is both that of Jesus and that of the church. Already in antiquity, the sower was interpreted both as Jesus (Clement of Alexandria, *Strom.* 1.7.37; cited by A. Jülicher, *Gleichnisreden* 2.534) and as the Christian preacher (*Herm. Sim.* 9.20.2; Justin, *Dial.* 125; *Clem. Rec.* 3:14). Theophylact (PG 123.797) seems to recognize the continuity between the two levels in his comment on our parable: "But the Son of God never ceases to sow in our hearts."

parable is not understandable without its interpretation, so the clash between God's kingdom and that of Satan which occurred in the ministry, death, and resurrection of Jesus, cannot be understood by the Markan community except as that community recapitulates Jesus' way. Mark's hearers themselves comprehend the "mystery of the kingdom of God" as they sustain the brunt of Satan's assault, and find themselves empowered by the life of God's kingdom which bursts forth wondrously in the midst of tribulation. As they face this assault and receive this empowerment, they see what was utterly incomprehensible before, the necessity of Jesus' suffering and death (8:31-33; 9:30-32; cf. 10:32-34).

Our text, then, evidences a certain melding between the time of Jesus and the time of the church, and yet those two periods maintain their distinctiveness. The relation of these periods to each other and to the parousia will be studied more closely below, in chapters 4, 5, and 6.

3

The "Parable Theory"
(Mark 4:10–12, 33–34)

TRANSLATION

4:10a   And when he was alone,

4:10b   those around him with the Twelve asked him the parables.

4:11a   And he said to them, To you the mystery of the kingdom of God has been given,

4:11b   but to those outside all things happen in parables

4:12a   in order that looking they may look, but not see,

4:12b   and hearing they may hear, but not understand,

4:12c   lest they turn and it be forgiven them.

* * * * *

4:33a   And with many such parables he used to speak[1] to them the word,

4:33b   as they were able to hear.

4:34a   Without a parable he would not speak to them,

4:34b   but privately, to his own disciples, he used to explain all things.

---

[1]I translate the imperfects in vv 33–34 as repeated, rather than continuous, actions in the past, because of the generalizing nature of v 34b; see especially the word *panta*, "all things."

LITERARY ANALYSIS

Structure

The structure of Mark 4:10-12. The importance of Mark 4:10-12 is rhetorically highlighted by the change of scene in 4:10a; the passage occupies a position of honor as one of the "secret teachings" of Jesus.[2] The passage falls into two unequal parts: the disciples' question (4:10) and Jesus' reply (4:11-12). Thematically, the focus passes from Jesus (4:10a) to the disciples (4:10b-11a) to "those outside" (4:11b-12).[3]

In 4:10-11a, the subject switches from Jesus (4:10a) to "those around him with the Twelve" (4:10b) and back to Jesus (beginning of 4:11a). Even when the subject switches to the disciples, however, they are described in relation to Jesus: they are "those about *him*," and they ask *him* about the parables. Jesus' prominence in relation to them is also emphasized by the singular verb *egeneto* ("he was") in 4:10, whereas a plural would be more logical: Jesus is *not* alone; the disciples are with him.[4] The second half of 4:10 is also awkward, in view of the redundancy of its subject, "those around him with the Twelve"; "those around him" could be assumed to *include* the Twelve, Jesus' closest disciples.

Jesus' saying in 4:11-12 has two different subjects: "the mystery of the kingdom of God" and "all things." It thus falls into two parts, 4:11a and 4:11b-12, which are unified by the divine passives *dedotai* (4:11a) and

---

[2]Already, this observation challenges the contention of E. Schweizer ("Frage" 4-7) in which he is followed by H. Räisänen (*Die Parabeltheorie im Markusevangelium* [Schriften der Finnischen Exegetischen Gesellschaft 28; Helsinki, 1976] 27-33) that the esotericism of the pre-Markan 4:11-12 is in conflict with Markan theology. We have already supported the opinion that Mark 4:11-12 was introduced into its present context by *Mark.* More importantly, we question the sort of redaction criticism that takes its bearings almost exclusively from those verses identified as editorial, at the expense of the present literary shape of the chapter. See B. Childs (*Introduction to the Old Testament as Scripture* [Philadelphia: Fortress, 1979] 300) on the necessity of attempting "to understand the effect of a redactional layer on the text itself."

[3]If we count words, the third group receives the lion's share of the attention (26 words), as much as Jesus and the disciples combined (5 + 21 words).

[4]Contrast 6:32, where the disciples are included in Jesus' being alone by the plural verb *apēlthon,* "they went away."

aphethē (4:12b).[5] The two parts are contrasted, however, by the adversative *de* in 4:11b and the inclusion between the dative plurals *ekeinois* and *autois*, which set 4:11b-12 off from 4:11a. As V. Fusco has observed,[6] 4:11-12 is not evenly balanced; its second part (vv 11b-12), which contains one main clause and two dependent clauses, is much longer than its first part (v 11a).

4:11 by itself, on the other hand, is nicely balanced. J. A. Baird[7] has diagrammed its elements as follows:

1. the mystery of the kingdom of God	all things
2. has been given	happen
3. to you	to those out-side
4. (with explanations)	in parables

Our only major reservation about Baird's schematization is the phrase in parentheses. In chapter 2 we have followed J. L. Martyn's lead in claiming that the parentheses should contain the words "in parables." In 4:11 "explanations" have not yet been given, whereas "parables" *have* been given, so that the perfect *dedotai* makes more sense according to Martyn's hypothesis than according to Baird's.[8]

A minor limitation of Baird's diagram is that, following common English word order, it puts the subject first. In both main clauses of Mark 4:11-12, however, the dative plurals "to you" and "to those outside" are in the first place; this order emphasizes the *division* between the disciples and the outsiders. The latter group is described in an extremely "distancing" way; already *ekeinois* implies distance, and this impression is heightened by *tois exō*.

The separation (not conveyed in English translations) of the subject of

---

[5]On these verbs as "circumlocutions for divine activity," see J. Jeremias, *Parables* 15.

[6]"L'áccord mineur Mt 13,11a/Lk 8,10a contre Mc 4,11a," *Logia. Les Paroles de Jesus. Memorial Joseph Coppens* (ed. J. Delobel; BETL 59; Leuven University: Peeters, 1982) 355.

[7]"A Pragmatic Approach to Parable Exegesis: Some New Evidence on Mark 4:11, 33-34," *JBL* 76 (1957) 201-207. Baird's diagram is helpful in correcting J. Jeremias' assertion (*Parables* 16) that the words "mystery" and "parables" correspond; the parallel to "mystery" is not "parables" but "all things."

[8]On the plural *parabolas* in 4:10, see above, chapter 2, n. 107.

4:11a, *to mystērion* ("the mystery") from its genitive *tēs basileias tou theou* ("of the kingdom of God") by the verb *dedotai* ("has been given") emphasizes the importance of "the mystery of the kingdom";[9] it also balances what would otherwise be an unwieldy nominal phrase.[10] 4:11a contains one of the so-called "minor agreements" of Matthew and Luke against Mark. Both Matt 13:11 and Luke 8:10 read, *hymin dedotai gnōnai ta mystēria tēs basileias*, "to you has been given to know the mysteries of the kingdom," rather than Mark's *hymin to mystērion dedotai tēs basileias*, "to you has been given the mystery of the kingdom." Thus both Matthew and Luke have "mystery" in the plural as opposed to Mark's singular, and both have the infinitive "to know" which Mark lacks. Furthermore, Matthew and Luke agree in keeping "mysteries" together with its genitive "of the kingdom," rather than splitting the genitive off from "mystery," as Mark does. Various ways of assessing this "agreement" will be discussed below. In the citation of Isaiah 6:9-10 in Mark 4:12 the order "hearing" and "seeing" found in the OT texts (MT, LXX, Targum) is reversed. The citation agrees with the Targum in the phrase "and it be forgiven them" and in the use of third person verbs in 4:12ab, as opposed to the second person verbs of the MT and the LXX.[11] In Mark's version, all the finite verbs of 4:12ab are in the subjunctive, controlled by the *hina* at the beginning of 4:12.

All three clauses in 4:12 show the same overall pattern, although vv 12a and 12b are closer to each other than to 12c. The overall pattern is:

conjunction   + verb in   + *kai*   + verb in
                 subjunctive   subjunctive

V 12c, however, departs from the pattern of v 12ab in lacking participles and the negative particle *mē*,[12] and in having the pronoun *autois* at its end. The more exact correspondence of v 12a and v 12b can be schematized:

---

[9] See *BDF* §473: separation of elements that belong together, such as nouns and their dependent genitives, gives greater effect to the separated elements.

[10] V. Fusco, "L'accord" 359.

[11] A convenient chart of all the OT versions of Isa 6:9-10, together with Synoptic citations, is given in J. Gnilka, *Verstockung* 14-15. On the reversal of "hearing" and "seeing," see H. Koester, "Test Case" 44. The first commentator to notice the congruence between Mark 4:12 and the Targum was T. W. Manson, *Teaching* 75-80.

[12] Cf. however *mēpote* at the beginning of v 12c.

conj.	+ present	+ same verb	+ *kai mē*	+ related vb.
	participle	in present		in aor.
	m. pl. nom.	subjunctive		subj. 3 pl.
		3 pl.		

V 12a and v 12b are also closely connected by the *kai* at the beginning of
4:12b. According to H. Koester, the departure in 4:12c from the exact
parallelism of 4:12a and 4:12b gives particular emphasis to the last
clause,[13] which on the basis of content alone (the intention that the
outsiders should neither repent nor be forgiven) is striking enough.

The structure of Mark 4:33-34. These verses, which conclude Mark's
"parable chapter," consist of three clauses (4:33, 34a, and 34b) that are
linked by two instances of *de*. Each clause contains a verb in the imperfect denoting Jesus' speaking (*elalei* ["he would speak"] in vv 33a, 34a,
epelyen ["he would explain"] in v 34b), but the clauses are dominated by
adverbial phrases that modify these verbs ("with many such parables,"
"without a parable," "privately to his own disciples"). The verbs take two
objects: *ton logon* ("the word," v 33a) and *panta* ("all things," v 34b).

Vv 33a and 34a parallel each other closely, *ouk elalei autois* ("he would
not speak to them") in 34a corresponding to *elalei autois* ("he would speak
to them") in v 33a, and both clauses being introduced by adverbial phrases
having to do with parables. V. Fusco[14] asserts that vv 33b and 34b also
correspond to each other, so that overall the passage has an ABA'B' structure. We think Fusco is right, although the correspondence is not as close
as that between vv 33a and 34a, and for a significant reason: the crowd's
hearing is contrasted, not with the disciples' hearing, but rather with
Jesus' revelation to them. As Fusco observes,[15] v 33b interrupts a series
of propositions whose subject is Jesus (vv 33a, 34a, 34b).

Turning now to the individual clauses in our passage, we notice first the
structurally prominent place assigned to parables in v 33a. Not only are
parables the first thing mentioned in the clause, but they are also emphasized by the number of words assigned to them (three out of the eight in v
33a) and by the emphatic word "many."

Two peculiarities about v 33a attract notice. First, as H. Koester

---

[13]"Test Case" 44.
[14] *Parola* 167-68.
[15] *Parola* 165.

points out, the phrase for speaking in parables, *lalein parabolais,* departs
from the usual Markan *lalein en parabolais* (3:23; 4:2; 12:1).[16]

Second, the referent of *autois* ("to them") is not at first clear. The
initial impulse of the hearer of Mark's Gospel would probably be to identify "them" as the disciples, since the scene change at 4:10 restricted
Jesus' following words to the disciples, and there has been no specific
reintroduction of the crowd. By the time the reader reaches 4:34, however, he has to change his mind, since the *autois* in v 34a (which corresponds to that in v 33a) is *contrasted* to Jesus' "own disciples" in v 34b.
For Mark, then, *autois* in v 33a, 34a must refer to the crowd.[17]

Turning our attention to 4:34, we see that, although the main structural
similarity is between vv 33a and 34a (see above), there is also a certain
degree of parallelism between v 34a and v 34b:

chōris	*de*	*parabolēs*		*ouk elalei*	*autois*
prep.	+ *de* +	noun	+	verb	+	ind. obj.

kat' idian de		*tois idiois mathētais*	*epelyen*	*panta*
adverb	+ *de* +	noun phrase	+	verb	+	dir. obj.

In v 34a, as in v 33a, the centrality of parables is accentuated by the
placement of the phrase about parables at the beginning of the clause.
This emphasis is heightened by the litotes, "Without a parable he did not
speak . . ."

Two words in v 34b, *de* and *idios,* deserve comment. Another *de* following the one in v 34a is surprising. Although the *de* in v 34b is adversative,
whereas that in v 34a is copulative, the combination of the two is still

---

[16]"Test Case" 47-48. 4:33 is the only instance to lack *en.*

[17]The private instruction begun in 4:10 probably comes to an end at
4:25; see below, chapter 4. The referent of *autoi* in 4:21, then, is the same
as in 4:11, 13 (the disciples), but different from the referent in 4:2, 33.
(*Autoi* in 4:33 is not *identical* with *autoi* in 4:2, though they are related;
see below, n. 52.)
Although it is possible that Mark's lack of specificity about when the
crowd reenters is inadvertent, it is also possible that he did not *wish* to
make the transition back to public discourse too clear, since the impression of mystery, in a chapter which has as its main theme "the mystery of
the kingdom of God," is thereby enhanced.

awkward.[18] By using this adversative *de* in v 34b, Mark contrasts Jesus' behavior vis-à-vis the disciples with his behavior vis-à-vis those from the crowd who do not become disciples. This contrast is further brought out by the repetition of *idios* in v 34b; Jesus speaks to his "own" (*idiois*) disciples "privately" (*kat' idian*). This repetition serves to identify the disciples in a programmatic way as the recipients of Jesus' special instruction.

The "law" of end-stress leads interpreters to give special attention to v 34b,[19] as do the adversative *de* and the emphatic phrase "his own disciples."[20] The focus in v 34b on the disciples corresponds to that of v 11a, whereas the focus on the crowd in vv 33-34a corresponds to that of 4:11b-12. Overall, then, if one juxtaposes the "parable theory" passages, one notes an ABB'A' structure:

4:11a	disciples
4:11b-12	"outsiders"
4:33-34a	"outsiders"
4:34b	disciples

The disciples are mentioned first and last, yet many more words are devoted to the outsiders than to them. This proportion and arrangement is similar to that in the Parable of the Sower and its interpretation: more attention is given to the bad soil than to the good soil, yet the good soil occupies the emphatic position at the end of the parable.

* * * * *

Our analysis of the structure of the "parable theory" passages has turned up several surprising or awkward constructions. We have noted the singular verb in v 10a and the awkward subject in v 10b, the accord of Matthew with Luke against Mark in v 11, and the agreement of Mark with the Targum in v 12. We have also seen the unusual phrase for speaking in

---

[18]On the difference between these two usages of *de*, see H. W. Smyth, *Greek Grammar* (Cambridge, Mass.: Harvard University, 1956; orig. 1920) §§2835 and 2836.

[19]V. Fusco, *Parola* 141.

[20]Contrast E. Schweizer ("Frage" 4-7), whose interpretation of vv 33-34 puts all the emphasis on the "positive" message of v 33b. Furthermore, as we will show below, in *Mark's* mind at least, the import of v 33b is negative.

parables, the unclear referent of "to them," and the two instances of *de* in vv 33-34. All of these features will prove to be relevant in the following discussion of the composition history of vv 10-12, 33-34.

Composition History

The composition history of Mark 4:10-12. We have demonstrated in chapter 2 above the probability that before Mark the Parable of the Sower was joined to its interpretation by some earlier form of 4:10, probably in conjunction with 4:13a. In this earlier form of 4:10, Jesus was asked, not about the parables, plural, but about the parable, singular. Up to the present point, however, we have left open the question of the earlier form of 4:10, as well as the question of the provenance and tradition history of 4:11-12.

The subject of 4:10 in its present form, "those around him with the Twelve," is awkward. It is probable that either "those around him" or the Twelve were present in 4:10 before Mark, and that Mark added the other group. The great majority of scholars, following R. Bultmann's lead,[21] have seen the mention of the Twelve (along with all references to the Twelve in Mark) as Mark's work; thus in the putative original of 4:10, "those around him" asked Jesus about the Parable of the Sower.

In an important article, however, E. Best has challenged this consensus, showing that reference to the Twelve probably occurred often in traditions incorporated by Mark into his Gospel.[22] In the specific case of 4:10, Best thinks it probable that the Twelve were present in the pre-Markan verse, which read: *kai hote egeneto kata monas syn tois dōdeka, ērōtōn auton tas parabolas* ("and when he was alone with the Twelve, they asked him about the parables").[23]

Best's proposal has much to commend it. He points out that the phrase *syn tois dōdeka* ("with the Twelve") runs on smoothly after *kata monas* ("alone"). His reconstructed form of 4:10 has the advantage of explaining the singular verb *egeneto*, which we noted above might more logically be a plural. The singular is a vestige of the earlier form of 4:10, when Jesus was "alone with the Twelve."[24]

---

[21] *History of the Synoptic Tradition* (New York/Hagerstown/San Francisco/London: Harper & Row, 1963; orig. 1921) 345-46.

[22] "Mark's Use" 11-35.

[23] Ibid., 17-18.

[24] In Bultmann's reconstruction of the pre-Markan 4:10, on the other hand, the singular verb is as illogical as in the present form of 4:10.

According to Best's hypothesis, then, Mark's redaction of 4:10 has changed its grammatical structure. Whereas, before his work, *syn tois dōdeka* ("with the Twelve") modified the adjectival phrase *kata monas* ("alone"), in his redaction it modifies the subject, "those around him" (see Chart 3). Mark has placed the new subject *hoi peri auton syn tois dōdeka* ("those around him with the Twelve") after the verb, in accordance with usual NT word order,[25] and he has split up the double accusative by placing half of it ("him") before the subject and half of it ("the parables") after the subject, In the interests of clarity and balance.

Best suggests that the phrase "those around him," which *ex hypothese* Mark has introduced into 4:10, was transferred from the original version of 4:11-12, which he thinks was addressed to *tois peri auton*; perhaps, he hypothesizes, it began, "Jesus said to those around him . . ." He reasons that the pre-Markan logion now found in 4:11-12, although independent of its present context, must have had a defined audience; the distinction between "you" and "those outside" would have made little sense without some specification of who "you" was. "Those around him" would have contrasted very effectively with "those outside."[26]

This suggestion is intriguing and plausible, but it does not move beyond possibility to probability. It is also possible that Mark took the phrase "those around him" from the tradition in 3:31-35, where it is integral to the story.[27] In this apophthegm, at least, we can be reasonably sure that Mark heard about "those around him," whereas with Best's reconstruction of the original form of 4:11-12 we are in the realm of speculation.

Best's hypothesis about the origin of the phrase "those around him" is based on the presupposition that there was a pre-Markan form of 4:11-12, and although we are not convinced by the hypothesis, we agree with Best on the presupposition.[28] Evidence that in 4:11-12 Mark incorporated a previously-existing logion includes the antithetic parallelism, redundant *ekeinos*, circumlocutions for divine activity, and agreement of the citation of Isa 6:9-10 with the Targum, all of which point toward an origin for

---

[25] *BDF* §472.

[26] "Mark's Use" 17-18.

[27] J. Lambrecht, *Astonished* 141.

[28] Earlier writers such as A. Jülicher (*Gleichnisreden* 1.121) and W. Wrede (*Messianic Secret* 55-66) supposed 4:11-12 to be entirely Mark's creation, since they saw the "parable theory" it expressed as a conception that was alien to Jesus and that had been imposed on the parables by Mark, either out of misunderstanding (Jülicher) or to further dogmatic ideas (Wrede).

CHART 3

1. Original form of Mark 4:10 according to E. Best

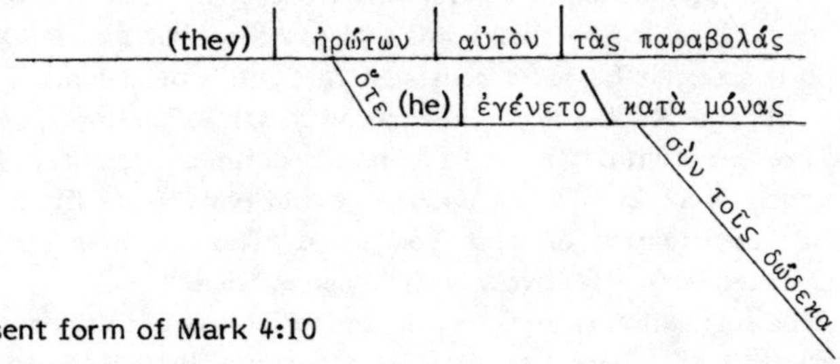

2. Present form of Mark 4:10

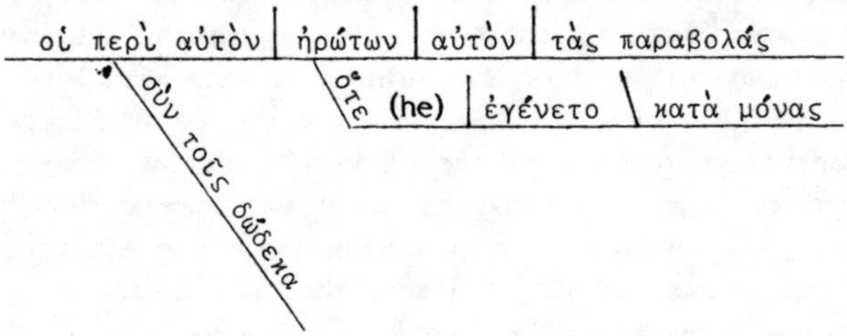

the logion in Jewish Aramaic-speaking circles in Palestine.[29] Mark himself, on the other hand, is probably not from Palestine, as his numerous
geographical errors about Palestinian geography suggest;[30] also, upon
occasion, he seems to err with regard to details of Palestinian Judaism.[31]
In addition, most of the Semitisms in his Gospel are to be found, not in
editorial passages, but in traditional material.[32] Mark may not even have
been a Jew.[33]

---

[29]A. Ambrozic (*Hidden Kingdom* 47-53), citing T. W. Manson, J.
Jeremias, and J. Gnilka.

[30]H. C. Kee, *Community* 102-103; W. G. Kümmel, *Introduction* 97; J.
Gnilka, *Evangelium* 1.33.

[31]His statement in 7:3 (the explanatory *gar* clause indicates Markan
redaction) that "all the Jews, . . . observing the tradition of the elders,"
require washing of hands before they eat, is unhistorical; the Sadducees
did not observe Pharasaic traditions, and they opposed the extension of
priestly purification rules to the general populace (see J. Gnilka, *Evangelium* 1.281). There is also some question about whether or not Jewish law
provided for a woman divorcing a man, as in Mark 10:12. See the contrary
opinions of, on the one hand, V. Taylor (*Gospel* 419-20), E. Schweizer
("Scheidungsrecht der jüdischen Frau? Weibliche Jüngen Jesu?" *EvT* 42
[1982] 294-300), and H. Weder ("Perspektive der Frauen?" *EvT* 43 [1983]
175-78), who clam they could not, and B. Brooten ("Konnten Frauen im
alten Judentum die Scheidung betreiben? Uberlegungen zu Mk 10,11-12
und 1 Kor 7,10-11," *EvT* 42 [1982] 65-80; "Zur Debatte über das Scheidungsrecht der jüdischen Frau," *EvT* 43 [1983] 466-78), who claims they
could.

[32]See V. Taylor, *Gospel* 65 and E. J. Pryke, *Redactional Style* 8.

[33]Mark's main concern seems to be, not mission to the Jews, but to the
Gentiles; see 7:24-30 and 13:20. Paul also, however, was a missionary to
the Gentiles, and *he* was a Jew; but there is nothing in Mark corresponding
to Romans 9-11. Rather, Mark thinks that the privileged place of the Jews
has been transferred to the church; see 12:1-12, esp. 12:9.

E. Schweizer (*Good News* 148) sees in the "distancing" description of
Jewish practices in 7:3-4 indication that Mark is a Gentile: J. Gnilka
(*Evangelium* 1.281), however, disagrees on this conclusion, and indeed
Mark's distance alone does not necessarily indicate a non-Jewish back-
ground.

W.-G. Kümmel (*Introduction* 97) writes that Mark "does not know that
the account of the death of the Baptist (6:17ff.) contradicts Palestinian
customs," apparently referring to Salome's public dance. Herod and his
family, however, are not presented in Mark as models of Jewish Law
observance.

In 4:11-12, therefore, as throughout his Gospel, Mark provides evidence that, although he himself is not an Aramaic-speaking Jew, he has, by some process of transmission, become the inheritor of numerous Aramaic Jewish-Christian traditions.[34] Although Semitic traits in themselves do not prove authenticity,[35] the saying found in 4:11-12 may, indeed, go back to Jesus himself, as its closeness to another probably authentic *Jesus-logion*, Matt 11:25-27 par. Luke 10:21-22, suggests.[36] In any case, it was probably not created by Mark.

The "minor agreement" of Matthew and Luke against Mark 4:11a also may support the conclusion that Mark was not the originator of the logion in 4:11-12. The most plausible explanation of that agreement[37] is that

---

[34]V. Taylor expresses very well this paradox about Mark's Gospel: "The sympathies of Mark are Gentile in their range, but his tradition is Jewish Christian to the core" (*Gospel* 65).

[35]See the justified criticism by A. Ambrozic (*Hidden Kingdom* 48) of T. W. Manson and J. Jeremias for jumping to the conclusion of authenticity from observation of Aramaic traits in 4:11-12.

[36]Both Mark 4:11-12 and Matt 11:25-30 par. speak of God's revelation of mysteries to Jesus' disciples and his hiding of them from outsiders. On the relation between the two logia, see B. W. Bacon, *Beginnings* 46-49; L. Cerfaux, "La connaissance des Secrets du Royaume d'après Matt XIII.11 et parallèles," *NTS* 2 (1955-56) 238-49; D. Nineham, *The Gospel of Mark* (Pelican New Testament Commentaries; London: Penguin, 1969; orig. 1963) 136-37; H. Schürmann, *Das Lukasevangelium* (HTKNT 3; Freiburg/ Basel/Wien: Herder, 1969) 1.458-61; D. Flusser, *Gleichnisse* 235-42, 275-77. H. Koester ("The Structure and Criteria of Early Christian Beliefs," *Trajectories through Early Christianity* [eds. J. M. Robinson and H. Koester; Philadelphia: Fortress, 1971] 220-21) accepts Matt 11:25-30 as a saying of Jesus, adding that it is this sort of saying that gave rise to Matthew's identification of Jesus with Wisdom.

[37]Admittedly, no certainty can be claimed for this or any other solution to the problem represented by Mark 4:11 and the other "minor agreements." They pose a problem for the two-source hypothesis, and are the major argument for the revival of the Griesbach hypothesis; see W. R. Farmer, *The Synoptic Problem: A Critical Analysis* (New York: Macmillan, 1964) passim. The overwhelming weight of evidence, however, is still on the side of Markan priority (see most recently J. A. Fitzmyer, "The Priority of Mark and the 'Q' Source in Luke," *To Advance the Gospel* [New York: Crossroad, 1981] 3-40). Indeed, H. Koester has subjected the very chapter under study, Mark 4:1-34, to detailed analysis as a "test case" of synoptic relationships, and has summarized his results in one sentence: "Mark 4:1-34 was one of the sources which Matthew used in

Matthew and Luke preserve the original version of the logion, which Mark also knew from tradition, and which he edited into its present Markan form. Matthew and Luke knew the Markan version, but they also knew the original version, perhaps as an oral tradition;[38] and they preferred this

---

13:1-54, and the only source which Luke used in 8:4-18" ("Test Case" 85).

Koester's early solution to the problem posed by the minor agreement against Mark 4:11a ("Test Case" 36-38), combined redaction- and textual criticism. Matthew and Luke independently introduced *gnōnai* because "to give the mystery" is obscure, and Mark's original text had the plural "mysteries." (B. H. Streeter [*The Four Gospels: A Study of Origins* (London: Macmillan, 1924) 313] thought Matt 13:11 originally had the singular "mystery.")

While possible, the text-critical component of this argument seems improbable; as V. Fusco points out ("Accord Mineur" 356) the poorly-attested texts upon which critics such as Streeter and Koester rely are probably to be explained as harmonizations. Fusco's own solution seems more logical: the minor agreement under consideration, while it does not discredit the two-source hypothesis, indicates that source criticism alone is insufficient to solve the synoptic problem ("Accord Mineur" 360). See the following note on the continued influence of oral tradition even after the composition of Gospels.

Koester has now revived in new form an old solution to the problem of the minor agreements, the *Ur-Marcus* hypothesis ("History and Devlopment of Mark's Gospel [From Mark to Secret Mark and 'Canonical' Mark]," *Colloquy on New Testament Studies: A Time for Reappraisal and Fresh Approaches* [ed. B. Corley; Macon, Georgia: Mercer University, 1983] 35-57). This hypothesis, however, is still open to the objections summed up by W. G. Kümmel (*Introduction* 61-63). Especially questionable is Koester's argument, advanced several times, on the basis of awkward Markan phrases that are not reproduced by Matthew or Luke. Koester concludes that these Markan phrases are secondary intrusions in the text, but it seems more likely that Matthew and Luke read the phrases but deliberately omitted them due to their awkwardness. Even J. D. Crossan, who otherwise follows Koester's reconstruction of the relation between "Canonical Mark" and "Secret Mark" (*Four Other Gospels: Shadows on the Contours of Canon* [Minneapolis: Winston, 1985] 91-121), does not go along with Koester's resort to the *Ur-Marcus* hypothesis (ibid., 119-120). On "Secret Mark," see below, n. 41.

[38] W.-G. Kümmel (*Introduction* 63) lists the passage under discussion as one of "a small number of agreements which can scarcely be depicted as accidental," and adds that "these few instances may be explained through the influence of the oral tradition." The continuing vitality of that tradition in the first Christian centuries, even after the composition of the

version to Mark's because of its greater coherence and its emphasis on understanding.[39]

Although we will go into greater detail on this subject later, the following outline of the reasons for Mark's changes in the Matthew/Luke form of 4:11-12 can be presented: 1) Mark did not wish to ascribe understanding to the disciples in the period before the crucifixion and resurrection, so he removed the verb "to know."[40] 2) Mark wished to bring the logion he introduced in 4:11-12 into connection with the paradoxical division of God's kingdom depicted in the Parable of the Sower, so he changed the plural "mysteries" to the singular "mystery."[41] 3) He placed

----

Gospels, is sometimes ignored by source critics. Papias, although he knows the Gospels of Matthew and Mark, prefers "the living and abiding voice" of the oral tradition (see M. Hornschuh in E. Hennecke and W. Schneemelcher, *New Testament Apocrypha* 2.78), and most of the sayings of Jesus cited by the Apostolic Fathers have probably been transmitted orally, as H. Koester's own earlier work showed (*Synoptische Überlieferung bei den Apostolischen Vätern* [TU 65; Berlin: Akademie, 1957]). On the whole subject of oral and written tradition, see most recently W. H. Kelber, *Oral and Written Gospel*.

As J. L. Martyn has pointed out to me in conversation, if the theory advanced here is correct Mark 4:11a par. would be analagous to the instances of overlap between Mark and Q, on which see Kümmel, *Introduction* 70-71.

[39]"It has been given to *know* the mysteries" is more readily comprehensible than "the mystery has been given." The plural "mysteries" would have made more sense to Matthew and Luke because they did not have in mind a specific mystery, the divided kingdom pictured in the Parable of the Sower, as Mark did. Especially in Matthew, the disciples are presented as basically understanding Jesus during his ministry; see J. D. Kingsbury, *Jesus Christ in Matthew, Mark, and Luke* (Proclamation Commentaries; Philadelphia: Fortress, 1981) 86.

[40]As V. Fusco points out ("Accord Mineur" 358), the *gnōnai* that is missing in 4:11 is used as a reproach in 4:13. It is especially 4:13b which makes 4:13 into a reproach, and we have ascribed 4:13b to Markan redaction.

[41]J. D. Crossan, following M. Smith, thinks that "the mystery of the kingdom of God" refers to baptismal instruction (*Four Other Gospels* 118; cf. M. Smith, *Clement of Alexandria and a Secret Gospel of Mark* [Cambridge, Mass.: Harvard University, 1973] 178-84), and that Mark has taken the phrase from the "Secret Gospel of Mark." In the latter, a young man whom Jesus has raised from the tomb comes to him by night, "wearing a linen cloth over his naked body. And he remained with him that night, for

to *mystērion* before *dedotai*, thus splitting "the mystery" off from its genitive "of the kingdom of God," in order to compensate for the omission of *gnōnai* and to give greater stylistic balance to the logion,[42] as well as to emphasize "the mystery of the kingdom."

The composition history of Mark 4:33-34. Considerations of style and content support the conclusion that 4:33-34a is pre-Markan, whereas 4:34b is Markan.

Mark 4:33, if taken by itself, presents uninterpreted parables as having a pedagogical purpose, whereas 4:34b presents them as requiring explanations in order to be understood.[43] 4:33 accords with the emphasis on

---

Jesus taught him the mystery of the kingdom of God." According to Crossan, Mark found the esotericism of this passage problematical because the Carpocratians had exploited it; he therefore neutralized the inference of private instruction "by situating the instruction not within secret ritual but after public parable."

The following points render this hypothesis unlikely: 1) The Carpocratian connection would require a late second century date for Mark, but all the other evidence points to a composition around A.D. 70 (see above, chapter 1). Contrary to Crossan, in Mark the implication of esotericism is not "safely neutralized"; rather, the *contrast* between public instruction (4:1-9) and private explanation (4:10-25) emphasizes the importance of secret teaching even more than in the Secret Gospel passage. 3) The phrase "mystery of the kingdom of God" fits better into the Markan setting than into the Secret Gospel setting. Smith's baptismal interpretation of the phrase can only be established by loosening the phrase from its Markan setting (as Smith acknowledges, *Clement* 178) and citing passages from other NT books where baptism is referred to as a mystery. Baptism is never, however, referred to as the mystery *of the kingdom* in the NT, and there is nothing *in Mark* to support Smith's contention that "Christian baptism is 'the mystery of the kingdom of God' because it enables those to whom it is given to enter the kingdom" (ibid., 183). On the contrary, the genitive "of the kingdom of God" makes more sense within the Markan setting of chapter 4, which consists of parables *of the kingdom of God;* the mystery of the kingdom is its paradoxical character as depicted in those parables.

[42]V. Fusco, "Accord Mineur" 359. We have also observed a concern for stylistic balance in Mark's redaction of 4:10; see above.

[43]J. Gnilka (*Verstockung* 52) maintains the unity of 4:33 and 4:34, both of which he assigns to the pre-Markan parable source, by interpreting 4:33b in a negative sense ("in accordance with their inability to hear"). While this is evidently the way in which *Mark* wished 4:33b to be under-

"hearing" that we have observed in 4:3a, 4:9, and the interpretation of the Parable of the Sower, all of which we have identified in the previous chapter as pre-Markan; 4:34b, on the other hand, accords with the esotericism of 4:11-12, which we believe was introduced into the "parable chapter" by Mark himself.

Furthermore, we have noted above a confusion about the referent of *autois* in 4:33a, 34a. This confusion would be explained if the chapter previously ended with 4:34a. In this previous form of the chapter, *autois* would have referred to the disciples; only the addition of 4:34b has changed its referent to the "outsiders," and introduced the confusion.

Stylistic considerations reinforce our analysis. We have noted above that finding the *de* twice in 4:34 is strange, and that the two instances of *de* differ in meaning. If the chapter ended at 4:34a, these problems would not exist, and 4:34a is an appropriate ending for a "parable chapter." We have further noted that the expression found in 4:34a, *lalein parabolais*, differs from the usual Markan *lalein en parabolais*; the former usage appears to be pre-Markan, while the latter is Markan.[44] On the other hand, the expression *kat' idian*, which occurs in 4:34b, is Markan terminology.[45]

Mark 4:33-34a probably was the conclusion of an intermediate stage in the development of the collection of parables.[46] The conclusion was added at the same time that the interpretation of the Parable of the Sower (4:14-20), along with 4:13a and the word "listen" in 4:3a, was intercalated into a previous collection of three seed parables;[47] concurrently 4:9 may have been moved from the end of the collection to its present position.

All of these pre-Markan additions would have had a similar theme: hearing the word is of vital importance, but not all human beings are given this ability to hear. At this intermediate stage, 4:33 would have

---

stood, it is a strained way of reading 4:33b which probably is not original, as H. Raïsänen points out (*Parabeltheorie* 54-55).

[44] H. Koester, "Test Case" 47-48.   Koester identifies the three instances of *lalein en parabolais* (3:23; 4:2; 12:1) as Markan redaction.

[45] E. Best, "Mark's Use" 18.

[46] According to our reconstruction, then, in the pre-Markan stage the parable collection ended with the statements, "And with many such parables he would speak the word to them, as they were able to hear; and without a parable he did not speak to them."

[47] Cf. J. Jeremias (*Parables* 13-14), who points to the absolute use of *ho logos* in 4:14 and 4:33.

meant, "In this manner he spoke to the disciples, in accordance with their ability to hear, to be good soil." Mark's addition of 4:34b to 4:33-34a has transformed both the human objects of Jesus' parabolic teaching and its purpose.

EXEGESIS

The "In" and "Out" Groups

As noted above, in 4:11-12 the contrast between the two groups to which the parables are addressed, "you" and "those outside," is emphasized by the placement of the dative plurals at the beginnings of the clauses. An exegesis of the "parable theory" must begin by determining exactly how Mark conceived each group.

The "in" group. The group whom Jesus addresses in 4:11a as "you," to whom the mystery of the kingdom has been given, has been described in 4:10 as "those around him with the Twelve." This same group is denominated "his own disciples" in 4:34. Thus for Mark the group of disciples includes both the Twelve and another, more indefinite set of persons. This association of the Twelve with a larger group would come as no surprise to the reader of Mark. In 3:13-14 Jesus has called to himself "whom he wished," and *out of their number* he has appointed the Twelve.[48]

How would Mark's readers have interpreted the phrase "those around him" in 4:10? The reader of chapter 4 has just seen Jesus surrounded by a group called "those around him" (*tous peri auton*) in chapter 3 (3:34); cf. 3:32, where we read that "there sat around him (*peri auton*) a crowd." "Those around him" are contrasted to another group made up of those "standing outside" (*exō stēkontes*, 3:31; cf. *exō zētousin se*, 3:32), the members of his biological family; Jesus looks not at these "outsiders" but at the members of his true family, who are sitting around him inside the house. The similarity to the contrast in 4:11-12 between "those around him" and "those outside" is obvious.

This linkage between the groups in 3:31-35 and those in 4:10-12 makes especially relevant the description in 3:32 of a crowd sitting around Jesus, and the denotation of this group in 3:34 as "those around him." These

---

[48]In 8:34 there is a further widening of the addressees; here Jesus calls to himself "the crowd with the disciples," a phrase whose grammatical structure recalls that of 4:11a, "those around him with the Twelve."

verses establish a relation between *the crowd*, or at least a portion of it,
and "those around him."[49] The latter phrase denotes those from the crowd
who have been drawn by Jesus' teaching and who, in directing all their
attention to his word, are doing the will of God (3:35). They are not "official" disciples like the Twelve; if they were, they would not be described
by the word "crowd." Moreover, the description of them in 3:35 is very
general.[50] They are people who have been attracted to Jesus on this
particular occasion, yet are serious about their adherence to him (3:35).
Jesus' encomium, "Behold my mother and my brothers!", suggests that this
group of "unofficial" disciples may include women.[51]

Mark's addition of *hoi peri auton* to 4:10, therefore, has widened the
"in" group so that it includes not only the Twelve, but also those from the
crowd who have been stimulated by Jesus' teaching to further inquiry.[52]
In asking Jesus for illumination about the parables, they have demonstrated that they are "good soil" and people who have ears to hear; cf. the
juxtaposition of 4:8, 4:9, and 4:10. In the Parable of the Sower and its
interpretation, therefore, the contrast between "good soil" and "bad soil"
is equivalent to that in 4:10-12 between "those around him" and "those
outside." If this is true, however, the receptivity and desire for further
clarification on the part of "those around him" must be traced back to
God, who has made them to be "good soil" (see above, chapter 2).[53]

---

[49]Thus the crowd is not exclusively "outside" in Mark; it includes both
future insiders and future outsiders. See E. Best's characterization of the
crowd, cited below.

[50]"Whoever (*hos an*) does the will of God . . ." Cf. the general formula-
tions of 8:35-38 and 10:29-31, on which see S. Freyne, "Disciples" 20.

[51]Cf. the description in 15:41 of a group of women who followed Jesus
and ministered (*diēkonoun*) to him when he was in Galilee, and of others
who came up with him to Jerusalem. E. Schweizer's reluctant dismissal of
the idea of women disciples in Mark ("Scheidungsrecht" 297-300) is based
mainly on the presumption that the Twelve and the disciples are coexten-
sive groups, but this is not always the case; see E. Best, "Mark's Use of
the Twelve," *ZNW* 69 (1978) 11-35, esp. 32. On the question of women
disciples in Mark, see most recently W. Munro, "Women Disciples in
Mark?" *CBQ* 44 (1982) 225-41.

[52]Thus *autois* in 4:1-2 and in 4:33-34 refers to slightly different groups,
since in the latter case those who have been stimulated to inquiry have
been subtracted.

[53]We disagree with C. F. D. Moule ("Mark 4:1-20" 98-103) who denies
that 4:11-12 has any "predestinarian" implications. If "those around him"
ask questions of Jesus, they do so because they have been chosen by him;
cf. 3:13-14, which introduces this whole segment of the Gospel.

For Mark, then, part of faithful listening is asking questions appropriate to Jesus' teaching;[54] and this Markan idea, we would suggest, arises from Mark's apocalyptic outlook, and has its counterpart in Jewish apocalyptic literature, especially the QL. In 1QH 4:23-24, the hymnist thanks God that "you . . . have not covered with shame the face of all them that inquired of me"; conversely, in 1QS 5:11-12 the wicked are those who "have not inquired nor sought Him . . . in order to know the hidden things in which they have guiltily strayed." In a world dominated by the Spirit of Falsehood, the truth is hidden from all but those who inquire of the community's leader, and through him of God, about the hidden secrets of the Law. It is a sign of divine favor to know, and culpable not to know, the necessity of this inquiry.

Similarly, in Mark, the hiddenness of the kingdom makes inquiry necessary. Because Satan opposes God's action and blinds human beings (4:15-19), only those who penetrate beyond surface appearances can see the kingdom's advent. Similarly, only those who penetrate by inquiry beyond the prosaic surface of the parables can see them as a picture of that advent. Those who perceive that matters worthy of the most searching inquiry have been broached in the parables, and who know where to turn with their questions, have already been drawn into the mystery of God's kingdom.

"Those around him with the Twelve," then, denotes not only the Twelve, who are the nucleus of the post-Easter community,[55] but also

---

[54] The Church Fathers and later Christian commentators emphasize the importance of the disciples' inquiring of Jesus about the parables. Origen (*Hom. Jer.* 12.13) writes that, while all hear the parables, only the apostles question Jesus and thus come to hear "in a secret way" (*kekrymmenōs*). Later writers see the incitement of such questioning as the purpose of the parables (e.g. Cyril of Alexandria, cited in J. A. Cramer, *Catenae in Evangelia s. Matthaei et S. Marci* [Oxonii, 1840] 311), and both praise the apostles for inquiring of Jesus (e.g. Theophylact [on Matt 13:10-12, PG 123.290] and Maldonatus [on Matt 13:11]) and blame the Jews for not doing so (Chrysostom, *Hom. Matt.* 45.2).

[55] On the disciples as the nucleus of the future community, see V. Fusco, *Parola* 135; we would identify this nucleus more especially as the Twelve. See above, chapter 2, on the groups of people in 4:15-20; cf. R. Pesch, *Markusevangelium* 1.237. *Contra* T. J. Weeden and W. H. Kelber (see chapter 2, n. 188) who think that Mark wishes to distance his readers from Peter and the other disciples; indeed, for Weeden, the Twelve represent Mark's *opponents*. Mark 14:28 and 16:7 present insuperable difficulties for this interpretation.

those who have been drawn to Jesus from the crowd, which E. Best rightly describes as symbolizing "the vague amorphous mass of men which is the object of evangelization."[56] The latter component of the group would have had special significance for Mark's readers, for they, too, had once been part of the "crowd," but now had been drawn into the circle of "those around Jesus." Now the reader, like the disciples, hears the announcement that is withheld from outsiders, "To you has been given the mystery of the kingdom of God . . ."[57] Indeed, throughout the Gospel the reader hears the secret instruction that Jesus gives to the disciples but withholds from outsiders. The position of the reader as an "insider" is explicitly recognized by an aside that occurs in one of these secret teachings: "Let the reader understand" (13:14).[58]

Thus, in the description of the "in" group as "those around him with the Twelve," Mark has his eye both on those who followed Jesus during his lifetime and on the hearers in his own community. Neither for Jesus' disciples during his earthly life, however, nor for Mark's contemporary hearers, is a position as an "insider" a guarantee that one has attained to a complete and permanent gnosis. As, during his lifetime, Jesus' disciples frequently misunderstood him, so in the Markan community there is the danger that hearers will be led astray by false Christs and false prophets (13:22). Furthermore, Mark's readers will be tempted to react in puzzlement and incomprehension to the strange scenes he paints, such as that of the young man who runs away naked (14:51-52), the cry of dereliction (15:34), and the abrupt ending of the Gospel (16:8).[59] It is only by a

---

[56]E. Best, "Role" 392.

[57]Cf. W. Schmithals, *Das Evangelium nach Markus* (Ökumenischer Taschenbuchkommentar zum Neuen Testament 2; Gütersloh/Würzburg: Mohn/Echter, 1979) 1.237-42.

[58]The bond that links the reader and the disciples as insiders is further strengthened by the parallel between God's announcement in 1:1, "You are my beloved son," which (aside from Jesus) only the reader hears, and God's announcement in 9:7, "This is my beloved son," which only the three disciples hear. In some ways the reader is *more* of an insider than the disciples are. From the very beginning of the Gospel (1:1) he is aware of Jesus' full identity as Son of God, knowledge that is withheld from the human characters in the story until the centurion's confession in 15:39 (see D. Juel, *Messiah and Temple: The Trial of Jesus in the Gospel of Mark* [SBLDS 31; Missoula, Montana: Scholars, 1977] 46-47; D. Rhoads and D. Michie, *Mark as Story*, 57-58).

[59]The shock value of scenes such as these leads J. R. Donahue ("Jesus as the Parable of God in the Gospel of Mark," *Int* 32 [1978] 368-86) and,

continual exercise of faith after the last word of the Gospel has ceased to reverberate that its hearers will be enabled to resist the temptation to turn away in bafflement.

The "out" group. Turning our attention now to the group in 4:11-12 that is excluded from "the mystery of the kingdom," we note first the scene change in 4:10; Jesus secludes himself with his disciples. Thus the reader's first impulse would be to take "those outside" in 4:11b as the group that has just been left behind, namely those from the crowd who have not been stimulated by Jesus' parables to further inquiry, the unreceptive members of the crowd.[60] The hypothesis that "those outside" means those who stand outside the circle of disciples is strengthened by the history of the term, which is used in the Pauline corpus to refer to non-Christians.[61] 3:31-32 reveals that even members of Jesus' family can belong to this group, at least temporarily (see above).[62] For Mark's hearers, this

---

following him, W. H. Kelber (*Oral and Written Gospel* 123-24) to identify the entire Gospel as "parabolic"; see our discussion of the wider meaning of *en parabolais* below.

[60]See V. Fusco (*Parola* 227) who asserts that *ekeinois* is not superfluous; it makes the reference apply not only to unbelievers in the abstract (*hoi exō*) but specifically to the large crowd described in 4:1-2. *Contra* A. Ambrozic (*Hidden Kingdom* 66), who categorically denies a link between the "outsiders" and the crowd. It is relevant that in the Passion Narrative the "crowd" turns against Jesus (15:11-15). Yet the crowd is not *identical* with "those outside," at least in the early part of the Gospel; see above, n. 49.

[61]J. Behm, "*exō*," *TDNT* 2 (1964; orig. 1935) 575-76. In rabbinic literature, *hhyṣwnym* means "those condemned as heretics." The citations from the Pauline corpus are 1 Cor 5:12-13; 1 Thess 4:12; Col 4:5. Cf. *hoi exō-then* in 1 Tim 3:7 and *hoi exō anthrōpoi* in 2 Clem 13:1.

[62]In 3:21 Jesus' relatives "go out" (*exēlthon*) and say that Jesus is insane (*exestē*); then they are described as "outside" (*exō*) in 3:31-32. Perhaps the repetition of the *ex-* prefix is ironic. Jesus' relatives say that he is "standing outside normal human sanity" (the literal meaning of *exestē*), but they themselves are the "outsiders" (3:21, 31-32). It is possible that this passage is anti-James or directed against the idea of a Christian caliphate (the latter is suggested by E. Schweizer, *Good News* 87), but such hypotheses are impossible to prove, and the members of Jesus' family may not ultimately be "outsiders" in Mark's mind; see R. E. Brown et al., *Mary in the New Testament: A Collaborative Assessment by Protestant and Roman Catholic Scholars* (United States Lutheran-Roman Catholic Dialogue; Philadelphia/New York: Fortress/Paulist, 1978) 53.

description of family members as outsiders would have had a familiar ring, for some members of their community had probably been handed over to death by relatives (cf. 13:12). The link in 3:21-22 between Jesus' family and the scribes (both groups think Jesus insane) suggests that the latter may also be "outsiders." This suggestion is confirmed by another line of reasoning. We have observed above that the juxtaposition of 4:8, 4:9, and 4:10 implies that "those around him with the Twelve" are equivalent to the good soil in the Parable of the Soil. Conversely, "those outside" should be equivalent to the bad soils in the parable.

This equivalence is established when we remember that the outsiders of 4:11 are people who hear and hear, but never understand. According to 4:15-19, however, this is exactly what happens with the bad soils; they hear, but their hearing never comes to fruition. By the time Mark's readers reached 4:20, then, they would have made the connection between the two groups in 4:11-12 and the two groups in 4:13-20. Therefore, since *hoi exō* = the bad soils, and our previous work has linked the Pharisees with the pathway soil of 4:15,[63] the Pharisees are among *hoi exō*.

The connection of the outsiders with the bad soils of the parable means that Mark's readers would have interpreted the outsiders, as they interpreted the bad soils, on two levels, the level of the story itself and the level of the Markan community.[64] We have already seen how resonant the descriptions of family members as outsiders would have been for the Markan community. Similarly, "those outside" would include people in Mark's own day who were pathway soil, who, like the scribes and Pharisees in Jesus' time, were determined opponents of the gospel from their very first hearing of it, and were subjecting its proclaimers to persecution. They would also include those among Mark's contemporaries who were rocky and thorny soils, who, like Judas during Jesus' ministry, at first received the gospel message gladly but afterwards apostasized.[65] If the

---

[63]See above, chapter 2, on groups in 4:15-20.

[64]See above, chapter 2, on the kerygma of the Parable of the Sower for the Markan community.

[65]On Judas as thorny soil, blinded by the deceitfulness of riches, cf. the reference to his greed in 14:11. Judas is thus ultimately one of *hoi exō*, although according to strict logic he should be among the audience of 4:11a.

Erstwhile disciples are thus included among *hoi exō*. W. Kelber (*Kingdom* 32-36), however, goes too far when he interprets *hoi exō* solely in terms of a Christian conflict *intra muros;* the outsiders also include people like the pathway soil, who have *never* responded positively to the word.

rough outline of Judas' story applies to the apostates from the Markan community,[66] the latter may have joined in the persecution of their former Christian brothers and sisters.[67] In any case, *hoi exō* would include the people who were persecuting Mark's listeners.

"Those outside," then, denotes those who stand outside the circle of disciples, both on the level of the Gospel narrative and on the level of the Markan community. The sharp dualism in 4:11-12 between this group and "those around him" poses a difficult hermeneutical problem for many modern interpreters.[68] For Mark there is no neutral ground. Ultimately one either becomes a disciple, or one is among "those outside"; and it is not an adiaphoron whether or not one ends up adhering to Jesus. The words "ultimately" and "ends up" in the last sentence, however, are important. In 9:38-41 Mark's Jesus rebukes his disciples for forbidding an exorcist to cast out demons in Jesus' name, adding, "He who is not against us is for us." Although this pronouncement does not mitigate the seriousness of whether or not one is ultimately drawn to Jesus,[69] it does warn against

---

[66]Such a link is suggested by the juxtaposition of the usages of *paradidōmi* ("deliver up," "betray") in chapter 13, referring to the persecution the Markan community is undergoing, with its usages in chapter 14, referring to Jesus' betrayal by Judas (13:9, 11, 12; 14:10, 11, 18, 21, 41, 42, 44). Cf. L. Schottroff, "Die Gegenwart in der Apokalyptik der synoptischen Evangelien," *Apocalypticism in the Mediterranean World and the Near East. Proceedings of the International Colloquium on Apocalypticism, Uppsala, August 12-17, 1979* (ed. D. Hellholm; Tübingen: Mohr/Siebeck, 1983) 114.

[67]If the Markan community is being betrayed by apostates, then the prophecy in 13:12 that "brother will deliver brother to death" takes on added poignancy because of the Christian usage of *adelphos* to mean "fellow Christian." R. E. Brown (*Antioch* 124) cites *1 Clem* 5:2; Tacitus, *Annals* 15:44; and Matt 24:10 to show that such betrayal of Christian by Christian did take place in the first century.

[68]The problem is illustrated by the title of H. Boer's book *Theology out of the Ghetto: A New Testament Exegetical Study concerning Religious Exclusiveness* (Leiden: Brill, 1971). Boers wants to see theology come out of the ghetto, but passages such as ours seem to lead back into the ghetto. (H. Räisänen [*Parabeltheorie* 118] also sees 4:11-12 as reflecting a "ghetto" mentality.) Boers's solution is to say that Mark 4:11-12 represents a pre-Markan understanding, which is at odds both with the historical Jesus and with Mark (ibid., 10-18, 107-118); for a criticism of this view, see above, n. 2.

[69]9:39 does not deny the cruciality of whether one is "against us" or "for us," only that the disciples know who ultimately belongs in which

a premature judgment about who is in which group.

The Effect of the Parables on the Two Groups

We have now to ask how the parables function when they intersect these two groups.

The effect of the parables on the "in" group. We have argued in chapter 2, following J. L. Martyn, that 4:11-12 contains not only a statement about the effect of the parables upon "outsiders" (4:11b-12), but also, by implication, a statement about their effect upon "insiders" (4:11a). According to our interpretation of 4:11a, it is the parables themselves that give the mystery of the kingdom of God to these insiders.

We have also noted, however, that although the mystery of the kingdom is *given* in the Parable of the Sower, it is not *understood* until the explanation has been appended. Indeed, throughout Mark's Gospel, the pattern seems to be that for the disciples explanation is necessary before the parables can be understood (see Chart 4).[70] This qualification, however, does not negate the apocalyptic function of the parables, since they are an essential component in a revelatory discourse consisting of parable and interpretation.[71]

---

group. POxy 1224 (cited by J. Gnilka, *Evangelium* 2.61) follows 9:40 with, "He who is far away today will be close to you tomorrow."

If "in your name" in 9:38 is read in the light of "in my name" in 9:41, the man is not merely using Jesus' name for magical purposes, since those in 9:41 have some sort of commitment to Christ, although they are not "official" disciples. Cf. our description above of "those around him" as people who have been drawn by Jesus' power although they are not among the Twelve. W. L. Lane comments on 9:40 (*The Gospel of Mark* [NICNT; Grand Rapids: Eerdmans, 1974] 343-44): "It was not necessary to be a direct follower of Jesus to share in a conflict which has cosmic dimensions; opposition to Satan unites the man to Jesus in his distinctive mission (cf. 3:27)." Lane's mention of 3:27 is insightful, since the same line of reasoning is used there as here: since Jesus (or the exorcist) is casting out demons, he is on the same side as God (or Jesus).

[70]This is the implication of 4:34b. Cf. also 4:10-20; 7:18-23, where the disciples receive an explanation of the "parable" that has been given in 7:14-15, and 13:29, where the short parable of the fig tree in 13:28 is interpreted (see J. Lambrecht, *Astonished* 140).

[71]Cf. E. Schweizer (*Good News* 100): "Even if a parable is not understood it will still fulfill its purpose, and that purpose is to reveal God."

CHART 4

The "Parable Theory"

Insiders	*Outsiders*
3:23-27		Jesus' enemies seem to understand import of parables
4:1-2		Jesus teaches the crowd in parables
4:10	In private, "those about him with the twelve" ask Jesus the parables.	
4:11-12	Same group as above has been given the mystery of the kingdom of God [in parables].	To those outside all things happen in parables so that they may look but not see, hear but not understand, lest they turn and be forgiven.
4:13	Same group rebuked for not understanding Parable of Sower.	
4:14-20	Same group given explanation of Parable of sower.	
4:33-34	In private, Jesus' own disciples given explanations of all things.	Those who are not Jesus' own disciples are taught solely in parables, "as they were able to hear."
7:14-15		Crowd exhorted, "Hear me all of you and understand," and given a "parable."
7:17	In private, Jesus' disciples ask him the parable.	

Chart 4 (cont.)

	Insiders	Outsiders
7:18a	Disciples rebuked for not understanding the parable.	
7:18b-23	Disciples given explanation of the parable.	
12:1-12		Jesus' enemies understand import of parable; this increases their hostility.
13:28	In private, four disciples exhorted to "learn the parable" from the fig tree.	
13:29	Parable explained?	

As instruments of revelation to the insiders, the parables are channels of a divine gift; this is indicated by the "divine passive" *dedotai* ("has been given") in 4:11.[72] Mark, like other apocalyptic thinkers, views knowledge as God's gift;[73] cf. 6:2, where Jesus' auditors exclaim, "What is the wisdom that has been given (*hē dotheisa*) to him?"[74] In the future this divine *dosis* will continue in the disciples' teaching, because of their close association with Jesus;[75] see 13:11: "Whatever is given you (*ho ean dothē hymin*) in that hour, that say."[76] What will be crucial in this testimony

---

[72]See J. Jeremias (*Parables* 15 n. 15) on *dedotai* as a circumlocution for divine activity.

[73]See my "Mark 4:10-12" 558-59. Cf. 1QS 3:15; 11:10: Man does not establish his way; it is God who establishes human thoughts.

[74]Cf. A. Ambrozic's comment on the phrase "not as the scribes" in 1:22: It tells the reader that the source of Jesus' teaching is God ("Teaching" 135).

[75]This association is suggested by the repetition of the pronoun *auton* ("him") in 4:10b.

[76]On the gift to the disciples, see 4:25a. On their post-Easter teaching, see 6:7-11, 30, which foreshadows that teaching. Cf. S. Freyne ("Disciples" 9) on the association of Daniel with other *maskilim* who "instruct the many."

will be, not human intellectual activity, but the speaking of the Spirit.[77]

The epistemological status of the disciples. By God's grace, then, the disciples have been given the mystery of the kingdom of God in the parables. Yet this conception is in a certain tension with 4:13 and 7:18, where Jesus rebukes the disciples for not comprehending parables. *Part* of the solution to this paradox can be found in the observation made above, that the mystery has been *given* although it has not yet been *understood.*[78]

Yet this explanation does not solve the entire difficulty posed by the clash between the privilege ascribed to the disciples in the "parable theory" and the incomprehension for which they are rebuked in 4:13 and elsewhere. The problem is not just one of intellectual consistency but also of tone. After hearing Jesus upbraid the disciples for their lack of understanding and hardness of heart in such harsh terms in 8:17-21, for example, would a reader be inclined to think that "the mystery of the kingdom" had been given to them? Would he not, on the contrary, think that they were among "those outside," given the closeness between the language of 8:17-18 and that of 4:12?[79] Furthermore, if, as we have maintained above, the disciples' inquiry in 4:10 is so commendable, why does Jesus rebuke them in 4:13 for not knowing the parable?

In attempting to answer these questions, it should first be remarked that the disciples occupy an *intermediate* position in Mark:

> Unlike the "outsiders," they are granted "the mystery of the kingdom of God" and a certain perception of who Jesus is. Unlike the demons, however (and the centurion at the cross) they do not during his lifetime recognize Jesus' full dignity as the Son of God, and they are bewildered and repulsed by his references to his approaching Passion.[80]

---

[77]Cf. my "Mark 4:10-12" 559 on 12:34: The scribe who answers intelligently is "not far from the kingdom"; it is the advent of God's kingdom that makes true perception possible.

[78]If Mark has eliminated *gnōnai* from 4:11, as we have hypothesized, this redaction has lessened, but not eliminated, the tension under consideration.

[79]Cf. K.-G. Reploh, *Markus, Lehrer der Gemeinde* (SBM 9; Stuttgart, 1969) 83-86.

[80]J. Marcus, "Mark 4:10-12" 562 n. 18.

In 8:27-38, for example, on the one hand the disciples, who perceive Jesus' messiahship, are contrasted with the mass of uncomprehending humanity (hoi anthrōpoi . . . hymeis de, 8:27-29). On the other hand, however, they are rebuked for not understanding the necessity of Jesus' passion, and thus thinking on a purely human level.[81] The closeness to 4:10-13, where the disciples are both contrasted with "the outsiders" and rebuked for incomprehension, is evident.

This mixture of comprehension and incomprehension within the elect community is known to us from other apocalyptic texts,[82] where part of its function is to point to the *penultimate* nature of the present time.[83] Similarly, in Mark, the disciples' mixture of comprehension and incomprehension emphasizes that the time of Jesus' earthly ministry is a penultimate time. Although, with Jesus' first appearance in the Gospel, God's mysteries have begun to be revealed, no human being can possess wholeness of sight until after Jesus has been crucified (cf. 9:9; 15:39). Insight, like salvation, is not a human capacity, and its definitive arrival must await God's definitive action in Jesus Christ; "with human beings it is impossible, but not with God" (10:27).[84]

The motif of the disciples' incomprehension, however, does not merely dramatize the difference between the time of Jesus and that of the church.[85] It probably also suggests that within the Markan community there is incomprehension of the same matters that baffle the disciples in the Gospel: the present age as a time of hiddenness (4:10-13),[86] the necessity of the way of the cross (8:31-33; 9:32; cf. 10:32), and the way in which Jesus shatters old categories (3:21-22; 7:17-23; 10:10-12). Thus the uncomprehending disciples perform at least two different narrative functions in Mark's Gospel: 1) they are representatives of the benightedness of

---

[81]V. Fusco, *Parola* 130.

[82]See my "Mark 4:10-12" 567-79; *contra* H. Räisänen (*Parabeltheorie* 118-25), who sees the incomprehension motif of 4:13b as contradicting the "Qumran-like" dualism of 4:11-12.

[83]Cf. M. Hengel, *Judaism and Hellenism: Studies in their Encounter in Palestine during the Early Hellenistic Period* (Philadelphia: Fortress, 1974) 1.207-208.

[84]We recall that in 4:33-34 the crowd's hearing is contrasted, not with the disciples' ability to hear, but with Jesus' revelation to them.

[85]*Contra* V. Fusco, *Parola* 136-37, 148.

[86]That this hiddenness is a stumbling-block for some in the Markan community is suggested by 13:6-7, 21-22, which speak of the temptation to believe prematurely that the hiddenness is over.

even the most perceptive people in the pre Easter world, and 2) they exemplify problems that continue to afflict Jesus' disciples after Easter.

The picture in 4:10-13 is thus consistent with the rest of the Gospel, in which the disciples fall between the incomprehension of the outsiders and complete understanding. In 4:10-20 they begin on a level similar to that of the outsiders, the "merely human" level of incomprehension, where they "look without seeing" (cf. 4:12), and therefore receive rebuke; but unlike the outsiders, they are at least aware that there *is* another level, which they seek to penetrate by inquiry.

Furthermore, it is helpful to observe that rebukes, such as the one in 4:13, do not necessarily imply rejection. As A. Ambrozic points out, the parallel between 4:12 and 8:18 breaks down because the latter lacks the "damning conclusion" of the former.[87] The *purpose* of Jesus' rebuke in 4:13 must be considered. In chapter 2 we demonstrated that 4:13 functions analogously to the word "listen!" in 4:3a; both direct attention to the importance of understanding what is to follow, suggesting that the rebuke in 4:13 has a pedagogical purpose.

This reading of 4:13 is confirmed by E. E. Lemcio's discernment of a dialogue form in Mark 4:1-20; 7:14-23; and 8:14-21: ambiguity, incomprehension, surprised or critical rejoinder, and explanation.[88] In this form, which Lemcio traces back to OT roots (e.g. Ezek 17:1-24; Zech 4:2-14), the hearer cannot really be expected to understand the initial statement, which is ambiguous, and the revealer's rebuke ("surprised or critical rejoinder") functions as a prelude to the full explanation.[89] As V. Fusco points out, Mark's sequence is always incomprehension/explanation, never explanation/incomprehension; his theme is not blindness, but blindness which has been overcome.[90]

---

[87] *Hidden Kingdom* 69.

[88] "External Evidence for the Structure and Function of Mark iv. 1-20, vii. 14-23 and viii. 14-21," *JTS* 29 (1978) 323-38.

[89] In drawing these conclusions from the form we are going beyond what Lemcio explicitly states.

[90] *Parola* 138. We might rephrase Fusco's statement, Mark's theme is blindness that has been, *or will be,* overcome, because of the one apparent exception to his formulation, 8:17-21; here Jesus' last word is a rebuke. (The subject of Fusco's assertion, however, is the instances where Jesus instructs the disciples privately after a public discourse: 4:1-20; 7:14-23; 9:14-29; 10:1-12). As K.-G. Reploh points out (*Lehrer* 80), the phrasing of 8:21, "Do you not *yet* understand?", implies that the disciples' misunderstanding is only temporary.

A pedagogical purpose for Jesus' rebukes would be in line with the apocalyptic viewpoint of the Gospel of Mark. To cite an apocalyptic parallel, in the QL chastisement (*mwsr*) seems to be a prerequisite for, and a sign of, membership in the covenant community, and is thus a cause for rejoicing.[91] Indeed, one text offers a parallel to the double role of Jesus in 4:11a and 4:13 (revealer, rebuker); the author of 1QH 2:13-14 has been a revealer of mysteries for men of truth, although he tests and tries them by chastisement.[92]

The rebuke of 4:13, then, is not a *revocation*, but rather a *confirmation*, of the statement about the disciples' privilege in 4:11a. Jesus asks why they do not understand, not *in spite of*, but *in view of* their having been given the mystery of the kingdom. Mark understands the rebuke to function as a challenge to the insiders to attain to a deeper level of perception; to them that have, more will be given (cf. 4:25). The rebuke does not imply that the disciples should not have asked the question of 4:10, for without that question the explanation, which is portrayed in such a positive light in 4:34, would never have taken place.[93]

_____

[91]1QS 6:14-15: The postulant is examined, "and if he receives *mwsr* ('chastisement' or 'discipline') he brings him into the covenant." 1QH 2:13-14: The function of the hymnist is "to test (*lbḥwn*) [men of] truth and to try (*lnswt*) lovers of instruction." 1QS 10:12-13: Judgment is a cause for rejoicing; "I will choose that which he teaches me and I will rejoice as he judges me." Indeed, chastisement of the elect by God may be part of the mystery of the kingdom, as 1QH 9:23 suggests: "For in the mystery of your wisdom you have chastised (*hwkḥth*) me." (Translations mine.) Much of this vocabulary (discipline, testing, chastisement) is borrowed from Israelite Wisdom literature, especially Proverbs.

[92]This parallel lends plausibility to our compositional analysis above, according to which Mark is responsible for both 4:11-12, which emphasizes the privilege of the disciples, and for 4:13b, which turns 4:13 into a rebuke. (4:13a without 4:13b is not reproachful.)

The parallel of 1QH 2:13-14 to Mark 4:10-13 extends even further, because in the continuation of the passage the author contrasts his function vis-à-vis the members of the community with his function vis-à-vis outsiders in a way analogous to Mark 4:11-12: "And I was a man of dispute for the interpreters of straying, [but a man of pe]ace for all who seek true things; and I became a spirit of jealousy to all who seek sm[ooth] things" (1QH 2:14-15).

[93]Jesus reprimands the disciples not for their question, but for not at first understanding the parable. Since they do not understand, the question is a good and necessary thing, leading as it does to the explanation.

The rebuke of 4:13, then, does not alter Mark's conviction that to Jesus' disciples, both before and after Easter, Jesus' parables (of which the explanations form an inseparable part) reveal the mystery of the kingdom of God.

The effect of the parables on the "out" group. Contrasted to the revelatory effect of the parables upon the "insiders" (4:11a) is their effect upon the "outsiders": to the latter all things "happen in parables" so that they might become blind (4:11b-12).

One of the main exegetical questions in 4:11-12 is the meaning of *en parabolais ta panta ginetai*. J. Jeremias, relying on his reconstruction of "the Aramaic original" of 4:11-12, translates the latter phrase "all things are imparted in riddles, i.e. they remain obscure."[94] As far as *Mark* is concerned, however, such a meaning, which separates the logion from its immediate context, is not evident; whatever *en parabolais* might have meant *before,* for *Mark* its most immediately obvious meaning is "in the linguistic form of parables." As V. Fusco points out, throughout chapter 4 *parabolē* means "parable" (4:2, 10, 13ab, 30, 33a, 34a), a linguistic form that Jesus chooses in distinction to other forms (4:33-34).[95]

According to 4:11b-12, the effect of parables so defined upon the outsiders is blindness, lack of understanding, and hardness of heart. Commentators have frequently objected that this theory is not consistently maintained by Mark, since, they claim, in 3:23-27 and 12:1-12 Jesus' enemies *do understand* his parables.[96] It is doubtful, however, that Mark would have regarded the enemies' reaction in these passages as "understanding." Rather, the passages are precisely examples of "looking without seeing, hearing without understanding," because in them the enemies "look" (*blepein*) and "hear" (*akouein*), i.e. grasp the parables in a superficial manner, without being admitted to the deeper level of insight indicated by the words "see," "understand," and "repent."[97] In order to substantiate this point, it is helpful to look at the verbs of perception used in 4:12.

---

[94] *Parables* 16-17.

[95] *Parola* 239-40. Fusco adds that Mark would not have intended a meaning for the word different from that in the verses immediately preceding and following 4:11-12 (4:10, 13).

[96] See e.g. H. Räisänen, *Parabeltheorie* 27-33; J. Lambrecht, *Astonished* 139-43.

[97] Cf. J. M. Robinson, *Problem* 125.

The verbs of perception in 4:12. In classical Greek *blepein* means "see, have the power of sight"; it puts a stronger emphasis than *idein* on the function of the eye, and is often opposed to being physically blind. On the other hand, *horan* (of which *idein* forms the second aorist), generally means "perceive, be aware of."[98] In the LXX and Philo *blepein* usually has a connotation of sense perception, whereas *idein* is often used for spiritual insight.[99] Similarly, in the NT *blepein* usually denotes the ability to see as distinct from physical blindness; the word is most at home "to denote seeing processes in the world of empirical phenomena as distinct from religious certainty, which has to do with things invisible."[100] In our passage these processes seem to include intellectual perception that remains outside the realm of faith, since those outside "look and look," but a parable cannot be physically *seen*.[101] In 4:12a, then, *idōsin* indicates true comprehension (see the parallel with *syniōsin*) and *blepontes blepōsin* all perception that falls short of it.[102]

Similarly, in 4:12b, *syniōsin* indicates true comprehension and *akouontes akouōsin* all perception that falls short of it. *Synienai* always has a very full meaning in Mark, indicating a profound grasp of the inner meaning of what Jesus has done (6:52; 8:17, 21) and said (7:14).[103] As for

---

[98]"*blepō*," LSJ, 318.

[99]W. Michaelis, "*horaō*," *TDNT* 5 (1967; orig. 1954) 325-27, 334-35.

[100]Ibid., 343-44, citing Rom 8:24-25; 2 Cor 4:18; Heb 11:1; 3:7.

[101]Cf. V. Fusco, *Parola* 179 n. 21. On *blepein* applied to mental perception in the NT, see BAG, 143 [7b]. Mark's lumping of a certain kind of intellectual perception with "mere seeing," and its separation from true comprehension, is reminiscent of Philo's partially Platonic epistemology, in which sensation and rational knowledge are mutually dependent, but distinct from the higher knowledge of the ideas which is the vision of God; see H. A. Wolfson, *Philo: Foundations of Religious Philosophy in Judaism, Christianity, and Islam* (Cambridge, Mass.: Harvard University, 1947) 2.3-11. Philo's desacralization of rational knowledge stems from his conviction, which Mark shares, of the transcendence of God over all human knowing. Mark, however, relativizes the first two kinds of perception more radically than Philo does.

[102]Mark's use of *blepein* is not consistent; elsewhere in his Gospel it can denote spiritual insight (8:18; cf. 4:24; 8:15, 12:38; 13:5, 9, 23, 33). In these instances, however, *blepein* is not contrasted with *idein*, as it is in 4:12.

[103]Three of the five Markan usages of *synienai* have to do with the significance of the feeding miracles (6:52; 8:17, 21). On 6:52, see Q. Quesnell, *The Mind of Mark: Interpretation and Method through the Exegesis of Mark 6:52* (AnBib 38; Rome: Pontifical Biblical Institute, 1969).

akouein, in 4:12 a more restricted definition of the word is used than in
4:3, 9, where it connotes true insight; the usage in 4:12, however, corresponds to that in 4:15, 16, 18. The variation in meanings of *akouein* is due
to Greek's having only *akouein* and its compounds to express the notion of
hearing, whereas a series of verbs for seeing exists.[104] Similarly, in
Hebrew the verb *šmᶜ* has both a restricted sense ("hearing *differentiated
from* understanding and doing") and a wide sense ("hearing effectively;
hearing, understanding, and doing").[105]

4:12ab, then, speaks both of the outsiders' comprehension of the parables on a superficial level and of their failure to penetrate beyond the
realm of appearance to that of true insight. This combination is especially
obvious in the case of 12:1-12, where, although Jesus' enemies intellectually grasp the message of the parable, this "perception" only increases
their opposition to him;[106] cf. 6:1-6a, where the crowd *sees* that there is
something astonishingly new in Jesus' wisdom and miracles, but they are
scandalized by it.[107] This perception of Jesus is a *hostile* perception,
which mirrors that of the demons.[108]

The latter, too, can be said to "look without seeing." Granted, they
have a clearer perception of Jesus' identity than any human character in
the story until 15:39; they know that he is the Holy One of God, who has

---

[104]W. Michaelis, "*horaō*" 316.

[105]See B. Gerhardsson, "Parable" 168 n. 1.

[106]See V. Fusco, *Parola* 178-79; J. D. Kingsbury, *Christology* 117, 121,
150-51. Fusco cites C. Masson, J. Gnilka, J. Schreiber, A. Ambrozic, R.
Pesch, and H.-J. Klauck as others who see in 12:12 a *confirmation* of the
parable theory. Fusco points out that 12:12 does *not* say that the enemies
knew the parable, only that they *knew that it was directed against them*.

[107]The healing story in 6:1-6a is closely parallel to that in 1:23-28 (see
esp. the crowd's expressions of amazement in 1:27; 6:2) except that in 6:1-
6a the crowd's response to the miracle is hostile. Mark may intend to
suggest by this changed reaction that the hardening spoken of in 4:11b-12
has now begun to set in.

[108] A. Ambrozic, *Hidden Kingdom* 61-62. It might be objected that
there is a difference between the *superficial* perception described in 4:12
and the *hostile* perception of Jesus' enemies in 12:12 and of the demons.
For Mark, however, this distinction seems not to exist; in 8:33 Jesus
rebukes Peter, calling him "Satan," for his incomprehension of the necessity of the crucifixion. On the surface, Peter's mistake is an honest one,
without malicious intent; yet Jesus reproves it as if it were an instance of
hostile, demonic refusal to perceive.

come to destroy them (1:24; cf. 1:34; 3:11; 5:6-7). Yet they still try to
resist him, not perceiving the folly of such an attempt. They attempt to
exorcise *him* by magical manipulation of his name;[109] they try to elude
him by haggling (5:10-12); most importantly, they endeavor to neutralize
the threat he poses to their kingdom by encompassing his death.[110] All of
these strategems, however, backfire.[111] The demonic forces, therefore,
can justly be charged with stupidity; their perception is a looking without
seeing because they do not understand that resistance to God's kingdom is
useless, and will only aid its triumph.

Between the sort of "knowing" manifested by Jesus' human and super-
human enemies, then, a knowing which leaves room for active hostility,
and the sort that Mark would designate "understanding," there lies a world
of difference. "World of difference" is not just a cliche; what distinguishes
the one sort of perception from the other is God's new world of understanding that has been inaugurated in Jesus' death and resurrection.[112]

The "blinding" theory of parables at first seems to be in tension with
4:33, where Jesus speaks to the outsiders in parables "as they were able to
hear." This tension indicates literary layers in 4:33-34, as we have maintained above; in a pre-Markan stage 4:33-34a referred to the disciples and
marked the end of the parable chapter, and *kathōs ēdynanto akouein*
meant "in accordance with their ability to hear." Mark's redaction of the
chapter, however, has changed the addressees in 4:33-34a to the outsiders,
and in this new context (because of the contrast to the insiders of 4:34b
and because Mark surely intends his readers to see that the two groups of

---

[109]R. Bultmann, *History* 209 n. 1.

[110]This demonic intention is implicit in the mirror effect just
described; Mark's readers would certainly have understood that behind the
human plot against Jesus there stood demonic enmity. They might even
have seen the incitement of the crowd by the chief priests (15:2) as parallel to the incitment of Jesus' enemies by the demons.

[111]The demons' attempt to exorcise Jesus by shouting his true identity
only serves to manifest that identity, at least to the Markan community;
the implication of 5:13 may be that the legion of demons has been
swindled (see R. Bultmann, *History* 210); and the crucifixion that the
demons plot does not put an end to Jesus' attack on them, but rather
brings it to completion. Cf. 1 Cor 2:8: if the rulers of this age had known
God's hidden wisdom, they would not have crucified the Lord of glory.

[112]We might contrast to this "looking without seeing" of Jesus' enemies
the picture of "true seeing" found in 10:51-52, which is structurally similar to 4:12a (10:51, like 4:12a, contains *hina* + *blepein* in the subjunctive).
10:52 implies that true seeing involves *following* Jesus "in the way."

4:33-34 = the two groups of 4:11-12) *kathōs ēdynanto akouein* can only mean "in accordance with the outsiders' hearing without understanding," i.e. with their inability to hear effectively.[113] The outsiders are not totally responsible for the way they hear; *ēdynanto* in 4:33 recalls to the reader a theme that was implicit in 4:9, 11-12, 14-20, 23: one is able or unable to hear only as God wills.

The outsiders and the explanations of the parables. Although the "outsiders" do not truly comprehend the parables, they understand them superficially; in 3:23-27; 12:1-12 they get Jesus' parabolic point *without an explanation*. Why, then, does Jesus withhold from them the explanations that are given to the disciples (4:10-20, 33-34; 7:17-23; 13:29)? 4:33-34, taken in conjunction with 4:10-12, seems to imply that the purpose of this withholding is to harden them in their blindness,[114] but how can this be the case if they understand the surface meaning of the parables *without* the explanations?

Mark, apparently, works out the parable theory of 4:11-12 in two different ways. The first way has nothing to do with the explanations of the parables; the outsiders are hardened in that, although they understand the parables superficially, this "understanding" makes them more hostile to Jesus (3:23-27; 12:1-12).

The second way does have to do with the explanations. The juxtaposition of the scene change in 4:10 with 4:11-20, causes the reader of 4:10-20

---

[113]Cf. J. Gnilka (*Verstockung* 51-52) and Q. Quesnell (*Mind* 75, 85); the latter renders 4:33b "according as they were able to listen (namely, without understanding)." Our interpretation of 4:33-34 in the light of 4:11-12 contrasts with the assertion e.g. in the work of A. Jülicher (*Gleichnisreden* 1.119, 143) and E. Schweizer ("Frage" 4-5) that 4:33b *contradicts* 4:11-12.

[114]In 4:33-34, it is part of the *privilege* of the disciples that they receive the explanations, without which the parables are meaningless to them. Therefore, in being excluded from the explanations, the "outsiders" are missing out on something very important; and, with 4:11-12 in mind, the reader would conclude that they were being "hardened" by exclusion from the explanations.

Withholding vital knowledge from outsiders is characteristic of Jewish apocalyptic literature. See 1QS 9:21-22, where the proper attitude toward the "men of perdition" is "everlasting hatred in a spirit of secrecy," and 1QS 4:6, where it is said that God's is a spirit of "faithful concealment of the mysteries of truth" (translations from G. Vermes, *The Dead Sea Scrolls in English* [2d ed.; Middlesex: Penguin, 1975; orig. 1962] 76, 88).

to suspect already what is confirmed in 4:33-34: the outsiders are *further* hardened by being deprived of the explanations of the parables. With Q. Quesnell, then, we might paraphrase 4:33, "With many such (uninterpreted) parables, he spoke the word to them, in accordance with their hearing-without-understanding." *As Mark understands them,* 4:33 and 4:11-12 are perfectly consistent, and can be connected by means of the thought found in 4:25: In view of the outsiders' limited and even hostile listening, Jesus spoke to them in such a way that their incomprehension was increased.[115] Mark 4:11b-12 therefore encompasses two hardenings, an initial hardening through the divinely-willed negative reaction to parables whose point is superficially understood, and a further hardening through exclusion from the interpretations of other parables.[116]

Although parables harden the outsiders in these two different ways, the "parable theory" is a consistent feature of Mark's Gospel. Exactly *how* the outsiders are affected does not seem to be as important to Mark as the general point that Jesus' parables are active speech, and that insofar as they encounter the outsiders, they are effective weapons of blinding in the apocalyptic war.[117]

The wider meaning of "in parables." We have asserted above that, as the immediate context shows, the most obvious meaning of *en parabolais* in 4:12 is "in the linguistic form of parables." The equation of *parabolē* with a linguistic form, however, is not the *entire* story.

---

[115]This interpretation of the Markan parable theory does not change the *hina* of Mark 4:12 to the *hoti* of Matt 13:13, since the initial lack of receptivity of the outsiders is in accordance with God's will, as the receptivity of "those around him" is. On the other hand, Matthew's *hoti* is not such a divergence from Mark as is sometimes assumed; those who are further hardened have previously shown themselves to be unreceptive.

[116]In 3:23-27 and 12:1-12 Jesus' enemies are aided in deciphering the elements of the parables, and thus attaining a superficial comprehension of them, by the controversial settings in which the parables occur; they do not receive the same aid in chapter 4. Intellectual comprehension of the surface meaning, which is withheld from the outsiders in chapter 4, is a necessary part of full understanding; the latter also, however, involves existential appropriation of what has been intellectually comprehended. Probably we are meant to understand that even if Jesus had explained the parables of chapter 4 to the "outsiders," they would have "looked without seeing" in the way that is apparent in chapters 3 and 12.

[117]I have derived the idea of parables as apocalyptic weapons from the lecturing of, and discussions with, J. L. Martyn.

In Mark not *all* of Jesus' public discourse is in parables.[118] Therefore, in interpreting 4:11b ("all things happen in parables"), either the meaning of *ta panta* must be limited or the meaning of *en parabolais* must be stretched. W. Kelber,[119] who adopts the latter course, writes that *panta* in 4:11 "stretch[es] parabolic dynamics across the Gospel."

Similarly, as we have noted above, in the structure of 4:11 the expression "all things" (*ta panta*) is parallel to "the mystery of the kingdom of God." Therefore 4:11b might legitimately be rephrased, "To the outsiders the mystery of the kingdom is delivered in 'parables' in such a way that they look without seeing, etc."[120] In Mark, however, the mystery of the kingdom is transmitted not only by means of parables, strictly defined, but by Jesus' entire ministry, including his death and resurrection, as we have seen in our discussion of the mysteriousness of the kingdom in chapter 2.

Finally, as we have noted above, parables cannot literally be *seen*, but 4:11b-12a implies that the *parabolai* affect the outsiders in such a way that they "look without seeing." In our exposition above we suggested that the solution to this problem may be that *idein* in 4:12 refers not to literal seeing but to mental perception. The difficulty, however, might also be resolved by broadening the meaning of *parabolē* to include an *event* to which there clings an element of the marvelous or the obscure.[121] Such a

---

[118]*Contra* V. Fusco (*Parola* 178) who cites 3:23-30; 4:1-34; 7:14-23; and 12:1-12, but leaves out of consideration 8:34-38 and 11:17, in both of which Jesus teaches "outsiders" without parables; and the controversy stories in 2:15-28; 7:1-13; 10:2-9; 11:27-33; 12:13-17, 18-27, 28-34, 35-37, 38-40, none of which utilizes parables.

[119]*Oral and Written Gospel* 124.

[120]While synonymous parallelism does not always imply the identity of the parallel parts (see above, chapter 2, n. 130), the centrality of the theme of the kingdom of God in Mark suggests a very close relation between the kingdom's "mystery," on the one hand, and "all things" that are of vital concern to Mark, on the other.

[121]G. H. Boobyer, "The Redaction of Mark 4, 1-34," *NTS* 8 (1962-63) 63. This argument is not new; already Remigius (c. 438-c. 533) commented: ". . . Not only what he spoke, but also what he did, were parables, that is, signs of things spiritual, which he clearly shows when he says, 'That seeing they may not see'; but words are heard and not seen" (cited by Thomas Aquinas, *Catena Aurea: Commentary on the Four Gospels Collected out of the Works of the Fathers* [4 vols.; Oxford: Parker, 1842] on Matt 13:13). Cf. Bede (*In Marcum* on 4:11-12; CChrSL 120.482), who says that Jesus' parables included both words and deeds.

meaning for *parabolē* is found in the LXX (Deut 28:37) and the NT (Heb 9:9; 11:19); it corresponds to the broad meaning of the Hebrew *mashal*.[122]

If this broad meaning of "in parables" is accepted, then as G. Boobyer puts it, Dibelius' description of Mark as "a book of secret epiphanies" can be rephrased, "a book of parables."[123] Indeed, as Mark's Gospel progresses, more and more "parabolic" events accumulate.[124] J. R. Donahue points out that Jesus' miracles are parabolic, since they induce shock and surprise.[125] They also manifest the "mystery of the kingdom"; God's power is mightily at work in them, yet in a way that does not exclude powerful opposition (cf. 6:5-6).[126] The feeding miracles in particular are parabolic, as their significance is not immediately apparent.[127] The Gospel culminates in the Passion Narrative, which contains the most puzzling, astonishing, shocking happenings of all: Jesus' agony in Gethsemane; his allowing himself to be betrayed, arrested, tried and sentenced; his conduct before Pilate;[128] his mocking, crucifixion and death;[129] the scene at

---

[122]E. Lohmeyer, *Das Evangelium des Markus* (11th ed.; Göttingen: Vandenhoeck & Ruprecht, 1951; orig. 1937) 83-84. For a massive study of the Semitic background of the Gospel parables, see M. Hermaniuk, *La Parabole Evangélique: Enquête exégétique et critique* (Catholic University of Louvain Dissertation Series II, vol. 38; Paris/Louvain: Desclee, De Brouwer, Bruges/Bibliotheca Alfonsiana, 1947), and more recently P. Patten, "The Form and Function of Parable in Select Apocalyptic Literature and their Significance for Parables in the Gospel of Mark," *NTS* 29 (1983) 246-58.

[123]"Redaction" 59-70.

[124]C. H. Dodd's definition of a parable as a form "arresting the reader by its vividness or strangeness, and leaving the mind in sufficient doubt about its precise application to tease it into active thought," has been applied to Mark's picture of Jesus by J. R. Donahue ("Jesus as Parable" 376).

[125]Ibid., 380-82.

[126]Cf. H. H. Graham, "The Gospel According to St. Mark: Mystery and Ambiguity," *ATR* supp. 7 (1976) 43-55.

[127]K.-G. Reploh, *Lehrer* 83-86.

[128]Both by his cryptic reply in 15:2, and by his silence in 15:5, Jesus leaves Pilate in a state of obscurity; so that while Pilate *sees* that Jesus is called the king of the Jews, he does not *understand* the truth of that ascription. Thus Pilate becomes one who "looks without seeing."

[129]See my "Mark 4:10-12" 570-72 on Jesus' death as a "parable": to

the empty tomb; and the strange ending of the Gospel.[130]

Mark, therefore, probably meant *en parabolais* in 4:11 to have a *double* meaning.[131] While his hearers initially would have linked the phrase with parables strictly defined, as the Gospel continued to unfold they would have been led to apply 4:11-12 more generally to the whole story. Thus we are in basic agreement with J. R. Donahue and W. Kelber that *Mark's Gospel as a whole* functions as a parable; and we may add that Mark probably expected the Gospel's proclamation to have the same double effect as Jesus' parables: to some, a revelation of the kingdom's mystery, of the new space of forgiveness Jesus' advent has created *within* the old aeon; to others, an effect of perplexity, blindness, and hostility to God's purpose, of a firmer wedding than ever to the dying age.[132] Mark 4:11-12 thus turns out to be programmatic, not only for a few of Jesus' discourses, but for the Gospel as a whole.[133]

Mark 4:12ab and Markan irony. The programmatic nature of 4:11-12 is confirmed by an investigation of irony throughout the Gospel. R. A. Culpepper, relying on the work of D. C. Muecke and W. C. Booth, lists as

---

some (e.g. the centurion) it imparts the "mystery of the kingdom," others it leads to blindness. Cf. W. Kelber, *Oral and Written Gospel* 124.

[130]W. Kelber has rightly observed (*Oral and Written Gospel* 129) that the Gospel, like a parable, is open-ended.

[131]We do not believe that this is attributing to Mark more literary sophistication than he deserves; elsewhere in the Gospel he shows himself to be a literary craftsman capable of multiple meanings. In 13:32-36, for example, Jesus' exhortation to watchfulness is, on the most obvious level, a call to his four auditors to be alert for the coming of the parousia. As becomes evident from the remainder of the Gospel, however, it is also a call to the Markan community to pay close attention to what immediately follows chapter 13, namely the Passion Narrative.

[132]Cf. the similar apocalyptic dualism in 1 Cor 1:18; 2 Cor 2:15-16.

[133]Already J. Weiss (*Das älteste Evangelium. Ein Beitrag zum Verstandnis des Markusevangeliums und der älteste evangelischen Uberlieferung* [Göttingen: Vandenhoeck & Ruprecht, 1903] 57-58) emphasized the programmatic importance of the "parable theory" for Mark's Gospel, saying that, rather than the "hardening theory" of 4:11-12 being derivative of the messianic secret motif (as W. Wrede had asserted), the reverse was true. Cf. G. H. Boobyer ("The Secrecy Motif in St. Mark's Gospel," *NTS* 6 [1959-60] 225-35), who asserts that 4:11-12 is the "truly definitive account of the evangelist's point of view."

a basic feature of irony the "contrast of appearance and reality."[134] This contrast is also the theme of 4:12ab, where we hear of people who look and look but do not see, hear and hear but do not understand. Here the realm of appearance is suggested by the verbs "look" and "hear," that of reality by the verbs "see" and "understand."[135] Two other basic features of irony are "a confident unawareness . . . that the appearance is only an appearance" and "the comic effect of this unawareness."[136] This confident unawareness is perhaps suggested by the repetition of the words "look" and "hear" in 4:12ab (*blepontes blepōsin . . . akouontes akouōsin*);[137] similarly, throughout the Gospel Jesus' enemies are confident that their version of reality is true, and that Jesus' version is false (see e.g. 3:22-30).

Indeed, the contrast between the realm of appearance and that of reality is at the very core of Mark. The Gospel, with its mixture of styles, the abrupt movements of its story, and its "lack of descriptive detail and of information that may seem essential to the story," is evocative rather than sensory, signalling that Mark is interested, not in the surface level of the events he narrates, but in a deeper level.[138] In Mark's own phraseology, these two levels might be called "the things of human beings" (*ta tōn anthrōpōn*) and "the things of God" (*ta tou theou*; 8:33).

Our utilization of the literary category of irony, however, would be

---

[134]R. A. Culpepper, *Anatomy of the Fourth Gospel: A Study in Literary Design* (NT Foundations and Facets; Philadelphia: Fortress, 1983) 166-67.

[135]As we have noted above, Mark has reversed the order of the verbs from "hearing" and "seeing" to "seeing" and "hearing" in his citation of Isa 6:9-10. This reversal accentuates the link between 4:12ab and irony, since "appearance" is more closely related to the sense of sight than it is to the sense of sound.

[136]R. A. Culpepper, *Anatomy* 166-67.

[137]These repetitions are translations of the Hebrew form infinite absolute + finite verb (see F. C. Conybeare and St. George Stock, *A Grammar of Septuagint Greek* [Grand Rapids: Zondervan, 1980; orig. 1905] §81). This construction defines the verb more accurately or strengthens it. In Isa 6:9 specifically, the form expresses the long continuance of an action, and could be translated "hear ye continually" (*GKC* 342-43[l, r]).

[138]E. Auerbach, cited by D. Juel, *Messiah and Temple* 44-46. Auerbach contrasts Mark's evocative style with that of classical authors such as Homer, Petronius, and Tacitus; in the classical authors, everything is on the surface and the "intention is to present a thorough sensory impression of the events or persons to be described."

misleading if we did not make clear the distinctive features of the irony found in Mark's Gospel. In Mark, contrary to the impression that R. A. Culpepper's definition of irony cited above might give, "appearance" and "reality" are not two static realms. Rather, "reality" is that which is *coming*, and even now invading the present (cf. 1:15). True seeing, therefore, sees not the way things appear to be *now*, but the way they *will be*.[139] Such an epistemology is thoroughly apocalyptic; when we speak, therefore, of Markan irony, we must be aware of its being *apocalyptic* irony.[140]

The irony in the Gospel is also apocalyptic because inability to see beyond the "appearance" level is due to a blindness brought by Satan. This is clear from the rebuke in 8:33; concern for "the things of human beings" rather than "the things of God" comes from Satan; cf. 4:15-19, where the understanding of people who are "bad soil" has been blocked by Satan. More subtly, in 5:1-20 Mark seems deliberately to paint a picture of human opposition to Jesus which mirrors demonic opposition. The Gerasene townspeople, like the demon, are initially drawn to Jesus, almost against their will, and "see" him (vv 5, 14-15). This perception, however, is a "looking without seeing"; instead of welcoming Jesus they, again like the demon, are afraid (vv 7, 15) and plead with him to depart from them (vv 7, 17).[141]

"Looking without seeing, hearing without understanding" throughout the Gospel. Indeed, throughout the Gospel there are people who *do see something*, but whose vision does not go beyond the surface level. In 5:35-43

---

[139]For example, in 13:1-2, the disciples are directed away from their seeing (*ide, blepeis*) of the Temple as it now stands, and directed toward a vision of it in ruins.

[140]Platonists reading Mark 4:12 would think of Plato's distinction between *epistēmē* ("knowledge" = perception of the eternal forms) and *doxa* ("opinion," based on perception of the shifting appearances of everyday reality); cf. J. L. Martyn, "Epistemology" 276 n. 2. If they stayed totally within a Platonic way of thinking, however, they would miss the eschatological aspect of Mark's epistemology, which is also found in the joyful boast of 1QS 11:3: "For my eye has seen his wonders and the light of my heart *the mystery to come* (*rz nhyh*)." Trans. mine, following E. Lohse, *Texte*.

[141]See the use of *parakalein*, "to plead," in vv 10, 12, 17. In *contrast* to this pleading by the demon and the townspeople is that in v 18 by the man who was demon-possessed; he pleads to be allowed to be with Jesus.

the mourners have some justification for laughing at Jesus, for Jairus'
daughter *is* dead (v 35), even though Jesus says she is not (v 39). Jesus'
vision looks beyond the immediate appearance of death, perhaps to the
coming reality of the life he is about to bestow. Similarly, in 9:26 "looking
without seeing" leads to the (superficially justified) conclusion that Jesus'
exorcism of the epileptic has resulted only in death; but Jesus' resurrection power brings life out of death (9:27). In contrast to the limited perception of the crowd in these two healing stories is that of the Syro-
phoenician woman (7:24-30), who has an inkling of the kingdom's mystery;
she does not take at face value Jesus' rejection of her request to heal her
daughter, but sees the promise hidden in the rejection.[142]

The ruptured perceptivity described in 4:12ab leads to a rupture
between the *appearance* that Jesus' enemies present to the world and the
reality of their motives and inner thoughts; hence Jesus' repeated indict-
ment of their hypocrisy (7:6-7; 12:38-40). They are not interested in what
is true, only in what it is politic to say (11:31-32); contrast their (ironically true) statement about Jesus in 12:14: ". . . You are true, and care for
no person; that is, you do not look on the appearance of people, but truly
teach the way of God."[143] However, they are trapped by Jesus into an
admission that they *do not know* what is "from God" and what is "from
human beings" (11:33), thus giving the lie to their earlier assertion that
Jesus was from Satan (3:20-21).[144] As we have suggested above, however,
their "looking without seeing" is not just an intellectual deficiency, but
involves an *opposition* to the truth that has been revealed; they *see* something of Jesus' power manifested, but this partial perception only produces
hostility.[145]

---

[142]Cf. Martin Luther's discussion of this story, which emphasizes that
God's "yes" is deeply hidden under the appearance of a "no"; cited in P.
Althaus, *The Theology of Martin Luther* (Philadelphia: Fortress, 1966) 57-
58.

[143]On *gar* in 12:14 as explanatory, see E. J. Pryke, *Redactional Style*
126.

[144]Significantly Jesus, in his retort, does *not* parallel their "We do not
know," but rather says, "Neither do I tell you. . . ."

[145]Cf. A. Ambrozic (*Hidden Kingdom* 71-72), who defines *hoi exō* in
4:10-12 as people who have heard the Christian message and have understood it intellectually, but have refused to understand it in a manner that
leads to salvation.

"Looking without seeing" in the Passion Narrative. Mark's premier example for the phenomenon of partial perception combined with hostility is the reaction of Jesus' enemies to the Parable of the Vineyard (12:1-12); they grasp the intellectual point of the parable, but this only leads them to hate Jesus the more and to concoct a conspiracy for his arrest.[146] Indeed, their "looking at, without seeing" the Parable of the Vineyard results in Jesus' death, since the high priest's question in 14:61, which is the legal basis for Jesus' condemnation, picks up Jesus' allegorical reference to himself as the Son of God in 12:6.[147]

In the Passion Narrative itself, Mark's use of irony reaches a climax; as D. Rhoads and D. Michie put it:[148]

> When the opponents ridicule Jesus for claiming to be king of the Jews, the reader sees that the statements which they intend to be ironic sarcasm really are true: Jesus can prophecy [14:65]; he really is king of the Jews [15:2, 9, 12, 18, 26]; his death will secure the destruction of the temple [15:29]; and he cannot save himself except by losing his life [15:30; cf. 8:35].

Or, to use the vocabulary of 4:12, Jesus' opponents speak and hear the truth about him,[149] but their hearing is without understanding.

For example, the "Temple charge" of 14:58 is false testimony but also ironically true, because by his death Jesus will abolish the old religious order symbolized by the Temple; cf. the tearing of the Temple veil in 15:38.[150] The word order of the High Priest's question in 14:61, "You are the Christ, the Son of the Blessed?", ironically resembles an affirmation, and recalls other affirmations of Jesus' divine sonship that the reader (but not the characters in the story) has heard.[151] In 14:65, Jesus is mockingly

---

[146]Contrast to this "looking without seeing" the perception implied in the citation of Psalm 118 in 12:11: "This was the Lord's doing, and it is marvelous in our eyes." Thus another group, to whom the mystery of the kingdom of God has been given, is implied.

[147]J. D. Kingsbury, *Christology* 118-19.

[148]*Mark as Story* 60. We have added in brackets the verse numbers to which Rhoads and Michie seem to be referring.

[149]See *akouein* in 14:58, 64.

[150]D. Juel, *Messiah and Temple* 48, 169, 205-211.

[151]J. D. Kingsbury, *Christology* 119.

told to prophesy; at this very moment his prophecy of Peter's denial is
being fulfilled.[152]

The most complex tapestry of irony is woven around the title "King of
the Jews." J. D. Kingsbury has noted that the true meaning of this title is
transparent only to the readers.[153] To *them* is given the mystery of the
kingdom of God, but to almost all the characters in the story a looking
without seeing. Pilate's question about Jesus' kingship in 15:2, like the
High Priest's question about his divine sonship in 14:61, resembles an
affirmation, as Jesus' reply *sy legeis* ("you say it") suggests.[154] In 15:9,
12, Pilate calls Jesus "King of the Jews," though meaning to indicate
thereby that Jesus is an insurrectionist;[155] but the reader knows better.
The soldiers' mockery of Jesus in 15:18-21 adds further unintentional
testimony to his kingship.[156] He *is* a king, and royal cloaks and crowns
rightfully belong to him; but mockery is the sort of coronation that the
Messiah receives when the hidden kingdom is making its way into the
house of the Strong Man. Finally, the ridicule hurled at the crucified Jesus
(15:29-32) is the most profound, bitterly ironical truth of all those that his
enemies unwittingly utter. "He saved others, himself he cannot save";
indeed, *in order that* he might save others he cannot save himself.[157]

Thus, the events of Jesus' life and death turn out to be "parables" in the
broad sense. Those whom Mark's Gospel is meant to strengthen see that
they demonstrate the kingdom's mystery, its ability to burst forth glori-
ously even in the midst of the same contradictions and persecution that
they themselves, the members of the Markan community, are experiencing. To outsiders, however, these "parables" are aggravations inviting
hatred, ridicule, and even physical attack on their proclaimers. Yet even
the outsiders' ridicule, even their opposition to the kingdom, contains, for
those with ears to hear, a hidden testimony to its power; the blasphemies

---

[152]D. Juel, *Messiah and Temple* 71-72.

[153]*Christology* 125-28.

[154]This reply, however, is itself subtly ironic, since it is "an affirma-
tion which implies that the speaker would put things differently" (V.
Taylor, *Mark* 579). Jesus affirms Pilate's question, but not in the way that
Pilate intends it.

[155]Ibid.

[156]D. Juel, *Messiah and Temple* 47.

[157]Ibid., 48, calling attention to 10:45 and 14:21, 29. In *contrast* to the
"looking without seeing" of Jesus' enemies in the Passion Narrative is the
"true seeing" by the centurion in 15:39; see J. D. Kingsbury, *Christology*
129-31, and my "Mark 4:10-12" 571-72.

that they utter, like the cries of the demons, cannot help bearing witness to him whom they oppose. A change has taken place in the universe, and, though their perception is horribly distorted, even Jesus' enemies cannot fail to have their senses disturbed by this change. So powerful is the kingdom that it reaches down even into the hate-filled minds and venom-ous lips of its foes, drawing unwitting testimony from those who look without seeing.

The outsiders' incomprehension and their exclusion from repentance and forgiveness. Mark 4:12c, which is especially highlighted by its depar-ture from the pattern of 4:12ab, describes the result of the outsiders' incomprehension: they neither repent nor are forgiven. The link between insight, repentance, and forgiveness is clarified by the QL.[158] Basic to the idea of repentance at Qumran is the division of the cosmos into two mutually exclusive battle formations, the lot of God and that of Belial. Repentance (*šwb*, to which *epistrephein* in Mark 4:12 corresponds) means leaving the one formation for the other, *turning away* from the lot of Belial and *returning to* the lot of God.[159] If one cannot *see* where God is acting and where his enemy is at work, however, one cannot abandon the lot of Belial and return to Yahweh; consequently one cannot enter the sphere within which God's gracious forgiveness is experienced.

This link between insight, repentance, and forgiveness underlies several Markan passages. Since the outsiders do not believe the kerygma, they cannot *see* that the time has been fulfilled in Jesus' advent, and so they cannot *repent* and enter the sphere of the *forgiveness of sins* that God's action has created in the world (cf. 1:14-15; 1:4). Similarly, they cannot *see* in Jesus' exorcisms the inbreaking of God's power; rather, they persis-tently ascribe them to Satan. Therefore they do not align themselves with the divine power that is revealed in the exorcisms, and so they cannot be *forgiven* (cf. 3:28-30).[160] Perception leads to repentance, which leads to forgiveness; but since the first link in this chain is denied to "those out-side," so are the latter two.

Furthermore, those in 4:12c who do not receive forgiveness are people who have taken offense at the forgiveness that Jesus has bestowed upon others. The scribes in 2:1-17 take offense at Jesus' pronouncement of

---

[158]See my "Mark 4:10-12" 563. Not cited there is CD 20:32-34, where hearing and forgivness are linked.

[159]P. Parente, "Contributo" 695.

[160]V. Fusco (*Parola* 247) points out the parallel between the "terrible finality" of 3:29 and of 4:12.

forgiveness (2:5) and at his eating with sinners (2:16), thus thwarting his intention that they "may know" his authority to forgive sins (2:10).[161] Their perception is a hearing without understanding; they have seen neither that forgiveness is to be found in Jesus nor that *they themselves* stand in need of it (2:17).

Another type of perception, however, is also present in 2:1-17. When Jesus heals the paralytic, the crowd in amazement glorifies God, crying, "We have never yet seen thus (*houtōs*)." Although *houtōs* here may be construed as an adverb used as an adjective,[162] Mark may also have meant the adverb to be given its full force, suggesting that Jesus has brought a *new way of seeing*, to which some members of the crowd have been granted access.[163]

Mark 4:12c is a stern conclusion, and has contributed to our passage being described as "cruel," "perverse," and "monstrous."[164] Comparison with Jesus' words about Judas later in the Gospel, however, suggests that the tone of 4:12c is not primarily one of revengeful gloating.[165] Although the "outsiders" represent those who are subjecting the Markan community to persecution, Mark's basic attitude toward them is probably something approaching pity. The master they serve, and the fate in store for them, are dreadful; it would have been better for them had they never been born (cf. 14:21).[166] Mark's readers would have reacted with a shudder to the

---

[161]Note the structural similarity between 2:10 and 4:12: *hina* + a verb of perception, and mention of forgiveness.

[162]BAG 598 (5), *BDF* §434 (1).

[163]This new way of seeing is not a once-and-for-all possession; alertness is needed, lest one be led astray (cf. 13:21-23; 14:38). Neither, however, does an occasional lapse into "looking without seeing" plunge one irremediably into the lot of Belial. We have noted above that the otherwise parallel 8:17-18 lacks the "damning conclusion" of 4:12; the disciples can fall into "looking without seeing" *for a time* without ceasing to be disciples.

[164]C. A. Moore, "Mk 4,12: More Like the Irony of Micaiah than Isaiah," *Light unto My Path: Old Testament Studies in Honor of Jacob M. Myers* (Gettysburg Theological Studies 4; Philadelphia: Temple University, 1974) 335-36.

[165]J. L. Martyn has pointed out to me in conversation that Mark 13, unlike much of the apocalyptic literature contemporary with it, is extremely restrained in its description of the punishment meted out on the wicked.

[166]The interjection *ouai*, "alas," which introduces the saying about Judas in 14:21, denotes pain or displeasure (BAG 591), and the saying

destiny they foresaw for their persecutors: a remaining in the dark, dead world of the old age, where the movement to repentance never occurs, and sins are never forgiven.

The problem of the hina *in 4:12c.* Thus the same "parables" that impart the mystery of the kingdom of God to the disciples also cause blindness and obduracy in "those outside." Insofar as *en parabolais* in 4:11 refers to parables strictly defined (and this is the most immediate referent of the phrase), the double reaction to the parables attests that Jesus' word, like the word of Yahweh in the OT, is filled with *dynamis,* imparting life to some and death to others.[167] Jesus' words "will never pass away" (13:31), because they are filled with this divine power.

Looked at from one angle, the opposite effects of Jesus' words upon different groups of people reflect the warfare between God and Satan; the "outsiders," in whom the parables cause blindness, are people under Satan's domination, while the "insiders" are those who have been called by God. Ultimately, however, the division is due to God's will alone, just as at Qumran the struggle between the two Spirits is subsumed under the heading, "From the God of knowledge comes all that is and shall be" (1QS 3:15). This is demonstrated by the word *hina,* "in order that," in 4:12.

From the beginning of the Christian era commentators have attempted to soften the meaning of the *hina.* Some have interpreted Mark's *hina* as if it meant the same thing as Matthew's *hoti* ("because"),[168] while others, such as J. Jeremias, have translated it as "in order that the scripture

---

itself is in the form of a lament. Cf. the categoric command to forgive in 11:25; the outsiders are doubtless included. The Markan attitude toward outsiders is thus somewhat at variance with the attitude expressed in the QL; cf. for example 1QS 9:21-22, cited above, n. 114.

[167] On the word of God in the OT, see G. von Rad, *Old Testament Theology* (New York/Evanston/San Francisco/London: Harper and Row, 1965) 2.80-98. The life-giving aspect of the word can be seen in texts such as Deut 8:3; 32:47; the death-dealing aspect in Isa 9:8; Jer 5:14; both in Jer 1:9-10.

[168] Already Chrysostom (*Hom. Matt.* 45.2) interprets Mark's *hina* as meaning that Jesus talked to the Jews in parables *because* they saw without seeing. In our century Pernot and Hesseling asserted that in Mark 4:12, as in the later koine, *hina* is equivalent to *hoti;* their arguments are summarized and answered by H. Windisch, "Die Verstockungsidee in Mc 4,12 und das kausale *hina* der späteren Koine," *ZNW* 26 (1927) 203-209.

might be fulfilled that says. . . ."[169] These interpretations, however, cannot be supported exegetically. Throughout Mark's Gospel, *hina* always has a final sense and denotes intention; if Mark had wished to avoid a "hardening" theory, he would have avoided the *hina*.[170] Moreover, the intentionality of the *hina* is confirmed by the word *mēpote* ("lest") which follows in 4:12c.[171]

Neither does the observation that Mark 4:12 is a citation of an OT text, Isa 6:9-10, call for a softened interpretation of the *hina*. Throughout the NT the Isaian text is always interpreted in a severe manner; and in Mark 4:12 the *hina* belongs to, rather than introduces, the citation, thus excluding the translation, "in order that the scripture might be fulfilled that says. . . ."[172] Neither is the problem solved by saying that Mark's *hina* is a mistranslation of the relative pronoun *dě* found in the Targum;[173] aside from the objection that this theory tells us nothing about what *Mark* meant by his *hina*, M. Black has shown that, even in the Targum, *dě* followed by *dilěmā³* (= Mark's *mēpote*) would speak unambiguously of hardening.[174]

Thus the problem posed by the *hina* for our sensibilities remains, and indeed Mark probably *intended* it to remain. As we have shown in the previous chapter, Mark, in common with many Jewish apocalyptic thinkers, views the design according to which God enlightens some while blinding others as part of a *mystery*, the mystery of the kingdom of God. Since it is a mystery, however, it is not *meant* to be totally comprehensible by human beings on this side of the unveiling that will occur at the parousia.[175]

---

[169] *Parables* 17; cf. already Pseudo-Chrysostom (probably Victor of Antioch) on Mark 4:12; cited by Aquinas, *Catena Aurea* 2.75-76.

[170] H. Windisch, "Verstockungsidee" 203-209.

[171] *Mēpote* here means "in order that . . . not" (BAG 519) and is an example of "*mē* in an expression of apprehension" which is combined with the subjunctive "if the anxiety is directed towards warding off something still dependent on the will" (*BDF* §370), here God's will. It is true that *mēpote* can be an interrogative particle indicating an indirect question, as in 2 Tim 2:25, where it means "whether perhaps" (BAG 519). There is no indication in Mark 4:12, however, that an indirect question is involved.

[172] V. Fusco, *Parola* 246, 249, 255-57.

[173] T. W. Manson, *Teaching* 75-80.

[174] M. Black, *An Aramaic Approach to the Gospels and Acts* (Oxford: Clarendon Press, 1946) 154-57.

[175] Although Easter is the major epistemological watershed for Mark (9:9; 16:7), texts such as 13:26; 14:62 suggest that at the parousia a

An attempt to deal with the problem of the *hina* in 4:12, however, does not end with this admission. Although we have objected to J. Jeremias's translation of *hina* as "that the scripture might be fulfilled that says," it *is* significant that 4:12 is a citation from the OT. For Mark, God's mysterious hardening of human beings is similar to other paradoxical things he does through Jesus Christ, in that it has been foretold in the scripture. Jesus' death itself fulfills God's purpose as revealed in the OT; he is delivered over to his enemies "so that (*hina*) the scriptures might be fulfilled" (14:49; cf. 9:12). Similarly, Mark's readers would have seen their own history foreshadowed in the Isaiah passage which is quoted in 4:12. While 4:12 refers most immediately to the strange opposition encountered by *Jesus*, Mark's readers, experiencing similar opposition in their own time (13:9-13), would also have interpreted the *hina* as an indication that the opposition *they* were experiencing was no cause for alarm; rather, it fulfilled a purpose that God had announced, in a mysteriously veiled fashion, many centuries before.

Yet the harsh *hina* of 4:12, like the other citations of OT scripture, does not completely negate human responsibility; Mark sees a delicate interplay between God's overarching will, as expressed in the scripture, and human will. The Son of Man goes "as it has been written of him," yet this does not provide an excuse for the man by whom he is betrayed (14:21). John the Baptist was killed "as it had been written of him," yet it can also be said that his murderers "did to him whatever they pleased" (9:13). How the matter is described depends on whether one views it from the level of "the things of human beings" or from level of "the things of God" (cf. 8:33). Although the latter has a certain priority, in order to get the full picture *both levels* must be viewed simultaneously.[176] The *hina* of 4:12 circumscribes, but does not eliminate, human responsibility.

Further light will be shed on the *hina* in 4:12 when we discuss the instances of *hina* in 4:21-22 in chapter 4 of this work.

THE KERYGMA OF MARK 4:10-12, 33-34
FOR THE MARKAN COMMUNITY

The "parable theory" is meant by Mark to be understood on two

---

further unveiling will occur: what now is perceptible only to disciples will then become visible to all, even to Jesus' enemies.

[176]Cf. J. L. Martyn, "Paul" 10-17.

levels.[177] On one level, Jesus addresses the characters in the story, his companions during his earthly ministry, and tells them that in the Parable of the Sower they have been given a picture of the mysterious interpenetration of the old and new ages. On another level, Jesus addresses the Markan community that has come to believe through those first disciples.

In order to understand the kerygma of the "parable theory" for that community, it is helpful to turn once more to Jewish apocalyptic literature for comparison. At Qumran, the members of the elect community are called "children of the eternal mystery" (*bny swd 'wlmym*, 1QS 2:25);[178] thus a *mystery* is determinative for the identity of the community. Furthermore, in the QL and other Jewish apocalyptic literature, knowledge of mysteries *upholds* the elect community in the eschatological testing[179] and *saves* it from destruction.[180]

Similarly, knowledge of the "mystery" that is revealed in the parables and in the parable theory of 4:10-12 is central to the community's identity, since the community is a group that lives, and knows it lives, at the collision of the ages, in other words in the "mystery of the kingdom." This knowledge is vital for the community, enabling it to endure the eschatological tribulation with hope, since it sees *in that tribulation* a confirmation that God is powerfully at work in the world and is therefore provoking a powerful counter-reaction. As in Jewish apocalyptic, the purpose of the bestowal of the mystery on the elect people is not simply to *comfort* them,[181] but literally to *save their lives* (cf. 13:13b).[182]

---

[177]Cf. the conclusion of chapter 2 above, on Mark as a "two-level narrative."

[178]Translation mine. *Swd 'wlmym* could also be translated "the mystery of the ages," making the secret that has been given to the Qumran community a close approximation to Mark's "mystery of the kingdom of God."

[179]See 1QM 17:8-9: "And you, the sons of his covenant, be strong in the ordeal of God! His mysteries shall uphold you until he moves his hand for his trials to come to an end" (trans. G. Vermes, *Dead Sea Scrolls* 146).

[180]Cf. S. Freyne, "Disciples" 9: In Dan 2:20-23 a *mystērion* is revealed to Daniel, "knowledge of which will save him and his friends from destruction."

[181]*Contra* V. Fusco, *Parola* 231. J. L. Martyn has pointed out to me that apocalyptic writings aim at something more than "consolation."

[182]The lives of the members of the Markan community, however, will be saved *as they lose their lives* (8:35). Cf. S. Freyne ("Disciples" 12), who points out that in Wisdom 2:11-22; 3:3 the death of the just is genuine wisdom.

The relation between the elect community and the "mystery of the kingdom of God," however, is not just that the former *knows* the latter. As we have noted, the verb *gnōnai* ("to know") is missing in 4:11. On the level of the story of Jesus' ministry, we have suggested, this absence may imply that the mystery has been *given* to the disciples, but cannot be *known* by them until after the resurrection. For the Markan community, however, the absence of *gnōnai* may have a positive sense: to the community it has been given, not merely to *know* the mystery of the kingdom, but to *participate* in it through the suffering it endures at the hands of "those outside."[183]

For the Markan community, the opposition of "those outside" is a reality that cannot be ignored, and indeed, as we have pointed out above, most of the words in the "parable theory" passages are devoted to the outsiders. Yet we have also noted above that the first and last concern of those passages is the "insiders." The structure of the "parable theory" passages suggests that God's "last word" is not blindness, but sight; not the hiding of the truth from the outsiders, but its revelation to the insiders. Indeed, Mark 4 taken as a whole implies that light rather than darkness is God's "last word"; as we will demonstrate in the remainder of this study, the overall movement of the chapter is from hiddenness to revelation (4:21-25, 26-29, 30-32). This movement is expressed programatically in 4:21-25, to which we turn next.

---

[183]One is reminded of Lear's beautiful speech to Cordelia, in which he invites her to go away to prison with him, where they will "take upon's the mystery of things/ As if we were God's spies . . ." (*King Lear* 5.3).

4

The Sayings about the Lamp and the Measure (Mark 4:21–25)

TRANSLATION

4:21a   And he said to them, Does the lamp come in order that it may be put under the bushel or under the bed?

4:21b   Does it not (come) in order that it may be put on the lampstand?

4:22a   For there is nothing hid, except in order that it may be manifested,

4:22b   nor did anything become hidden, but in order that it might come into manifestation.

4:23   If anyone has ears to hear, let him hear!

4:24a   And he said to them, Take heed what you hear!

4:24b   With the measure you measure, it shall be measured to you,

4:24c   and it shall be added to you.

4:25a   For he who has, it shall be given to him,

4:25b   and he who has not, even what he has shall be taken from him.

LITERARY ANALYSIS

Structure

Mark 4:21-25 consists of two similarly-structured pairs of sayings (vv 21-22, 24b-25), connected by a central pair of commands to hear (vv 23, 24a). Vv 21-22 and vv 24b-25 are alike in being introduced by *kai elegen autois* ("and he said to them") and in consisting of a metaphorical

saying (vv 21, 24bc)[1] followed by an explanatory saying (vv 22, 25) introduced by *gar* ("for").[2] Furthermore, the metaphorical sayings use the
related images of the bushel and the measure,[3] which are drawn from
indoor, domestic life, as opposed to the outdoor, agricultural setting of
the seed parables.[4] The structure of our passage, then, is as follows:[5]

4:21	"And he said to them . . ."	A
	metaphor	B
4:22	explanation (*gar*)	C
4:23	call to hear	D
4:24	"And he said to them . . ."	A'
	call to hear	D'
	metaphor	B'
4:25	explanation (*gar*)	C'

All four of the main sayings (vv 21, 22, 24bc, 25) make use of parallelism, all except v 24bc employ antithesis,[6] and all four are bound together
by the assonance of the -*thē* sounds from the passives. The individual
parts of vv 21-22 and 24b-25, however, are especially closely linked with
each other by assonance.[7]

---

[1] Does Mark intend his readers to understand these metaphors as *parabolai*? R. Pesch (*Markusevangelium* 1.248) asserts that he does, pointing to
the wake-up call of 4:23, which has previously been applied to the Parable
of the Sower (4:9). On the other hand, J. Dupont ("La transmission des
paroles de Jésus sur la lampe et la mesure dans Marc 4,21-25 et dans la
tradition Q," *Logia. Les Paroles de Jésus—The Sayings of Jesus. Memorial
Joseph Coppens* [BETL 59; ed. J. Delobel; Leuven University: Peeters,
1982] 206 n. 12) asserts that in chapter 4 Mark alternates seed parables
(vv 3-9, 13-20, 26-32) with general statements about parable purpose (vv
10-12, 21-25). Dupont's analysis, which implies that vv 21-25 do not contain parables, is supported by the structural similarities between vv 10-12
and vv 21-25, on which see below.
[2] V. Taylor, *Mark* 262; J. Dupont, "Transmission" 202.
[3] R. Bultmann, *History* 325.
[4] See B. Standaert, *L'Évangile selon Marc. Composition et genre litté-
raire* (Brugge: Zevenkerken, 1978) 210.
[5] G. Lindeskog ("Logia-Studien" 158-60) calls this structure chiastic, but
it is so only in a very rough way.
[6] J. Dupont, "Transmission" 202.
[7] Vv 21-22: *tethē* . . . *tethē* . . . *phanerōthē* . . . *elthē eis phaneron*;
vv 24-25: four verbs ending in -*thēsetai* (ibid.).

Vv 21-22 are characterized by a movement from negative to positive. The saying in v 21 progresses from *mēti*, which expects a negative answer, to *ouch*, which expects a positive answer; similarly, v 22 moves twice from negation (*Ou . . . oude*) to affirmation (*ean mē . . . alla*).[8] The most striking feature of vv 21-22, however, is the four *hina* ("in order that") clauses. These clauses would probably remind Mark's readers of the *hina* clause in 4:12, and two other features of vv 21-22 recall vv 10-12: the words "hid" (*krypton*) and "hidden" (*apokryphon*) are related to the meaning of *mystērion* (v 11a), and the becoming hidden (*egeneto apokryphon*) in 4:22b is reminiscent of vv 11b-12, where for the outsiders all things happen (*ginetai*) in parables so that they might neither see nor understand.[9]

Two rhetorical devices in v 21 accentuate the appropriateness of the lamp being placed on the lampstand: the closeness to each other of the words "lamp" (*lychnos*) and "lampstand" (*lychnia*); and the phrase "or under the bed" in v 21a, which makes v 21b stand out in sharper relief.[10] We might paraphrase, "A *lychnos* is made to be put on a *lychnia*, not under a bushel or under a bed or anywhere else where it cannot be seen!"

The two commands to hear in vv 23 and 24a simultaneously link and separate vv 21-23 and 24-25. The first of these, 4:23, repeats 4:9, but the relative construction of the latter has been replaced by a conditional construction. As in 4:9, the wake-up call of 4:23 directs the attention of the readers to what has just preceded; the command of 4:24a, on the other hand, directs their attention to what will immediately follow.[11] The combination of verbs in the command, "Look what you hear!", however, is unusual, and recalls 4:12ab, where *blepein* and *akouein* occur together.[12] The beginning of a new sub-unit in v 24 is indicated by the introductory

---

[8]J. Dupont, "Transmission" 203.

[9]Ibid. 206.

[10]On the latter, ibid. 203 n. 3.

[11]The *Weckruf* ends the section 4:3-9, since a new scene is introduced in 4:10; some manuscripts also introduce it in 7:16 to underline 7:14-15. The call to attention in 4:24a, on the other hand, is analogous to *akouete* in 4:3, which *introduces* a passage. 4:24a cannot refer to what precedes, since 4:23 has this function; by process of elimination, then, it *must* refer to what follows. Cf. R. Laufen, *Die Doppelüberlieferung der Logienquelle und des Markusevangeliums* (BBB 54; Bonn: Königstein, 1980) 167, 170.

[12]B. Standaert, *Évangile* 212 n. 1.

formula "and he said to them" and by the switch from a third person singular subject in v 23 to a second person plural subject in v 24.[13]

After the call to attention, vv 24-25 comprise three simple conditions with the protasis in the present indicative and the apodosis consisting of a future passive indicative plus a personal pronoun:

24b	in the measure you measure	it shall be measured to you
24c		and it shall be added to you
25a	for he who has	it shall be given to him
25b	and he who does not have	even what he has
		shall be taken from him

As the diagram makes clear, the symmetry of this section is broken by v 24c, "and it shall be added to you."[14]

The symmetry is also broken, although less drastically, in v 25b. Now the dative of the personal pronoun (*hymin . . . hymin...autǭ*), becomes a genitive preceded by a preposition (*ap' autou*).[15] The stylistic detachment of v 25b is accentuated by its description of a type of action (taking away) that is opposite to the type described in vv 24b-25a (measuring to, adding, giving). This detachment emphasizes the harsh v 25b, which is also emphasized by the repetition of sounds in its first two phrases (*kai hos ouk echei . . . kai ho echei*). The rhetorical emphasis on a harsh feature is reminiscent of 4:12, where the most drastic clause in the parable theory, 4:12c, is accented by its detachment from the pattern of 4:12ab.

Nor is this the only link between 4:24b-25 and the parable theory of 4:10-12. J. Dupont notes that there is an inclusion between *hymin . . . dedotai* ("to you has been given") in v 11a and *dothēsetai autǭ* ("it shall be given to him") in 4:25a.[16] We may add that the two apodoses of v 24bc might be paraphrased with *dothēsetai hymin* ("it shall be given to you"), so

---

[13] J. Dupont, "Transmission" 203.

[14] Some manuscripts have attempted to remedy this imbalance by either omitting v 24c or by adding *tois akouousin*, so that v 24c reads "and it shall be added to you who hear"; see C. E. Carlston, *Parables* 157 n. 8. Recently J. B. Bauer ("Et adicietur vobis credentibus Mk 4,24f.," *ZNW* 71 [1980] 248-51) has argued that the original version of 4:24 lacked *kai prostethēsetai hymin*; J. Dupont ("Transmission" 221), however, replies that the texts that omit 4:24c are not impressive and that the principle of *lectio difficilior* favors its retention.

[15] J. Dupont, "Transmission" 202 n. 4.

[16] Ibid. 206.

that these clauses are part of the inclusion.[17] Moreover, both passages contrast the group that "has been given" with a group that "has not been given."

Indeed, throughout the entire section 4:21-25, as we have seen, Mark's readers probably would have been reminded of the parable theory of 4:10-12, and would have begun to see its enigmas in a new light (cf. 4:21). The instances of *hina* and the motif of hiddenness in 4:21-22 would have reminded them of the *hina* and the motifs of mystery and blindness in 4:11-12; the combination of *blepein* and *akouein* in 4:24a would have been reminiscent of 4:12ab; and the idea of giving to some while taking away from others in 4:25 would have brought to their minds 4:11-12. These links between the two passages will prove important in the following analysis of the composition history of 4:21-25.

Composition History

Pre-Markan arrangement? The verbal and thematic links just mentioned make it likely that Mark, who introduced 4:10-12 into the parable source, also introduced 4:21-25. Like vv 10-12, vv 21-25 break up the unity of the three seed parables; and the Markan formula *kai elegen autois* introduces vv 21-23, 24-25, as it introduces vv 10-12.

The association of these logia is secondary, as is shown by their presence in different contexts in Q[18] and by tensions between the individual sayings in vv 21-22 and vv 24b-25. V 21 implies that hiding the lamp is senseless, but v 22 implies that the hiddenness has a purpose, albeit a penultimate one, namely to promote manifestation.[19] Similarly, in v 24 one receives according to the way one measures; the person in v 25b, however, does *not* receive according to the little he has, but rather has it taken away from him.[20] Although not conclusive in themselves (one must not try to make ancient teachers and writers too logical), these tensions *in combination with* the evidence from Q make it fairly certain that vv 21, 22, 24bc, and 25 originally circulated independently.

Is *Mark*, however, the person who brought them together? The links

---

[17]The rough equivalence of "shall be measured/added" to "shall be given" is suggested by the first clause in 4:25a.

[18]H. Zimmermann, *Neutestamentliche Methodenlehre. Darstellung der historisch-kritischen Methode* (3d ed.; Stuttgart: Kath. Bibelwerk, 1970) 184-85.

[19]V. Fusco, *Parola* 284.

[20]C. E. Carlston, *Parables* 156-57.

noted above between vv 21-25 and vv 10-12 suggest Markan responsibility; and since, further, Mark introduced the complex vv 21-25 into its present position, the burden of proof is on those who would deny that Mark also brought the logia together. The main argument for a pre-Markan collection is that the individual sayings are connected with each other by catchwords and solely by *gar*, and "both of these features already occur in the earliest transmission of sayings."[21] H. Schürmann replies, however, that the association of sayings in vv 21-25 is not only by catchword but also by content,[22] and J. Dupont points out that Mark himself often uses *gar* to relate material of different origins.[23]

As we proceed we shall observe evidence that Mark sharply revised the individual logia within vv 21-25; also, when we come to the exegesis of our passage, we will see evidence supporting Schürmann's assertion that the combination of logia is not just by catchword but also by theological content. These observations will strengthen the hypothesis that Mark is responsible for the arrangement of the logia in vv 21-25.[24]

Composition history of Mark 4:21. The various forms of the saying about the lamp (Mark 4:21) are schematized in Chart 5.[25] The two basic versions are the Q form (Luke 11:33[26] par. Matt 5:15) and the Markan form, since both Luke 8:16[27] and *Gos. Thom.* 33 seem to be secondary.[28]

---

[21] H. Koester, "Test Case" 75-77; cf. V. Taylor, *Mark* 262.

[22] *Lukasevangelium* 1.469.

[23] "Transmission" 219 n. 65.

[24] Holders of the contrary opinion are split between those like V. Taylor (*Mark* 262) and H. Koester ("Test Case" 75-77) who believe that Mark found all of vv 21-25 combined, and those like J. Jeremias (*Parables* 91) who believe that he found v 21 attached to v 22 and v 24bc to v 25, but not combined with each other.

[25] Charts 5, 6, 7, and 8 are basically English translations (with some rearrangement and a few emendations) of the charts of the Greek versions given by H. Koester, "Test Case" 70, 72, 76, 78.

[26] On the text of Luke 11:33, see B. M. Metzger, *A Textual Commentary on the Greek New Testament* (London/New York: United Bible Societies, 1971) 159; V. Fusco, *Parola* 290; J. Dupont, "Transmission" 211.

[27] Luke 8:16 is dependent on Mark 4:21, although Luke has brought in the ending ("in order that those going in may see the light") from Q; cf. H. Koester, "Test Case" 71.

[28] The *arrangement* of logia in *Gos. Thom.* 32-33 seems to follow Matt 5:14-15 and Matt 10:26-27 par. Luke 12:2-3, although the *text* of the saying about the lamp in *Gos. Thom.* 33 is closest to Luke 11:33. The

Which is more nearly original, the Markan form or the Q form? The Markan form differs from that of Q in the following respects: 1) It is expressed as a question. 2) It does not mention the lighting of the lamp. 3) It is not impersonally expressed, as the Q logion was (see *kaiousin* in Matt 5:15; Matthew probably preserves the Q form almost intact).[29] 4) In Mark the lamp is the subject, rather than the object of the action; furthermore, the lamp is personified; it "comes," and purpose is attributed to it (*hina*).[30] 5) Mark has the alternative "or under the bed." 6) Mark lacks the statement about the lamp giving light to those in the house.

Many of these differences point to the secondary nature of the Markan logion. First, *hina* is a preferred Markan conjugation,[31] and it plays an especially prominent role in chapter 4 (vv 12, 21-22); on the other hand, the impersonal form of the Q version is a Semitism and argues for its relative antiquity.[32] *Contra* J. Jeremias, the personification of the lamp is not a specifically Semitic feature.[33] Rather, the lamp's "coming" is best explained as Markan vocabulary; it corresponds to the "coming" of Jesus in the previous chapters (1:7, 9, 14, 24, 29, 39; 2:17; 3:20).[34] The lamp is very important for Mark; his redaction of 4:21 has eliminated every other protagonist in order to make the lamp the subject.[35]

Jeremias also argues for the originality of Mark on the basis of the "Semitic" question form. Mark himself, however, seems to have a pre-deliction for rhetorical questions and double questions, so the point is

---

secondary nature of the *Gos. Thom.* text is shown not only by its dependence on the Synoptics but also by the ending, "in order that everyone coming in and going out may see the light," which is probably a reference to the soul of the gnostic coming into and leaving the world (see F. Hahn, "Die Worte vom Lichte Lk 11, 33-36," *Orientierung an Jesus. Zur Theologie der Synoptiker. Für J. Schmid* [Freiburg: Herder, 1973] 113-114; *contra* H. Koester, "Test Case" 71).

[29] See G. Schneider, "Das Bildwort von der Lampe," *ZNW* 61 (1971) 184-86; J. Dupont, "Transmission" 210-211.

[30] V. Fusco, *Parola* 290.

[31] See H.-J. Klauck (*Allegorie* 228 n. 206) who gives the statistics for its usage in the Gospels: 41/65/46/15.

[32] J. Jeremias, "Die Lampe unter dem Scheffel," *ZNW* 39 (1940) 238.

[33] *Contra* J. Jeremias, "Lampe" 238; as J. Jülicher already pointed out (cited by C. E. Carlston, *Parables* 150 n. 7), such personification is also found in classical and koine Greek.

[34] H.-J. Klauck, *Allegorie* 228 n. 204; cf. G. Schneider, "Bildwort" 188, 197-98.

[35] V. Fusco, *Parola* 290-95.

CHART 5

Mark 4:21	Luke 8:16	Luke 11:33	Matt 5:15	Gos. Thom 33
Does the lamp come in order that it may be put under the bushel	For no one having lit a lamp covers it with a vessel	No one having lit a lamp	Neither do they burn a lamp and put it under the bushel	For no one lights a lamp and puts it under the bushel
or under the bed? Does it not come in order that it may be put on the lampstand?	or puts it under a bed but on a lampstand	puts it in a hidden place but he puts it on the lampstand	but on the lampstand	nor does he put it in a hidden place but he puts it on the lampstand
	in order that those going in may see the light	in order that those going in may see the brightness	and it gives light to all those in the house	in order that everyone going in and coming out may see its light

moot;[36] and in view of the other evidence Mark's question form can be safely ascribed to him, especially since, as we shall see below, there is a good rhetorical reason for it in the context of vv 21-22.[37]

Composition history of Mark 4:22. Chart 6 compares the forms of the saying about hiddenness and manifestation. Again, the two basic forms are Mark and Q (Matt 10:26 par. Luke 12:2), since Luke 8:17 follows Mark 4:22[38] and the P.Oxy. and *Gos. Thom.* versions are secondary and depend on the Synoptics.[39]

Comparison of the Markan and Q versions reveals the following differences: 1) Q uses a relative construction with *ouden . . . ho ouk* ("nothing . . . which not"), as opposed to Mark's *ou . . . ean mē, oude . . . all'* ("not . . . except, not . . . but"). 2) Mark's version employs two instances of *hina*. 3) The pairs of expressions used to describe hiddenness and manifestation are different. 4) In the second pair, Mark has a verb (*egeneto*, "became"), while Q lacks a verb.

As was the case with 4:21, here in 4:22 most of the differences cited point toward the Q version being primary, the Markan version secondary. Again, *hina* is a favorite Markan conjunction; and its use in 4:22 transforms a sensible observation about the difficulty of keeping anything

---

[36]G. Schneider, "Bildwort" 197.

[37]Mark's change of the saying about the lamp to a question would have provided him with an additional reason for omitting the Q ending ("and it gives light to all those in the house"); see J. Dupont, "Transmission" 218 n. 63.

[38]Luke has introduced the clause "which will not be known" from Q, just as he introduced the Q ending from 11:33 into 8:16.

[39]P.Oxy. 654.4, which is very close to *Gos. Thom.* 5, contains a secondary ending, "and buried which will not be raised" (H. Koester, "Test Case" 75). As for the *Gos. Thom.* versions, H. Koester ("Test Case" 73-75) argues that *Gos. Thom.* 5 is the oldest version of our logion, but he ignores the doublet in *Gos. Thom.* 6. The similarities and differences of these two *Gos. Thom.* versions are best explained by the hypothesis that both are derived from an amalgamation of Luke 8:17 and the Q saying (cf. H. Schürmann, *Lukasevangelium* 1.468; J. Fitzmyer, "The Oxyrhynchus Logoi of Jesus and the Coptic Gospel According to Jesus," *Essays on the Semitic Background of the New Testament* [Sources for Biblical Study 5; Missoula: Scholars' Press, 1974; orig. 1959] 381-384).

CHART 6

Mark 4:22	Luke 8:17	Luke 12:2	Matt 10:26	P.Oxy. 654.4	Gos. Thom 5	Gos.Thom. 6
For there is not anything hid except in order that it may be manifested nor that became hidden but in order that it might come into manifestation	For there is not anything hid which will not become manifest nor hidden which will not be known and come into manifestation	And nothing is covered which will not be revealed and hid which will not be known	For nothing is covered which will not be revealed and hid which will not be known	What is covered from you will be revealed to you for there is not anything hid which will not become manifest and buried which will not be raised	And what is hid from you will be revealed to you for there is nothing hid which will not be manifested	For there is nothing hid which will not be manifested and there is nothing covered which will remain without being revealed

secret, which has widespread parallels in the history of religions,[40] into a logical contradiction: the only purpose of hiding is to make manifest.[41]

While paradox should certainly not be denied to Jesus or to the earliest church, this particular paradox makes most sense in the context of Mark 4, and indeed is a key for deciphering Mark's purpose in writing that chapter. The presence in 4:22 of the verb *egeneto* (lacking in Q) suggests a definite event.[42] Both *egeneto* and *hina* take up loose ends from the earlier part of the chapter, and 4:21-22 answers a question that may be bothering the readers of 4:11-12: is the intentional hiddenness of the event described there (using *ginetai* and *hina*) to be God's last word? 4:21 already hints that the answer is no, and the *ouk . . . alla* construction of 4:22 helps drive the point home; the hiding described in 4:11-12 is seen now to have been only a penultimate occurrence, and one which served the purpose of eventual revelation.

This contrast between penultimate hiding and ultimate revelation links 4:22 with another Markan *proprium*, the messianic secret motif; and the latter helps to explain the inconsistency that hiding is senseless according to 4:21, but has a (penultimate) purpose according to 4:22. This inconsistency has its counterpart in the tension between two elements of the messianic secret motif:[43] 1) Jesus was the Messiah already during his lifetime, and his glory could not help constantly breaking through (1:45; 7:24, 36-37; cf. senselessness of hiding in 4:21). 2) Jesus' true identity had to be hidden while he was alive (9:9; cf. purposefulness of hiding in 4:22).[44] This consonance of the Markan form of 4:21-22 with the messianic secret motif is strong evidence for seeing Mark's hand in the arrangement and present form of those verses.

Other features of 4:22 also point toward redactional work. The phrase *elthē eis phaneron* ("comes into manifestation") is reminiscent both of Mark's use of *erchetai* ("comes") in 4:21, which we have taken to be redactional, and of his redactional use of words with the stem *phaner-* else-

---

[40]For history-of-religions background see R. Bultmann, *History* 95-96; Str-B, 1. 578-79; H.-J. Klauck, *Allegorie* 235 n. 249.

[41]Already J. Weiss (cited by V. Fusco, *Parola* 284 n. 27) termed Mark's formulation "intolerably artificial"; cf. C. E. Carlston, *Parables* 153-54; H.-J. Klauck, *Allegorie* 235-36.

[42]J. Dupont, "Transmission" 216.

[43]On these two elements see W. Wrede, *Secret* 124-29.

[44]4:22 and 9:9 are similarly structured; compare *ou . . . ean mē* in 4:22 with *mēdeni . . . ei mē hotan* in 9:9.

where in the Gospel in "messianic secret" passages (1:45; 3:12; 6:14).[45] It
seems likely, therefore, that the almost mechanical redundancy of the
synonyms in the Markan version of 4:22 (*phanerōthę̄* . . . *phaneron* as well
as *krytpon* . . . *apokryphon*) is a secondary feature (contrast the Q logion,
in which the synonyms are stylistically varied).[46]

Finally, the use in 4:22 of a favorite Markan construction, *ou* . . . *alla*
(also *ouk* . . . *ean mē*), as opposed to Q's relative construction, marks the
verse as redactional. F. Neirynck, however, notes that the Q version of
4:21 has this same *ou...alla* construction, while the Markan version lacks
it, and he plausibly concludes that Mark *transferred* the *ou* . . . *alla* construction from 4:21 to 4:22 when he turned the former into a question.
Both the transformation of 4:21 into a question and the introduction of
the *ou* . . . *alla* construction into 4:22 served the same rhetorical purpose,
to place greater emphasis on the affirmation in 4:22 that the sole purpose
of hiding is subsequent revelation.[47]

J. Dupont rightly notes, however, that Q seems to be secondary to
Mark in its use of *ouden*, "nothing," which smooths out of rockiness of the
Markan form.[48] Later we will see how Dupont accounts for this secondary
feature of the Q logion, while still maintaining its overall priority.

Composition history of Mark 4:23-24a. Vv 23-24a are probably Mark's
own work. V 24a shows definite signs of Markan redaction; both *blepein*
and *akouein* are Markan vocabulary, and their strange association together
("Look what you hear!") is reminiscent of v 12.[49] The *ei tis* ("if anyone")

---

[45]H.-J. Klauck (*Allegorie* 235-36) points out that the other Synoptics
use *phaneros* only in dependence on the three Markan references. Matthew
uses it only once (12:16), and Luke only twice (8:17); and neither of them
use the adverb *phaneros* (Mark 1:45) or the verb *phaneroō* (Mark 4:22).

[46]H. Koester ("Test Case" 73) says that the similarity of terms in the
Markan logion is unusual in sayings of this structure, and a sign of secondary growth.

[47]F. Neirynck, *Duality* 60-61; J. Dupont, "Transmission" 217-218.

[48]J. Dupont, "Transmission" 217. The Markan texts which add *ti* ("anything") after *estin* are trying to deal with the same roughness that Q deals
with by its construction with *ouden*. According to our reconstruction,
then, the pre-Markan version of 4:22 would be, "And there is not anything
(*oude estin*) covered that will not be revealed, and hid that will not be
known."

[49]On *blepein* and *akouein* as Markan vocabulary, see H. Koester, "Test
Case" 75-76, and R. Pesch (*Markusevangelium* 1.252), who points to the
redactional occurrences of *blepete* in 13:5, 9, 23, 33.

construction of v 23 is more elegant Greek than the relative construction of v 9, which may reflect Semitic influence.[50] This smoother version of v 9 in v 23 should be ascribed to Mark himself; for if v 24a is Markan redaction, v 23 probably is, too, as together they carefully structure the entire passage vv 21-25.[51]

Composition history of Mark 4:24bc. Chart 7 shows the two forms of the saying about measuring, that of Mark and that of Q, which links it with the saying about judgment (Matt 7:2; Luke 6:38). The only difference between the Markan and Q forms of the saying about the measure is the presence in Mark of the words, "and it shall be added to you." The note of imbalance that these words introduce does not necessarily mean that they are secondary;[52] the Q form might have eliminated this disturbing note, thus producing a saying more in line with parallel "measuring" sayings from the history of religions.[53]

However, the absence of the words *kai prostethēsetai hymin* from Q *together with* the function they perform in adapting v 24 to v 25 makes it plausible that they were added by Mark. We have shown above that vv 24 and 25 were probably originally independent, and we have noted the tension between the "correspondence" motif in v 24, and v 25, where the person who does not have does *not* receive according to the little he has. The words "and it shall be added to him" in v 24c decrease this tension

---

[50]R. Pesch, *Markusevangelium* 1.250; V. Fusco, *Parola* 289.

[51]Cf. J. Dupont, "Transmission" 219; R. Pesch (*Markusevangelium* 1.250), however, thinks it possible that 4:23 stood in the pre-Markan parable collection between 4:20 and 4:26.

[52]E. Neuhäusler ("Mit welchem Massstab misst Gott die Menschen? Deutung zweier Jesussprüche," *BLe* 11 [1970] 106-107, 111-112) points out that several Synoptic sayings correct an overly rigid correspondence between action and reward with the idea of the superabundance of the divine gift; see also V. Fusco, *Parola* 302.

[53]For these parallels, see Str-B, 1.444-46; M. Smith, *Tannaitic Parallels to the Gospels* (Philadelphia: Society of Biblical Literature, 1951) 135; B. Couroyer, "De la mesure dont vous mesurez il vous sera mesuré," *RB* 77 (1970) 366-370; H. P. Rüger, "Mit welchem Mass ihr messt, wird euch gemessen werden," *ZNW* 60 (1969) 174-82.

CHART 7

Mark 4:24b	Luke 6:38	Matthew 7:2
In the measure you measure it will be measured to you and it will be added to you	For in the measure you measure it will be measured again to you	And in the measure you measure it will be measured to you

CHART 8

Mark 4:25	Matt 13:12	Luke 8:18	Luke 19:26	Matt 25:29	Gos. Thom. 41
For he who has	For whoever has	For he who has	To everyone having	For to everyone having	He who has in his hand
it will be given to him	it will be given to him and he will be made to abound	it will be given to him	it will be given	it will be given and he will be made to abound	they will give to him
and he who does not have even what he has will be taken from him	but whoever does not have even what he has will be taken from him	and he who ever does not have even what he seems to have will be taken from him	but from the one not having even what he has will be taken	but of the one not having even what he has will be taken from him	and from him who has nothing even the little he has they will take it from his hand

by lessening the strictness of the correspondence motif; they are therefore most likely the work of Mark, who first combined vv 24 and 25.[54]

Composition history of 4:25. Chart 8 shows the forms of the saying
about giving and taking away. Both Matt 13:12 and Luke 8:18 are dependent on Mark 4:25; the Markan form is the simplest, and the additional
features in Matthew and Luke reflect those authors' respective redactional styles.[55] *Gos. Thom.* 41 is also secondary, as the phrase "in his
hand" indicates.[56] We come down again, then, to the Markan and Q (Luke
19:26 par. Matt 25:29) forms, which differ from each other in the following ways: 1) Mark uses relative constructions, while Q uses participial
constructions. 2) Mark lacks the word *panti,* "to everyone." 3) Both clauses
in the Markan version end with a pronoun in an oblique case, while only
the second clause in the Q form ends thus.[57]

This time, in contrast to the previous cases, the differences suggest
that the Markan form is primary, the Q form derivative. Most strikingly,
Q's avoidance of the Markan ending of the first clause, "it shall be given
to him," seems to be an amelioration of a Semitic construction that is
awkward in Greek.[58] Also more polished Greek, and therefore probably
secondary, is Q's participial construction; and the word *panti* at the beginning of the Q logion is probably a secondary strengthening.[59]

---

[54]Also, we have seen that Mark is probably responsible for the combination of vv 21-22; if so, however, he is also responsible for the combination of vv 24-25, since their structure parallels that of vv 21-22. See H.
Zimmermann, *Methodenlehre* 190; J. Gnilka, *Evangelium* 1.180; J. Dupont,
"Transmission" 221-22.

[55]The Matthean addition *kai perisseuthēsetai* ("and he shall be made to
abound") is also found in Matt 25:29; cf. also Matt 5:20, which is "a key
phrase for his Gospel" (H. Koester, "Test Case" 79). Luke has improved
Mark's Greek by changing the simple relative conditional into a future
more vivid relative conditional, and he has lessened the paradox in Mark
4:25b by changing "what he has" to "what he *seems* to have."

[56]H. Koester, "Test Case" 79.

[57]Luke's version of the Q saying (19:26) also avoids ending the second
sentence with a pronoun, but this is probably a redactional amelioration;
contrast Matt 25:29.

[58]H.-J. Klauck (*Allegorie* 239) citing K. Beyer and noting that many
texts of Mark 4:25 smooth out the awkwardness.

[59]J. Dupont, "Transmission" 226. The Q logion now stands at the conclusion of the Parable of the Talents; this position is itself secondary, as
J. Jeremias shows (*Parables* 62).

*   *   *   *   *

Our analysis produces somewhat conflicting conclusions: the Markan forms of 4:21, 22, and 24bc are secondary to the Q forms, but the situation is reversed in 4:25; also, the word *ouden* in the Q parallel to Mark 4:22 is a stylistic amelioration. J. Dupont's plausible explanation of these phenomena is that although there are links between the Q tradition and Mark 4:21-25, there is no *literary* relationship; this conclusion corresponds to that of W. G. Kümmel about the Mark/Q overlaps in general.[60]

The critical point, however, is that some of the most distinctive features of Mark 4:21-25, and especially those which tie our passage to vv 11-12, are the work of Mark himself. Having inserted the "parable theory" passage of vv 11-12 between the Parable of the Sower and its interpretation, Mark also inserted between that interpretation and the next seed parable a passage that he carefully shaped as an elaboration and enlargement of the parable theory.

EXEGESIS

The Addressees of 4:21-25

Our passage begins with the Markan introductory formula *kai elegen autois* ("and he said to them"). Who are *autoi*, to whom Jesus speaks in vv 21-25? In the previous verses (vv 10-20) he had been addressing the disciples, but by v 33 the audience has broadened to include the crowd that is outside the circle of disciples.

Mark provides several indications that the audience in vv 21-25 is still the group of disciples, and that the change back to public instruction does not come until 4:26. First, the main themes in vv 21-25 are hiddenness, revelation, and hearing, as in vv 10-20. The inclusion between 4:11 and 4:24-25 points in the same direction. 4:26-29 and 4:30-32, on the other hand, are seed parables, and the previous seed parable, the Parable of the Sower, was spoken to the crowd (4:1-9). Mark's conception is probably that "those outside" get only the outdoor, agricultural images of the seed parables, while the insiders get the indoor, domestic images of 4:21-25.[61]

---

[60]J. Dupont, "Transmission" 226; W. G. Kümmel, *Introduction* 70.

[61]J. Dupont, "Transmission" 205 n. 11. Thus the Markan saying about the measure differs from its rabbinic parallel, in that it speaks not of people in general but of the disciples; see M. Smith, *Tannaitic Parallels* 135.

Yet the disciples' privilege is balanced by responsibility. They are called to attention in 4:23, as the crowd was in 4:9; the changed audience of the wake-up call has been anticipated by 4:13, which implies that insiders too must pay attention.[62]

Mark 4:21-22

The images in 4:21. After the introductory formula, Mark brings forward his first pair of sayings (vv 21-22), beginning with the metaphor of the lamp that comes to be put, not under a bushel or a bed, but on a lampstand. As the explanatory *gar* clause in 4:22 makes plain, Mark sees the basic contrast in 4:21 as that between hiddenness and revelation.[63]

In postbiblical Judaism, a light or lamp can symbolize both a person and that person's teaching (see already Sir 48:1).[64] The personal nuance of the metaphor emerges clearly in *Sipre Num* 94:2-3, a commentary on the passage in Num 11:17 where God takes some of Moses' spirit and places it on the seventy elders. This *Sipre* passage contains some striking similarities to Mark 4:21:[65]

---

[62]J. Dupont, "Transmission" 206.

[63]Comparison with Judges 7:16 also suggests that Mark's readers would have thought the purpose of covering a lamp to be hiding its light (see H.-J. Klauck, *Allegorie* 230). As far as Mark is concerned, therefore, J. Jeremias's hypothesis ("Lampe" 237-40), that the main point of the parable is the contrast between lighting and extinguishing a lamp, cannot be maintained; in order to arrive at this interpretation, Jeremias has to eliminate the phrase "or under the bed" as secondary, and this surgery makes his analysis irrelevant for exegesis of Mark. The history-of religions parallels upon which Jeremias's work is based are of doubtful validity; see G. Schneider, "Bildwort" 191-93 and H.-J. Klauck, *Allegorie* 230. See also A. Dupont-Sommer, "Note archeologique sur le proverbe evangelique: mettre la lampe sous le boisseau," *Melanges Syriens offerts à Monsieur R. Dussaud* (Paris, 1939) 2.789-94.

[64]G. Schneider ("Bildwort" 192-93), citing also John 5:35; 8:12, and passages from rabbinic literature; cf. other citations in R. Pesch, *Markusevangelium* 1.249. See also 1QSb 4:27: "May God make of you . . . a great torch, a light to the world in knowledge, to enlighten the faces of many" (trans. mine, following E. Lohse, *Texte* 59).

[65]The beginning of this passage is cited by H.-J. Klauck (*Allegorie* 232). The translation is mine.

What was Moses like in that hour? He was like a candle placed
on a candlestick, from which many candles are lit, and its light
is not lacking at all; thus Moses' wisdom was not lacking at all.

Not only is a person compared to a light placed on a stand, as in Mark
4:21, but the comparison occurs in a context having to do with wisdom; cf.
the wisdom associations acquired by Mark 4:21 through its linkage with
the idea of revelation in v 22 and with the call to hear in vv 23-24a.[66]

Similarly, the lamp in Mark 4:21 symbolizes both Jesus' teaching about
the kingdom and the secret of his identiy. Vv 11-12 have portrayed a
parabolic message that is hidden from some people; this message is identical with "the word" of vv 14-20.[67] Therefore when Mark's readers heard
in v 21 about a hidden lamp, they probably would have linked it with the
hidden parabolic word of vv 11-20. This hypothesis is supported by a
rhetorical consideration, the assonance of *logos* ("word," vv 14-20) with
lychnos ("lamp," v 21).

If the lamp is the word in the parables, however, we must reckon with
both the narrower and broader meanings of *parabolē*, as we have analyzed
them in chapter 3. According to the narrower meaning, the lamp is the
message of the Parable of the Sower and the other seed parables in chapter 4, all of which, for Mark, concern the mystery of God's eschatological
kingdom. According to the broader meaning, the lamp is the secret of
Jesus' identity as it is revealed in his entire ministry, including his
miracles, teaching, and death.[68]

---

[66]The second-third century dating of *Sipre Numbers* does not vitiate
the interest of this passage for the exegete of Mark, since the comparison
of a sage with a lamp is also found before and during New Testament
times, and since the formal parallels between it and Mark 4:21 are so
striking.

[67]The two groups encountered by the parables in vv 11-12 are parallel
to the two groups encountered by the word in vv 14-20, and 4:33 ("in
parables he spoke the word") confirms that the parables contain the word;
see also the juxtaposition of "parable" and "my words" in 13:28, 31.

[68]To the coming of the lamp cf. the uses of *erchesthai* for Jesus in the
previous chapters of the Gospel; see R. Laufen, *Doppelüberlieferung* 169.

On the relation between the mystery of the kingdom of God and the
secret of Jesus' identity, see J. Marcus, "Mark 4:10-12" n. 36. The secret
of Jesus' identity has to do with the question, "Who is Jesus?"; the mystery of the kingdom has to do with the question, "Why don't people *see*
who Jesus is?" Thus the hiddenness of the kingdom is an extension of the
hiddenness of Jesus.

The *Sipre Numbers* passage to which we have compared Mark 4:21 implies that other people are illuminated through the enlightenment of Moses; this idea is also present in the Q form of the saying about the lamp ("and it gives light to all those in the house"), but it is omitted in Mark's version of the saying. The omission takes place not because Mark is uninterested in the enlightenment of his hearers, but because for him the saying about the lamp expresses a more basic although certainly interrelated reality, the difference between a world situation characterized by openness and one characterized by manifestation.[69] C. E. Carlston perceptively sums up the difference between the Markan and Q forms of the saying:[70]

> In Mark, the lamp is not brought in order that men may see the light (Luke), nor is it brought and put on a stand with the result that it gives light (Matthew); it is brought *in order to be put on a stand*. The public view of the lamp, not its light-giving function, is primary for Mark.

Mark's form of the saying stresses not the seeing subjects but the new objective environment created by the lamp's movement, although the latter certainly has *ramifications* for the seeing subjects. The lamp has moved into an open space in the cosmos, where nothing prevents it from being visible to all.

The movement from hiddenness to revelation in 4:22. This new situation of openness is taken up in v 22. As we have noted, however, there is some tension between the emphasis on the senselessness of hiding in v 21 and the emphasis on the purposefulness of hiding in v 22. Mark resolves this tension partly by causing v 21 to serve v 22 (see the *gar* in v 22); now v 21 means that a lamp does not come to be hidden *permanently* under a bushel or a bed, but in order to be placed on a lampstand *eventually*. The hiddenness which at first appeared to be senseless turns out to have its own strange logic.

The tension between vv 21 and 22, however, also corresponds to that

---

[69]That Mark understands 4:21 to apply on a cosmic scale is suggested by: a) the use of the definite article; it is not just a matter of any lamp and lampstand, but of *the* lamp and *the* lampstand, and b) the explanatory saying in v 22, which interprets v 21 in the broadest possible terms ("there is *nothing* hidden, except in order to become manifest").

[70]*Parables* 155.

between two elements of the messianic secret motif, as we noted in our analysis of composition history above. Jesus wishes not to be *phaneros*, manifest in public (3:12; cf. *phanerōthę* and *phaneron* in 4:22), yet he cannot escape detection (7:24; cf. 7:36-37). These "leaks" in the messianic secret are proleptic of the post-Easter state of openness, in which the Markan community lives.

For Mark, Easter is the point at which hiddenness gives way to revelation. This is most clearly indicated by 9:9, where Jesus commands the disciples to tell no one what they have seen (a vision of his transfigured glory) until the Son of Man is raised from the dead. This verse is similar to 4:22 in its theme of a hiding that gives way to revelation and in its grammatical structure.[71] As W. Wrede wrote, linking the two passages, 4:21-22

> refers back to the idea that something secret is being imparted in the parables. This is meanwhile received only by the disciples, but some day—more plainly, *after the resurrection*—they are to lift the veil from it and spread it abroad. For every secret is secret only for a season. It urgently seeks disclosure.[72]

Indeed, the very existence of Mark's Gospel points toward the changed post-Easter situation, for this production of a post-Easter community announces a message that Mark's Jesus forbids to be proclaimed during his lifetime. Jesus' divine sonship, which the demons were forbidden to confess during his earthly ministry, and which only they and God knew about,[73] is the content of the gospel that is now preached to all nations (1:1; 13:10).[74] Whereas previously secrecy was enjoined, and open proclamation was disobedience, now open proclamation is enjoined, and secrecy is disobedience (13:10; 16:7-8).[75]

The motif of the disciples' blindness also points toward the resurrection

---

[71]See above, n. 44.

[72]*Messianic Secret* 70-72.

[73]See 1:11, 24, 34; 3:11-12. The centurion at the cross recognizes that Jesus is the Son of God, but not until Jesus dies.

[74]This is true whether or not 1:1 includes the title "Son of God," since the confessions of Jesus' divine sonship cited in the previous note are overheard by Mark's readers, but not by the characters in the story. On the question of the text of 1:1, see B. M. Metzger, *Textual Commentary* 73.

[75]Cf. J. Gnilka, *Evangelium* 2. 344.

being a turning point, for Mark's clear implication is that this blindness will be healed after the resurrection. This inference emerges from the story about the two-stage healing of a blind man in 8:22-26, which Mark places between two episodes of apostolic misunderstanding (8:14-21, 31-33).[76] The formerly blind man's state of partial sight corresponds to the disciples' partial perception; cf. esp. Peter's true but incomplete confession of Jesus' messiahship in the misunderstanding story that follows the healing (8:29). The healing story, however, by its movement from partial to full healing of blindness, promises that this incomplete perception will yet be made whole. This promise is reinforced in the first of the misunderstanding stories, for there Jesus twice asks the disciples if they do not yet (*oupō*) understand (8:17, 21; cf. 4:40); he thereby implies that at a future point their vision will be perfected.

This point is the resurrection, as the redactional verses 14:28; 16:7 establish;[77] after it the disciples will *see* Jesus in a new way,[78] and this post-Easter seeing is *contrasted* to their being scandalized at his fate in the pre-Easter period.[79] The predictions of suffering for Jesus' sake in 13:9-13 leave the reader in no doubt that the disciples *did* see Jesus in Galilee and went on to follow him in the way of the cross.[80] The impression that Easter inaugurates an era of revelation is reinforced by the rising of the sun (16:2) and the appearance of the angel (16:5) in the narrative of the empty tomb. Since this is the only angel in Mark's entire narrative,[81] and since the sunrise scene contrasts starkly with the

---

[76]See E. S. Johnson, "Mark viii. 22-26: The Blind Man from Bethsaida," *NTS* 25 (1979) 370-83.

[77]*Contra* V. Fusco (*Parola* 128), who thinks that *oupō* in 4:40; 8:17, 21 points forward to Peter's confession in 8:29; if so the rebuke of Peter's misunderstanding in 8:32-33 is strange. On the redactional nature of 14:28; 16:7, see R. Fuller, *The Formation of the Resurrection Narratives* (New York: Macmillan, 1971) 53, and H. Paulsen, "MK XVI 18," *NovT* 22 (1980) 149.

[78]Cf. J. D. Kingsbury, *Christology* 136-37.

[79]See the *alla* at the beginning of 14:28.

[80]*Contra* J. D. Crossan, "Empty Tomb" 149.

[81]It is hard to accept the complicated and abstract theory of J. D. Crossan ("Empty Tomb and Absent Lord," *The Passion in Mark* [ed. W. Kelber; Philadelphia: Fortress, 1976] 147-48) that the young man of 16:5 is a symbol of Jesus, a neophyte in the Markan community, and the Markan community itself, all rolled into one. V. Taylor (*Mark* 606-607) rightly points to the use of *neaniai* for angelic beings in 2 Macc 3:26, 33, and to the descriptions of white-robed figures in Rev 7:9, 13; the average reader

darkness of 15:33, the reader is encouraged to think of Easter as a revelatory turning point.

Assuming that the Gospel ends at 16:8, however,[82] the last glimpse we have of this Easter morning paints a less than splendid picture of the post-resurrectional period. The women are stupefied by the angel's words about Jesus' resurrection, and they disobey the command to go and tell the disciples that Jesus is going before them into Galilee: "And they said nothing to anyone, for they were afraid" (16:8). Thus ends the Gospel.

This ending, however, does not refute our contention that Easter inaugurates a time of revelation. The women's disobedience will not thwart God's will that the truth of the resurrection should be spread abroad and that the disciples should see Jesus in Galilee. In the Gospel story of the empty tomb, Mark himself tells the tale that the women left untold. Somehow, the news has leaked out; it could not remain hidden. The abrupt ending of the Gospel would have left Mark's readers amazed, not that the divine will expressed in 16:7 had been thwarted, but that it had been fulfilled in spite of the disobedience described in 16:8.[83] Passages such as 4:21-22 (and 4:26-29, 30-32), with their description of hiddenness giving way to revelation, contribute to the reader's certainty of this fulfillment, for they "provide images that build momentum that leads to eventual disclosure, without which the ending of the Gospel makes no sense."[84]

Mark's presentation of Easter as the inauguration of a new age of revelation corresponds to OT, intertestamental Jewish, and rabbinic conceptions of the Age to Come. While the time just before the end is one in which "the truth will hide itself" (2 Bar 39:6), when the eschaton arrives this hiddenness will give way to an age of disclosure.[85] Especially interesting for comparison with Mark 4:11-12, 21-22 are texts from Isaiah (29:18, 24; 32:3; 35:5) that imply that the new age will bring a reversal of the sentence of insensibility found in Isa 6:9-10 and quoted in Mark

---

of Mark's Gospel would have assumed that the white-robed *neaniskos* in 16:5 was an angel.

[82]See A. Lindemann, "Die Osterbotschaft des Markus. Zur theologischen Interpretation von Mark 16.1-8," *NTS* 26 (1980) 300, and H. Paulsen, "MK XVI 1-8" 140-43.

[83]Cf. W. Lane, *Mark* 592: "The focus upon human inadequacy, lack of understanding and weakness throws into bold relief the action of God."

[84]Letter from D. Juel, 23 November 1983.

[85]J. Marcus, "Mark 4:10-12" 567-69; besides the Qumran texts cited there, see also 1QH 5:11-12. Cf. *1 Enoch* 90:35; *4 Ezra* 13:2.

4:12.[86] At that time, the blinded eyes of 6:9-10 will be opened, the closed ears unstopped; indeed, Isa 32:3 uses the same rare word that is found in 6:10, šʿʿ ("to be smeared over, blinded"),[87] to describe what will no longer be true of the eyes of those living in the messianic era. Thus, for Isaiah as for Mark the harsh sentence of Isa 6:9-10 is not God's final word about his revelation of himself to the world.

Hiding in order to make manifest. Mark 4:22, however, goes beyond the notion that hiddenness will yield to openness; it implies that hiddenness *serves the purpose* of openness. *Prima facie* this notion is nonsensical, but in the economy of Mark's Gospel it makes sense. God intends the outsiders to be blinded by Jesus' parables and his parabolic actions (4:11-12), so that they oppose him and eventually bring about his death;[88] in his death, however, the new age of revelation will dawn. Thus the hiddenness of Jesus' identity (cf. the *hina* clause in 4:12) leads to his death, which in turn results in the open manifestation of his identity (cf. the *hina* clause in 4:22). The *hina* clauses in vv 21-22, like the one in 4:12, refer to *God's* intention,[89] and all of these *hina* clauses intersect at the cross.

The crucifixion is a climax of human blindness, cosmic darkness, and divine revelation. The outsiders, in the persons of the chief priests and scribes, express the mocking wish that Jesus descend from the cross "in order that we may see and believe" (*hina idōmen kai pisteuōmen*; 15:32). Their mockery, which is reminiscent of 4:12 (*hina . . . mē idōsin*), shows that their perception is a looking without seeing;[90] thus the blind hostility described in 4:12 is the human cause for Jesus' ending up on a cross.

The crucifixion, however, is not only a climax of blindness; it is also a

---

[86]See J. Schniewind, *Evangelium* 42; A. Ambrozic, "Mark's Concept of the Parable. Mk 4, 11 f. in the Context of the Second Gospel," *CBQ* 29 (1967) 227. B. W. Anderson (*Understanding the Old Testament* [3d ed.; Englewood Cliffs: Prentice-Hall, 1975]447) asserts that God's call to the heavenly council to proclaim comfort in Isa 40:1-2 reverses the call to proclaim judgment in Isa 6:9-13.

[87]The only other OT usage of this verb is in Isa 29:9.

[88]Cf. to the *hina* of 4:12 the two uses of *hina* to express God's intention that Jesus die (9:12; 14:49); the three passion predictions (8:31; 9:31; 10:33-34) make a similar point.

[89]*Phanerōthę* in 4:22 is one of several "divine passives" in the chapter (vv 11, 21, 22, 24, 25).

[90]15:32 is the end of a redactional section of the Passion Narrative, 15:29-32; see J. Pryke, *Redactional Style* 23. Cf. also *idōmen* in 15:36.

turning point in God's disclosure of himself. The triumph of God that will become visible on Easter morning is already present, for those with eyes to see, in the midst of the weakness and suffering of the crucifixion.[91] This revelation is suggested not only by the centurion's confession in 15:39, but also by the tearing of the Temple veil in 15:38. That tearing is a partial fulfillment of Jesus' prophecy of the Temple's destruction (13:2), but it probably also would have suggested to Mark's readers a revelation of the divine glory hidden behind the inner veil.[92] In Jesus' death, then, God himself has ripped apart the barrier that shielded the holy of holies from profane sight, and has begun to flood the universe with the glorious radiance of the Age to Come.[93]

But before this radiance can stream forth, Jesus himself must enter

---

[91]Mark sees Good Friday and Easter as part of one event. On the relationship between the two stages of this event, see A. Lindemann, "Osterbotschaft" 311-312; J. Marcus, "Mark 4:10-12" 15-16.

[92]On the reference to the inner veil in 15:38 see C. Schneider, "katapetasma," TDNT 3 (1965) 629-30; also J. Gnilka, Evangelium 2.324; H. L. Chronis, "The Torn Veil: Cultus and Christology in Mark 15:37-39," JBL 101 (1982) 110. Chronis writes that this interpretation "modestly assumes only that Mark would have known what (whom!) the veil's destruction would have left exposed."

Mark's readers would not even need to be conversant with the OT in order to understand this implication. See Schneider ("katapetasma" 628) for evidence that also in non-Jewish Hellenistic religions katapetasma is one of the technical terms for the curtain hiding from profane sight the divine image in the shrine, and that therefore there would be an association in readers' minds between the removal of a temple curtain and the revelation of a divinity (CIG 2.2886; Ovid, Fasti 2.563; Clement of Alexandria, Paed. 3.2; Apuleius, Met. 11.20).

[93]Cf. H. L. Chronis, "Torn Veil" 97-114. Although there is no specific mention of the revelation of the divine glory hidden behind the veil, we believe that our interpretation is the most logical way of understanding the progression of events in 15:37-39: 1) Jesus dies, 2) the Temple veil is torn, 3) the centurion confesses Jesus as the Son of God. Note that in 14:57-65 three similar elements are present (Jesus' condemnation to death [14:64], the Temple charge [14:58], the Son of God title [14:61]) in conjunction with the motif of apocalyptic revelation (14:62).

The word houtōs ("thus") in 15:39, then, might refer not only to Jesus' death itself (15:37), but also to the event narrated in v 38, which accompanies the death.

into the darkness of death, which is characteristic of the old age.[94] This entrance is graphically depicted in 15:33-34:

> And when the sixth hour had come, there was darkness over the whole land until the ninth hour. And at the ninth hour Jesus cried with a loud voice, "Eloi, Eloi, lama sabachthani?" which means, "My God, my God, why have you forsaken me?"

The universal darkness of the day of judgment, covering "the whole land,"[95] presses down upon the crucified man, so that he cries out in the anguish of his abandonment by God. In accordance with God's purpose, however, he enters into this darkness, breathing out his spirit after a last, loud cry (15:37),[96] *in order that* humanity might live in the light of the new age (15:38-39); he gives his life as a "ransom for many" (10:45). God intends for Jesus' transcendent power to be revealed precisely in the midst of his powerlessness;[97] it is only in this context of manifestation in the midst of hiddenness that the *hina* of 4:22 makes sense.

Although the Markan motif of becoming hidden in order to become manifest is *sui generis,* the idea of God causing evil to reach a climax in order that the new age might come is familiar from Jewish apocalyptic.[98] In 4 Ezra 11:39, for example, God addresses the fourth beast from Daniel's vision, "Are you not the one that remains of the four beasts which I had made to reign in my world, *so that (ut) the end of my times might come through them?*" As W. Harnisch comments, here the terrible reign of the

---

[94]One of the mockeries to which he is subjected involves his face being covered with a blindfold (14:65); here already, perhaps, the reader sees Jesus beginning to be swallowed up by old-age darkness.

[95]Cf. Amos 8:9: "'And on that day,' says the Lord, 'I will make the sun go down at noon [the sixth hour], and darken the earth in broad daylight.'" Thus, in the Markan passion narrative, the darkness that begins at the sixth hour is a sign that the day of judgment has arrived. See J. Schreiber (*Theologie des Vertrauens* [Hamburg: Furche, 1967] 33-40) on other apocalyptic elements in Mark's crucifixion narrative.

[96]Since prior to this cry and the cry of abandonment in 15:34, only the demons have shouted with a loud voice (*phōnē megalē;* 1:26; 5:7; cf. Acts 8:7), it is possible that Jesus' death shout is understood by Mark as demonic. Such an exegesis would support our interpretation that at the crucifixion Jesus takes humanity's place in the darkness of the old age.

[97]H. L. Chronis, "Torn Veil" 106.

[98]See already Hab 2:13-14: the darkness of the peoples serves Yahweh's light.

beast is ascribed only a relative importance, since it serves the bringing in of the end.[99] The paradox is not strained to the breaking point, however, as it is in Mark, where the agent and symbol of God's triumph is an executed criminal.

The two clauses in 4:22. Although Easter is a revelatory turning point for Mark, the ending of the Gospel on the note of the women's disobedience implies that hiddenness continues in the post-Easter period; and many other features of the Gospel, such as the references to post-Easter persecutions in 13:9-13, point in the same direction. For this reason, F. Hahn and H.-J. Klauck refuse to see the point of manifestation alluded to in 4:22 as the resurrection; instead they think of a reference to the parousia.[100]

Resurrection and parousia, however, are not strict alternatives; Mark seems to have had *both* in mind as he edited 4:21-22. Easter and eschaton are intertwined in Mark's mind; J. Dupont rightly states that in Mark 4 "the present moment of the church's expansion after Easter is envisioned in the relation that unites it to its end, the eschaton."[101]

Furthermore, the wording of v 22 itself points to two different stages in the manifestation of God's kingdom. Although the clauses in vv 22a and 22b are in "synonymous parallelism," this does not necessarily mean that they are completely synonymous.[102] The first verb of v 22a is in the present tense (*estin*), while the first verb of v 22b is in the aorist (*egeneto*). Gnomic aorists being extremely rare in the New Testament,[103] we must assume that *egeneto* refers to a past event unless we are given a

---

[99]W. Harnisch, *Verhängnis und Verheissung der Geschichte. Untersuchungen zum Zeit- und Geschichtsverständnis im 4. Buch Esra und in der syr. Baruchapokalypse* (FRLANT 97; Göttingen, 1969) 254-55.

[100]F. Hahn, "Worte" 119; H.-J. Klauck, *Allegorie* 237. For a list of the scholars who take the two opposite sides in this debate, see V. Fusco, *Parola* 285-86. Fusco's own solution, that the reference is to the future point when Israel's blindness will cease (*Parola* 286-88), is based on passages from Paul, Matthew, and Luke, but conspicuously *not* from Mark. The *replacement* motif of Mark 12:1-12 contrasts sharply with the *restoration* motif of Rom 11:25-32.

[101]J. Dupont, "Transmission" 208 n. 21.

[102]On biblical parallelism see above, chapter 2, n. 130.

[103]L. Rademacher, *Neutestamentliche Grammatik. Das Griechisch des Neuen Testaments im Zusammenhang mit der Volkssprache* (HNT 1,1; Tübingen: Mohr/Siebeck, 1911) 124; N. Turner, *A Grammar of New Testament Greek* (Edinburgh: T. & T. Clark, 1963) 3.73-74.

good reason for thinking it gnomic; and no such reason presents itself. Indeed, if Mark had wished v 22b to have exactly the same meaning as v 22a, he probably would have omitted *egeneto* altogether, as Q did;[104] but on the contrary our literary analysis has shown that he has *introduced* the aorist verb in v 22b.

Thus v 22 might be paraphased, "Nothing is now hidden, except with the purpose of manifestation, just as in the past nothing became hidden except for the same purpose." As heard by Mark's first readers, this statement would refer to two times: the present of the Markan community (v 22a) and the past of the time of Jesus (v 22b).[105] The parallelism of these two acts in the "two-level drama" is accentuated by the redundancy of the pairs *phanerōthę . . . phaneron, krypton . . . apokryphon*, which is due to Markan redaction (see our analysis of the composition history of 4:22 above). Just as the time of Jesus was characterized by a hiddenness that gave way to, and served the purpose of, the revelation that occurred on Good Friday and Easter, so the present is characterized by a hiddenness that will lead to complete manifestation at the parousia.

Even after the resurrection, then, it remains part of the mystery of the kingdom that God's glory can only break forth in the midst of darkness (cf. 13:24-27). Because the truth of the gospel is hidden from the outsiders, they persecute the members of the Markan community as they once persecuted Jesus; but in the midst of this persecution, the Holy Spirit speaks (13:11) and a *martyrion* to Jesus Christ goes forth (13:9). The Markan community, then, finds its own story recapitulating what happens in Mark's passion narrative; it is driven to the uttermost state of powerlessness, suffering, and death, but discovers that in the midst of its weakness God's glory is revealed.[106]

Mark 4:23-24a

This revelation, however, is hidden from all those who cannot see the inbreaking of the new age in the crucifixion and resurrection of Jesus, and therefore Mark's readers must be called to attention. 4:23-24a is a

---

[104]V. Fusco, *Parola* 294.

[105]See G. Schneider, "Bildwort" 198; J. Lambrecht, "Redaction" 289; R. Laufen, *Doppelüberlieferung* 169.

[106]This revelation is proleptic of the full manifestation that will occur at the parousia, just as the revelation that occurred during Jesus' ministry was proleptic of the post-Easter state of openness.

progression; not only are the hearers called to listen (4:23), but to listen to something very particular: "Take heed *what* you listen to!" (4:24a).[107]

An antithesis is implicit in this exhortation; one is to listen to some things but not to others. In Mark's apocalyptic epistemology, the present age, insofar as it *is* the present age (10:30), is still subject to the influence of the Spirit of Falsehood; in such a world most of the voices that can be heard are deceitful. To listen to these voices is to be trapped in the realm of the old age, of appearances, of that which will not last; and ultimately to find oneself in a sphere of desolation, apostasy, and spiritual death (4:15-19). These other voices assume concrete form in the false Christs and false prophets of 13:5-6, 21-33, to whom are ascribed supernatural power ("they will give signs and wonders") and evil intent ("in order to deceive, if possible, the elect").[108] The relevance of the warnings against deceivers in chapter 13 for the exegesis of chapter 4 is reinforced by the presence within them of the word *blepete*, "take heed" (13:5, 23; cf. 4:24a).

Thus in 4:24a the Markan community is not just called to cut through the external word to the inner reality of the word.[109] It is also warned against a deceitful, Satanic word, which claims to be the word of God. Furthermore, the word of the gospel, which *should* be listened to, is not a word that proclaims timeless spiritual realities (as the outer word/inner word dichotomy might suggest). Rather, it is a word that announces an *event*, the coming of God's new world, which is even now breaking into the present (1:14-15). To listen to this word is to hear the reality of the new age which is coming, and which is already the hidden reality of *this* age.[110] Only those who take heed *what* they listen to, turning their

---

[107] Mark's *ti* emphasizes the *object* of hearing (contrast Luke's *pōs*); see V. Taylor, *Mark* 264. On 4:23-24a as a progression, see J. Dupont ("Transmission" 202-203), who points out that in Mark the second term of a double expression is usually more precise than the first.

[108] On this translation of *pros to*, see BAG, 710 (5e); also V. Taylor (*Mark* 516), who says that the construction indicates "subjective purpose."

[109] The external word/internal word dichotomy, propounded by J. Schniewind (*Evangelium* 46) and E. Schweizer (*Good News* 101) has some justification in the Markan text; see 4:12, where the outsiders "look without seeing, hear without understanding," i.e. comprehend in a merely superficial manner. It is *incomplete*, however, for it fails to reckon adequately with the apocalyptic basis of Mark's epistemology.

[110] Cf. T. S. Eliot, "Burnt Norton" 2, *Four Quartets:* "Both a new world/ And the old made explicit."

attention to where God is acting in a hidden way through Jesus Christ, will hear truly, and bear fruit a hundredfold (4:20).

Mark 4:24b-25

Relationship to 4:24a. Mark 4:24a introduces the sayings about measuring and giving (4:24b-25). It is not merely an introduction, however; it also announces the theme of those sayings, true and false perception.[111] One indication of this is the agreement in number of the verbs in v 24a ("take heed what you hear") and v 24b ("in the measure you measure"). Both are second person plurals, as opposed to the third person singulars of vv 21-23; this agreement suggests that, for Mark, hearing (v 24a) is the same as measuring (v 24b). More importantly, the inclusion between "to you has been given" in 4:11-12 and "shall be given to you" in 4:25, and the contrast in both passages between the group that "has been given" and the group that "has not been given," strongly suggests that 4:25, like 4:11-12, deals with epistemological questions.

This hypothesis is supported by background from the history of religions, especially the Qumran literature, where "measuring" and related concepts appear in epistemological contexts.[112] In 1QS 8:4, for example, the ruling council of the community behaves toward everyone "according to the measure of truth (*bmdt h'mt*) and the order of the time" (trans. mine). Other texts make clear that "measure of truth," "greatness of portion," and "weight" are synonymous images for the degree of insight possessed by a person, which is the basis upon which he is promoted at the yearly assize.[113] Not only these specific images but also the general idea

---

[111]J. Dupont ("Transmission" 204) poses the exegetical question of whether 4:24a is merely an introduction or also states the themes of 4:24-25.

[112]The closest *formal* parallel to the saying about the measure comes from the Palestinian Targum on Gen 38:26 where Judah, unmasked by Tamar, comments, "With what measure a man measures, in that same way it is measured to him, whether good measure or bad measure" (see M. McNamara, *The New Testament and the Palestinian Targum to the Pentateuch* [AnBib 27; Rome: Pontifical Biblical Institute, 1966] 138-42, and H. P. Rüger, "Mass" 174-82. This saying may take up a formula from grain repayment contracts (B. Couroyer, "Mesure" 366-70).

[113]Cf. for example 1QH 14:18-19: "I will cause each man to drawn near in accordance with his understanding, and according to the greatness of his portion (*krwb nhltw*) so will I love him" (trans. G. Vermes, *Dead Sea*

of reward in discrete degrees relates these texts to Mark 4:24. With this background in mind, v 24b means, "To the degree that you pay attention to what God has already revealed, to that degree will more revelation be bestowed upon you."[114]

History-of-religions parallels also support the assertion that Mark 4:25 relates to perception. While Mark's saying about giving ultimately stems from the mordant commonplace, found throughout the Greco-Roman world, that "the rich get richer while the poor get poorer,"[115] passages from rabbinic literature that place the saying in an epistemological context offer the closest parallels to the Markan logion. G. Lindeskog lists these parallels: 1) The rabbinic passages concern the relation between God and human beings. 2) They stress that God's way differs from human ways. 3) They speak of a divine gift, wisdom, and the quality one must have to receive it. 4) These ideas are expressed in parables.[116] Lindeskog's points are finely illustrated in b. Ber. 40a:[117]

> R. Zera, or some say R. Ḥanina b. Pappai [both c. 300] said: Observe how the character of the Holy One, blessed be he, differs from that of flesh and blood. A mortal can put something into an empty vessel but not into a full one. But the Holy One, blessed be he, is not so; he puts more into a full vessel, but not into an empty one; for it says, "If hearkening you will hearken" [Exod 15:26], implying, if you hearken you will go on hearkening, and if not you will not hearken."

The parallel to Mark 4:24-25 is especially close here because God's adding to a full vessel is related to *hearing*.[118]

Scrolls 193). Similarly, 1QS 9:12, 14-15 speaks of weighing the members of the community and promoting them according to their understanding. The latter text also speaks of *judging* the sectarians according to their spirits; cf. the association in Matt 7:2 between judging and measuring.

[114]Promotion according to one's understanding is also spoken of in 1QS 5:24; 6:14; CD 13:11-12; 1QH 10:27-28; 12:22-23; 14:18-19.

[115]G. Lindeskog ("Logia-Studien" 149) cites instances of this commonplace in pagan literature.

[116]G. Lindeskog, "Logia-Studien" 148-53.

[117]Cited in Str-B, 1.660-661. The other main passages cited by Billerbeck are *Midr. Qoh.* 1:7, on which see below, n. 124, and *Gen. Rab.* 20 par. The latter parallels Mark 4:25b: "What you desired is not given to you, and what belonged to you is taken away from you."

[118]As noted by H.-J. Klauck, *Allegorie* 239-40.

Although this particular passage is rather late, the ideas that it contains go far back in Israelite wisdom tradition. Already Proverbs 1:5 contains the theme of the sage hearing and learning more;[119] this passage also, like Mark 4:25, speaks of wisdom as a possesion ("he will *acquire* wisdom")[120] that is imparted in *mĕšālîm* (cf. Prov 1:1) and given by God (cf. Prov 1:7).

The wisdom imparted in Proverbs 1, however, has to do with matters of everyday experience, even though its source is God. In Daniel 2, on the other hand, as in Mark 4, wisdom ideas have undergone an apocalyptic transformation, and the wisdom granted to the wise is a secret that is contrasted with all human wisdom (cf. Mark's opposition of "the things of God" and "the things of human beings," 8:33). Dan 2:20-22, moreover, contains several other parallels to Mark 4:21-25:[121]

> 20) May the name of God be blessed from eternity and to eternity, for wisdom and might belong to him. 21) He changes the times and the seasons; he puts down kings and sets up kings; he gives wisdom to the wise and knowledge to those who know insight; 22) he reveals deep things and secret things; he knows what is in the darkness, and the light dwells with him.

Here we find the themes of "giving wisdom to the wise,"[122] the revelation of secrets (cf. Mark 4:22)[123] and God's power to establish and undermine whom he will (cf. Mark 4:25), as well as light imagery (cf. Mark 4:21)[124] and an eschatological context (changing times and seasons; cf. Mark 4:21-22). These are not just formal parallels; their combination in both Mark 4

---

[119]Cf. Prov 9:8-9.

[120]MT *yiqneh*, LXX *ktēsetai*.

[121]We have already drawn on Dan 2 in our discussion of the meaning of *mystērion* in Mark 4:11 in chapter 2.

[122]LXX: *didous sophois sophian kai synesin tois en epistēmē eisin*; cf. *dothēsetai* in Mark 4:25 and *syniōsin* in Mark 4:12.

[123]Theodotion renders 2:22 *autos apokalyptei bathea kai apokrypha*; cf. *apokryphon* in Mark 4:22.

[124]Daniel 2:21 evidently influenced the later development in Jewish circles of the motif "giving to the one who has" along epistemological lines. In *Midr. Qoh.* 1:7 (cited in Str-B, 1.660) R. Jochanan (d. 279) compares God's action in Dan 2:21 to that of a man lending money; he would rather lend money to a rich man whom he knows can repay it than to a poor man who perhaps cannot.

and Daniel 2 stems from the apocalyptic mindset of the two writers. When the power of God's new age breaks forth into the world, it brings eschatological insight to those whom God has chosen as its recipients, but an "eschatological reversal" to those predestined to be in the enemy ranks.

This apocalyptic interpretation helps to unravel a difficulty about v 25b: how can one both have and not have? To the apocalypticist such a combination is inevitable; since the Spirit of Darkness is still active in the world, the person who has "the things of God" often does not have "the things of human beings," and vice versa. The exegetical puzzle of v 25b is solved when it is realized that the person described there has the "things of human beings" but lacks the "things of God." 4:25 can be paraphrased: "He who has" the things of God, the mystery of God's kingdom, will be further enriched by new revelations of the glory that breaks forth in the midst of darkness; but "he who does not have" the things of God, who remains enmeshed in "the things of human beings," the realm of appearances associated with the old age, will in the end lose even the superficial perception that he possesses. We are back to the message of 4:11-12: enlightenment to one group, hardening to another.

The two groups in 4:24-25. The interpretation just advanced implies that the two groups of 4:11-12 (and 4:15-20) are also present in 4:24-25; "those who have" are the insiders of 4:11a, the good soil of 4:20, while "those who do not have" are the outsiders of 4:11b-12, the bad soil of 4:15-19. The latter group, we remember, includes both apostate Christians and people who have opposed the gospel from their first hearing of it (see chapter 2).

J. Gnilka and V. Fusco, however, assert that the import of 4:25b is that the insiders of 4:11 will themselves have their privilege revoked if they do not pay attention.[125] For Gnilka and Fusco the person being spoken of in 4:25b is the same as the addressee, namely the Christian disciple. Therefore vv 25a and 25b represent the two alternatives open to the disciples: they can either continue to be "those who have," in which case they will receive more, or they can become "those who do not have," and be stripped of their spiritual possessions.

While we recognize that the group in v 25b includes *former* disciples, it is clear from the structure of vv 10-25 that Mark means the two groups in vv 24-25 to correspond to the two groups in vv 11-12. We have noted above the inclusion between vv 11-12 and vv 24-25, and the presence in

---

[125] J. Gnilka, *Verstockung* 40; V. Fusco, *Parola* 300-302.

each of two groups, one of which receives a divine gift while the other does not. Furthermore, the structural detachment of v 25b from vv 24b-25a implies that the "you" addressed in v 24bc (= "he who has" in v 25a) is *different from* "he who does not have" in v 25b; therefore the addressees of vv 24-25a, the disciples, are a different group from the subjects of v 25b. Vv 24-25a refer to the disciples, while v 25b refers to the out-siders.[126]

This exegesis is confirmed by the placement of vv 21-25 immediately after the interpretation of the Parable of the Sower. With the latter still ringing in their ears, Mark's readers would probably have associated the multiplication of what one has in 4:24bc-25a with the fruitfulness described in 4:20, and the loss of what one has in v 25b with the imperma-nence of transitory growth described in vv 15-19.[127] The people described in v 20, however, are the faithful disciples, while those described in vv 15-19 are the outsiders, as we have shown in chapters 2 and 3.

Moreover, the interpretation advanced by Gnilka and Fusco does not correspond to the wording of v 25, which posits two strictly separated groups, whose separation from each other can only increase, rather than a fluid situation where members of one group can cross over into the other. Had Mark meant v 25 to bear the meaning suggested by Gnilka and Fusco, he would presumably have worded it something like: "He who has, let him take heed lest it be taken away from him!" (cf. 1 Cor 10:12).

According to our interpretation, then, there is a caesura between vv 24bc-25a and v 25b; v 25b brings into view the outsiders, who were not under consideration in vv 24-25a. In our entire chapter, then, the descrip-tions of insiders and outsiders alternate to form a double chiasm:

4:10-11a	insiders
4:11b-12	outsiders
4:15-19	outsiders
4:20	insiders
4:24-25a	insiders
4:25b	outsiders

---

[126]We can therefore resolve the apparent tension between the prin-ciple of v 24b (as you measure, it shall be measured to you) and that of v 25b (the one who does not have does not receive according to the little he has) with the observation that these two clauses refer to two different groups, to whom different rules apply.

[127]J. Dupont, "Transmission" 204.

4:33-34a   outsiders
4:34b   insiders

Contrary to Gnilka and Fusco, therefore, 4:24-25 does not say to the disciples, "Pay attention—or else." Its import for them is all promise (4:24b-25a);[128] God's kindness to them is contrasted with his severity toward those outside (4:25b). The disciples will be given *more* than they deserve (see esp. "and it shall be added to you"). In this context, the introductory call to hearing (v 24a) functions not as a warning or a threat but as a gracious demonstration of the way in which the disciples can enter into blessing upon blessing of eschatological insight.

The time-referent of the futures in 4:24-25. When will the disciples obtain this insight, however? In other words, what is the time to which the future tense verbs of vv 24-25 refer? Since the time of revelation referred to in vv 21-22 turned out to be *both* the post-Easter period *and* the parousia, we are led to ask whether the same may not be true of vv 24-25.[129] If the answer is yes, then on one level this passage would prophesy that the pre-Easter disciples will attain a more profound understanding after the resurrection. On a second level it would prophesy that the members of the Markan community will experience a complete unveiling at the parousia, although there would be a prolepsis of this apocalypse in the ever-increasing insight now given to them in the midst of their suffering and persecution.

Mark 10:28-30 supports this suggested exegesis. Here Jesus prophesies that the disciples will receive a hundredfold *in this time* (the post-resurrectional period), and *in the age to come* eternal life. This gift to them is contrasted to the judgment pronounced upon the rich young man, from whom it is taken away to enter the kingdom of God (10:23-25); this statement, too, has both a present and a future nuance, as we saw in chapter 2. The *dynamis* of the new age will increase abundantly, and already is increasing abundantly, the possession of those who have entered the kingdom of God; but the destructiveness of the old age is already at work in those who remain under its domination, stripping them of what

---

[128]In speaking exclusively of a good measuring, the Markan saying differs from the parallel in the Palestinian Targum (see n. 112), which refers to both a good measuring and a bad measuring.

[129]C. E. Carlston (*Parables* 157) and J. Dupont ("Transmission" 205 n. 8) pose the exegetical question of whether these sayings refer to reward and retribution in this world or at the eschaton.

they have; and their spiritual barenness will be terrifyingly evident at the last day. A similar point of view lies before us in the QL, where the ranking of community members according to their "measure of truth" in the present is proleptic of their rank in the messianic age.[130]

The roles of human attention and of God's will in determining insight. V 24b, in the context of v 24a, implies that one's insight depends on the attention that one pays. This emphasis upon human responsibility, however, is qualified by several elements in the surrounding context.

First, Mark has expanded the rule, "As you measure, it shall be measured to you," with the addition, "and it shall be added to you." This addition destroys both the structural balance of the original sentence and the tidiness of its thought that reward is commensurate with action.[131] The equilibrium of the pre-Markan *talion* has been shattered by the Markan emphasis on God's gracious action.

Secondly, the juxtaposition of v 24 with v 25 implies that the one who "measures" is the one who "has"; he *has*, however, because he has been *given* (v 11a; cf. Paul in 1 Cor 4:7). Therefore God's action in granting the mystery of the kingdom to the disciples has priority over their hearing. This point is reinforced when we consider that the parenetic vv 23-25 are sandwiched between kerygmatic passages that describe the irresistible movement of God's kingdom from hiddenness to manifestation (vv 21-22, 26-32). For Mark, it is the latter movement that *creates* the human ability to hear. This same divine priority over faithful human action is implicit in the QL, where "the *chosen ones*" and "the *choosers*" are interchangeable terms for the members of the elect community, but the former designation is by far the more frequent.[132]

According to 4:11-12, 14-20, 25, the extent of human knowledge depends upon the *group to which one belongs*, while according to 4:21-22

---

[130]Cf. 1QSa 1:17-18 with 1QSa 2:11-21.

[131]See E. Lohmeyer, *Evangelium* 85-86. In form the original sentence (without v 24c) corresponds to E. Käsemann's category of a "sentence of holy law"; see above, chapter 2, n. 139, and cf. R. Pesch, *Markusevangelium* 1.252.

[132]"Chosen ones" (*bhyry*) occurs in 1QpHab 10:13; CD 4:3-4; 1QM 12:1, 4-5; 1QS 8:6; 11:16; 1QH 2:13; 14:15; "choosers of the way" (*bwhry drk*) only in 1QS 9:17-18, where a later scribe has corrected it to *bhyry drk* ("chosen ones of the way"). Cf. A. Dupont-Sommer, *Essene Writings* 95 n. 5.

it depends upon *what time it is*.[133] This tension also bears witness to
Mark's apocalyptic viewpoint. For all their faults, the disciples, and the
Markan community which they foreshadow, are people who already live
"as if" in the new age (cf. 1 Cor 7:29-31); the outsiders, on the other hand,
are people who live as though the old age were the only reality. The
collision between the two ages, therefore, is incarnated in the clash
between the two groups. Since they are the place where God's power
breaks forth in the midst of weakness, the disciples show forth the strange
and wondrous shape of the new age before it has fully dawned (cf. 4:11);
the shrieks of hatred uttered by their persecutors, on the other hand, are
the dying gasps of the old age (cf. 15:13-14, 29-32).

The Kerygma of Mark 4:21-25 for the Markan Community

Vv 21-22 are a hinge in Mark 4; they connect the hidden presence of
the kingdom, described in vv 3-20, with the movement from hiddenness to
manifestation described in the rest of the chapter (vv 21-32).[134] Hiddenness cannot be understood by itself, but only in the light of the coming
apocalypse. The Markan community lives in a world charged with a presence that is about to explode into complete manifestation.[135] Just as
during his ministry the secret of Jesus' identity could not be hid, but kept
breaking out, although it was not fully revealed until the crucifixion and
resurrection; so now the kingdom is "gathering to a greatness" and already
beginning to burst forth. The flame rushes up the fuse toward the dyna-
mite; the sparks thrown off, the revelations granted to the Markan community, foreshadow the incandescent eruption that will occur at the
parousia.

Within vv 21-32, however, vv 24-25 stand apart from the consistent
theme of the movement from hiddenness to manifestation. Yet this parenetic passage is not out of place. Its placement here suggests that human

-----

[133]Cf. V. Fusco, *Parola* 284.

[134]V. Fusco is therefore correct to subtitle his chapter on 4:21-25,
"Toward the Future" (*Parola* 279-304).

[135]Gerard Manly Hopkins' poem "God's Grandeur" has a similar
message; it describes the divine glory hidden but present in the world,
pushing toward complete disclosure:
    "The world is charged with the grandeur of God.
        It will flame out, like shining from shook foil;
        It gathers to a greatness, like the ooze of oil
    Crushed..."

perception arises out of the irruption of God's kingdom.[136] Furthermore, the hearing of God's word is the link between the present, in which God is secretly at work, and the future, in which he will be manifestly at work. The word speaks *in* the present *of* the future, and thus brings the reality of the future into the present for those with ears to hear in the Markan community.

As we have explained above, "he who has" (v 25b) has the things of human beings, but not the things of God; or, as Chrysostom puts it, he "has a lie."[137] This lie, however, has a great existential urgency for the Markan community. At first glance, those outside seem to be the "haves." They appear to know something that Jesus' disciples do not know: how to save their lives, how to win in the world; the proof is in their power of life and death over the Markan community. Conversely, Jesus' disciples at first seem to be the "have-nots"; they lose their lives.

Mark 4:25, however, is an apocalypse of where the Markan community and its persecutors *truly* stand. Those who lose their lives save them, and thus are the real "haves"; those who save their lives lose them, and thus are the real "have-nots" (8:35). The enemies of the Markan community do not know it yet, but that upon which they have relied has been destroyed. A dynamited building stands for a moment after the blast, apparently unchanged, before coming down with a crash;[138] even so the Strong Man's

---

[136]The sandwiching of vv 24-25 between the passages that describe an irresistible movement toward revelation raises questions about the ultimate fate of those who "do not have." Will the taking away of what they have be God's last word about them, or does the placement vv 24-25 imply that *all* those described there, including the outsiders, will ultimately live in the light of God's new age? The same question is posed by the overall structure of Mark 4; the hiddenness of vv 10-20 gives way to the revelation of vv 21-32. In Mark's soteriology, Jesus gives his life as a ransom for "many" (10:45); the ransom concept implies that he gives his life for those who have nothing to offer on their own behalf, not just for "those who have" (cf. J. Jeremias *"polloi,"* TDNT 6 [1968; orig. 1959] 536-45 on the inclusiveness of the word "many" in 10:45). After their betrayal of Jesus, the disciples' own salvation is based solely on God's grace. Does Mark think that ultimately the outsiders, too, will share in this grace?

[137]Cited by Aquinas, *Catena Aurea* 2.81, in a passage that has not come down to us in Chrysostom's extant writings; see also R. Pesch (*Markusevangelium* 1.253), who calls this having a nullity, only an appearance of having.

[138]This striking image comes from K.-G. Kuhn (cited by O. Kuss, "Zur Senfkornparabel," *Auslegung und Verkündigung* [Regensburg: Pustet, 1963; orig. 1959] 83).

house seems to have absorbed the shock of Jesus' advent, but its appearance of establishment is a total lie. At the parousia the fragility of the structure will be instantaneously revealed. What the outsiders "know" will be taken away from them, because the facade upon which it is based will collapse into nothing.

Mark's hearers, on the other hand, although they have lost everything, are rich; and they will become richer as they persevere in hearing the word. They have heard the word of the crucifixion, that God's power is released at the nadir of theirs; and the parousia will reveal to the whole world the substantiality of that in which they have placed their trust.

Our interpretation of 4:21-25 has emphasized that both Easter and the parousia are revelatory moments for Mark; both the time of Jesus' ministry and the post-Easter period contain a mixture of hiddenness and revelation. Mark's two-level presentation, however, does not so blur the boundaries between the time of Jesus and that of the church that the distinction between these two periods is lost. In the next passage, the Parable of the Seed Growing Secretly, Mark indicates how he views the relation between these two times and their different mixtures of hiddenness and revelation.

5

The Parable of the
Seed Growing Secretly
(Mark 4:26–29)

TRANSLATION

4:26a	And he said, Thus is the kingdom of God
4:26b	as a man should throw seed upon the earth
4:27a	and should sleep and arise night and day
4:27b	and the seed should sprout and grow
4:27c	in what manner, he himself does not know.
4:28a	By itself the earth bears fruit
4:28b	first a blade, then an ear, then full grain in the ear.
4:29a	But when the fruit is ripe
4:29b	he immediately sends out the sickle
4:29c	for the harvest has come.

LITERARY ANALYSIS

Structure

Grammatically and thematically, the parable falls into three sentences:
vv 26-27, v 28, and v 29.

In the first sentence (vv 26-27), the introductory formula (v 26a) is
awkwardly connected to the rest of the sentence.[1] The sentence contains
three sets of verbs in the subjunctive ("throw," "sleep and arise," "sprout

---

[1] See BAG, 897(II4c) which suggests that an *an* has been lost. Some
manuscripts smooth out the awkwardness by adding *ean*, "if," after *hōs*, or
by adding *hotan*, "when," after *anthrōpos*, "man"; see A. Ambrozic, *Hidden
Kingdom* 106.

and grow"), governed by the word *hōs*, "as"; in this sentence, the man is the center of attention.[2]

The second sentence (v 28), while somewhat awkwardly connected to the first,[3] continues the motif of growth found near the end of the first sentence; this growth now becomes the exclusive theme. Both of the first two sentences contain a pattern of threes, i.e. the three sets of verbs in the subjunctive in vv 26-27 and the three stages of growth in v 28.[4] The latter are described in an emphatically linear manner in v 28.[5] The growth is now said to be due to the ground rather than the seed, and the most significant verbs are no longer in the subjunctive but in the indicative mood.

Finally, in the third sentence (v 29) the focus of attention shifts back to the man,[6] as in vv 26-27. V 29, however, is also closely related to v 28. It picks up the final element in v 28, the ripe grain, just as v 28 picked up the element of growth found near the end of v 27. Like the first and second sentences, the third contains a pattern of three (the three verbs).[7]

As H.-W. Kuhn has noted, the shift in focus from the man to the seed and back to the man again is reflected in two common names for the parable, The Seed Which Grows By Itself and The Patient Farmer.[8] Efforts to resolve this ambiguity in favor of either the seed or the man

---

[2]He is the subject of the first two sets of subjunctives, and while the seed is the subject of the third set, a dependent clause ("as he himself does not know") brings the man back into play, and in an emphatic way (*autos*).

[3]Note the asyndeton; some manuscripts supply *gar* or *hoti* after *automatē*.

[4]See B. B. Scott, *Symbol-Maker* 84.

[5]See especially the words "first . . . then . . . then" (*prōton . . . eita . . . eita*) in 4:28; cf. R. Pesch, *Markusevangelium* 1.255.

[6]A. Ambrozic (*Hidden Kingdom* 116-17), claims that the farmer is basically "a foil to the growing seed," and points out that 4:29b is flanked by clauses which suggest that his resumption of work is determined by the arrival of the harvest; thus "the farmer, though active, seems to be passive with regard to the ripe seed." This is unconvincing. The farmer is the focal point of 4:29; 4:29c does not shift attention away from him, but merely gives the reason for his conduct, while 4:29a sets the stage for his action. Cf. J. D. Crossan, "Seed Parables" 251.

[7]J. D. Crossan, "Seed Parables" 253.

[8]H.-W. Kuhn, *Sammlungen* 106-107.

are misguided; the man is not just a "foil for the seed,"[9] but neither is he the exclusive center of attention.[10]

Composition History

1 Clem 23:4; *Ap. Jas.* 12:22-31; and *Gos. Thom.* logion 21 seem to be related to Mark 4:26-29. We reproduce these passages here, along with their immediate contexts.[11]

1 Clem 23:4 (cf. 2 Clem 11:3)[12]

> Far be that Scripture from us which says, "Wretched are the double-minded, who doubt in their soul and say, 'These things we heard even in the time of our fathers, and behold, we have grown old, and none of them has happened to us.' *O foolish men, compare yourselves with a tree; take a vine; first it sheds its leaves, then there comes a bud, then a leaf, then a flower, and after these an unripe grape, then the full bunch."* You see how in a short space of time the fruit of the tree comes to *ripeness.* Truly his purpose will be *quickly and suddenly* accomplished . . ."

Ap. Jas. 12:22-31

> "For this cause I tell you this, that you may know yourselves. *For the kingdom of heaven is like an ear of grain after it had sprouted in a field. And when it had ripened,* it scattered its fruit and again filled the field with ears for another year. You also: *hasten to reap an ear* of life for yourselves that you may be filled with the kingdom!"

---

[9]See A. Ambrozic, *Hidden Kingdom* cited above, n. 6.

[10]J. Jeremias (*Parables* 151-53) dismisses 4:27-28 as merely a "retarding moment" in the parable, but as H.-W. Kuhn (*Sammlungen* 107 n. 41) points out, the parable is too short for two whole verses to be merely a "retarding moment."

[11]The sections compared with Mark 4:26-29 are italicized; it is to them that the verse numbers refer.

[12]Translation altered from R. M. Grant and H. H. Graham, *The Apostolic Fathers: A New Translation and Commentary* (6 vols.; New York/Toronto/London: 1964-67) 2.48-49.

Gos. Thom. logion 21

> "You, then, be on your guard against the world. Arm your-
> selves with great strength lest the robbers find a way to come
> to you, for the difficulty which you expect will (surely) mate-
> rialize. Let there be among you a man of understanding. *When
> the grain ripened, he came quickly with his sickle in his hand
> and reaped it.* Whoever has ears to hear, let him hear."

The structural elements of these passages, in comparison with the
corresponding elements in Mark 4:26-29, are summarized in Chart 9.
Several elements in the Markan parable are missing in all of the other
passages: the man's casting of the seed into the earth, his sleeping and
rising, his non-knowing, the "automatic" growth of the plant, and a specific allusion to Joel 4:13 (ET 3:13).

The 1 Clement passage is not based on Mark;[13] nor indeed is it directly
related to the Markan parable, since the only points of comparison are
with Mark 4:28, and even there the parallels are not close enough to
suggest dependence in either direction. 1 Clement 23:4 seems to come
from a lost Jewish apocryphal work, the Book of Eldad and Modad,[14] and
this suggests that the gradual unfolding of a plant was a fixed metaphor
for the certainty of the coming of the end in Jewish apocalyptic traditions.

As for the *Apocryphon of James* and *Gospel of Thomas* texts, C. W.
Hedrick[15] claims that the former may well represent the original form of
the saying found in Mark 4:26-29, but in view of the *Apocryphon*'s gnostic

---

[13] 1 Clement does not seem to have known the canonical Gospels (the
"words of Jesus" that it quotes probably come from oral tradition); see
R. M. Grant, *The Apostolic Fathers* 1.36-44.

[14] J. B. Lightfoot, *The Apostolic Fathers: Clement, Ignatius, Polycarp*
(Grand Rapids: Baker, 1981; orig. 1889-90) 2.80-81. Lightfoot thinks of
Eldad and Modad as a Christian apocryphon, but F. W. Beare ("Hermas,
Shepherd of," *IDB* 2 [1962] 584) describes it as a Jewish work. The latter
view is more plausible, given the lack of Christian elements in the
extracts that have come down to us, their closeness to Jewish apocalyptic
literature (particularly 4 Ezra) in content, and the great Jewish interest in
the period of the wilderness wanderings, in which the incident of Eldad
and Medad took place.

[15] "Kingdom Sayings and Parables of Jesus in *The Apocryphon of James*:
Tradition and Redaction," *NTS* 29 (1983) 1-24.

CHART 9

Mark 4:26-29	1 Clem 23:4; 2 Clem 11:3	Ap. Jas. 12:22-31	Gos. Thom. log. 21
1. thus is KOG as	8. Oh, fools	1. KOH is like	
	1. compare	15. ear of grain	
2. a man	2. yourselves		
	to a tree		
	take a vine		
3. throws seed			
4. on earth			
5. and sleeps and arises			
6. night and day		7. after had sprouted	
7. and seed sprouts (*blasta*)			
		4. in a field	
8. and grows			
9. as he himself does not know			
10. of itself			
11. earth bears fruit	12. first		
12. first	sheds leaves		
	then		
	7. comes bud (*blastos*)		
	then		
13. blade	13. leaf		
14. then	14. then		

Chart 9 (continued)

	Mark 4:26-29	1 Clem 23:4; 2 Clem 11:3	Ap. Jas. 12:22-31	Gos. Thom. log. 21
15.	ear	15. flower and after this unripe grape		
16.	then	16. then		
17.	full (*plērēs*) grain in ear	17, 21. full (*parestēkuia*) bunch		
18.	but when fruit is ripe	18. [fruit comes to ripeness]	18. and when ripened scattered fruit and filled field	18. when grain ripened
19.	immediately	19. [in a little time] 19. [quickly and suddenly shall his will be fulfilled]	19. hasten	19. he came quickly
20.	he sends forth sickle		20. to reap	20. w/sickle & reaped
21.	for harvest has come (*parestēken*)			

Brackets indicate from continuation of passage in 1 Clement 23:4-5, not from "Scripture" cited there.

coloring this claim is questionable.[16] Similarly, *Gos. Thom.* logion 21 has
de-eschatologized the motif of reaping and lessened the allusion to the
OT;[17] moreover, the portion of *Gos. Thom.* logion 21 which is similar to
Mark 4:29 gives the impression of being a fragment. Both the *Ap. Jas.* and
the *Gos. Thom.* versions go back either to Mark itself or to oral tradition,
but it cannot be claimed that they represent a more "primitive" version of
the latter; therefore, In tracing the history of the tradition now found in
Mark 4:26-29 they can be left out of the account.

The Markan parable may have undergone expansions during its transmission; the awkwardnesses noted in our discussion of its structure could
be cited in support of this hypothesis. Furthermore, the citation of Joel
4:13 in Mark 4:29 seems to link the man with God, who is the wielder of
the sickle in Joel,[18] but in 4:27 the man is pictured as being inactive in
making the seed grow and as not knowing how it grows, images that ill
accord with an identification with God.[19] Finally, the Old Testament
citation in v 29 follows the MT rather than the LXX version of Joel,[20]
whereas *karpophorei* in v 28a is possible only in Greek (contrast the
Semitic *edidou karpon* in v 8).[21]

Yet such expansion is by no means certain. The pattern of three "threesomes," and the fact that each succeeding sentence picks up an element in
the preceding one, suggest unity. The shift of focus from the man to the
seed and back to the man, as well as the shift in attribution of growth
from plant to ground to plant, may merely be narrative devices. The
"confusion" in the picture of the man may be resolved by the assertion

---

[16]See the concluding exhortation, "Hasten to reap an ear of life for
yourselves that you may be filled with the kingdom!" This has definite
gnostic overtones, *contra* H. Koester, "Three Thomas Parables" 200-201.

[17]In view of the OT and Jewish association of reaping with the
eschatological judgment, an association which is well attested in the
teaching of Jesus (see below on "the periods in the Gospel of Mark"), we
are justified in speaking of a "de-eschatologizing." *Gospel of Thomas*
regularly eliminates OT references; see below, chapter 6, n. 9.

[18]See J. Dupont, "La parabole de la semence qui pousse toute seule
(Marc 4, 26-29)," *RSR* 55 (1967) 379-83.

[19]Bede (CChrSL 120.486 §§1916-46) identifies the man in 4:26-28 as
the Christian, but in 4:29 as God.

[20]Like the MT, it speaks of a single sickle, whereas the LXX has the
plural; also like the MT, it speaks of a grain harvest (*therismos*), whereas
the LXX speaks of a wine harvest (*trygētos*). See R. Stuhlmann, "Beobachtungen und Überlegungen zu Markus IV.26-29," *NTS* 19 (1973) 161-62.

[21]J. D. Crossan, "Seed Parables" 252.

that he participates both in human action and in divine action, in a way that will be unfolded below. The linguistic evidence is not decisive; it is possible that one narrator could have had a knowledge both of the Masoretic Text of the OT and of Greek idiom,[22] or that the first translator of the parable into Greek rendered Semitic constructions with Greek idioms. As for the awkwardness of the introduction, perhaps some such word as *ean* is to be understood. The parable as it presently stands must be our starting point as we move on to exegesis.

EXEGESIS

Allegorical Interpretation

In interpreting our parable, we realize that each major feature of the parable has a referent which Mark expects his readers to recognize from the parable's structure and its relationship to its context. As we mentioned in our discussion of the interpretation of the Parable of the Sower, recent scholarship has shown Jülicher's sharp distinction between parable and allegory to be inaccurate, particularly with regard to OT and Jewish parables, which often use stock metaphors.[23] Aside from this general point, the interpretation of the Parable of the Sower clearly illustrates that *for Mark* the main elements of parables have allegorical significance.[24]

Moreover, both Mark 3:23-27 and 12:1-12 lend support to the point. In the former, the house/kingdom of 3:23-26 is the dominion of Satan, and the "strong man's house" in 3:27 is, by its juxtaposition with 3:23-26, implied to be the dominion of Satan also, while the "stronger one" is Jesus. In the latter, there are several allegorical details, such as the

---

[22]See M. Hengel's discussion of the Greek language in Palestinian Judaism in *Judaism* 1.58-65.

[23]See already P. Fiebig and A. Hunter, whose positions are summarized by W. Kissinger (*The Parables of Jesus: A History of Interpretation and Bibliography* [ATLA Bibliography Series 4; Metuchen, N.J./London: Scarecrow, 1979] 80-83, 148-49); more recently R. E. Brown ("Parable and Allegory" 254-64) and H.-J. Klauck, whose work is summarized and reviewed by C. E. Carlston ("Parable and Allegory" 228-42); see also D. Flusser, *Gleichnisse* 1.119-37.

[24]Cf. D. Rhoads and D. Michie, *Mark as Story* 55-56: Mark views all his parables as allegories.

"many others" (= the prophets, 12:5) and the "beloved son" (= Jesus, 12:6); and indeed, in 12:12 Jesus' opponents seem to make the allegorical equation that the wicked tenants = themselves.[25]

Thus, since Mark understood parables allegorically, and since our aim is to find out *Mark's* interpretation of 4:26-29, an effort must be made to discover the Markan referents for the main elements in that parable: the man, the seed and its growth, and the harvest.

The Identity of the Man

The man in Mark 4:26-29 is the sower of the seed, yet he is not responsible for the growth of the plant, indeed does not know how it grows; inactive during the time of growth, at the time of harvest he suddenly springs into action and reaps the grain. Three major candidates for the referent of the man have been suggested: God, Jesus, and the disciples.[26]

The man as God. As mentioned above, the citation of Joel 4:13 in Mark 4:29 supports the identification of the man with God.[27] Although the farmer's slumber seems at first inconsistent with identifying him with God,[28] V. Fusco has recently pointed in rebuttal to OT images which speak of God as sleeping and otherwise being absent. The problem addressed in such passages is God's apparent inactivity on behalf of his

---

[25]Bibliography on allegorical features in 12:1-12 includes J. D. Crossan, "The Parable of the Wicked Husband men," *JBL* 90 (1971) 451-65; J. D. M. Derrett, "Allegory and the Wicked Vinedressers," *JTS* 25 (1974) 426-32; J. A. T. Robinson, "The Parable of the Wicked Husbandmen. A Test of Synoptic Relationships," *NTS* 21 (1974-75) 443-61, and H. Koester, "Three Thomas Parables" 195-203.

[26]Several interpreters, including J. Weiss, C. A. Bugge, N. A. Dahl, R. H. Fuller, G. Bornkamm, and J. Jeremias, have suggested that the parable was addressed by Jesus to Zealots who were counseled to have patience (see J. Dupont, "Semence" 375 n. 28 for references). While this is a possible interpretation of the original meaning (*if* the parable really does go back to Jesus), on the *Markan* level there is no evidence for an anti-Zealotic front.

[27]J. Dupont ("Semence" 382-83) asserts that, since Mark 4:26-29 is a parable of the kingdom of God, God must be the chief actor in the parable; see our refutation of this argument in chapter 2, n. 72.

[28]See the succinct formulation of the problem by C. E. Carlston (*Parables* 208 n. 32): If the sower and the *reaper* are identical, so are the sower and the *sleeper*.

covenant people; God's sleeping speaks of "human history under the sign of the absence of God."[29] Another intriguing comparison is provided by 4 Ezra 4:37: "God will not move nor arouse [things? the times? the souls of the just?][30] until their measure is fulfilled." Although here God is the one who waits to *rouse from sleep*, rather than the person who *sleeps* as in Mark 4:27, the juxtaposition of the motif of sleep, and of the general impression of temporary inactivity, with that of sudden activity when the eschatological "measure" is fulfilled, is strikingly similar to our text.

Yet there are grave difficulties in identifying the farmer in Mark's parable with God, the most serious one being v 27c: the farmer does not know how the plant grows. The attempts by commentators who identify the farmer with God to gloss over this phrase merely underline their embarrassment.[31]

Furthermore, if the man corresponded to God, to what would the earth correspond? Verses 27-28a seem to make the point that the earth by itself (*automatē*), not the farmer, is the cause of the growth of the plant; so that the farmer is subordinate to the earth in this matter of growth. The difficulty of finding someone or something to which God would be subordinate is obvious.

Indeed, if there is any image in the parable that should be identified with the activity of God, it is the earth rather than the farmer. This conclusion emerges not only from the subordination just mentioned, but also from the history-of-religions background of *automatē*; this word

---

[29]V. Fusco, *Parola* 354-55: God is far from the wicked (Pss 13:1; 94:7), but he can also be experienced *by the faithful* as distant (Ps 22:1, 11, 19; 35:22; Job 23:8-9), as silent (Pss 22:2; 28:1; 35:22; 83:1; Job 30:20; Hab 1:13), or as hidden (Pss 13:1; 44:24; 88:14; Isa 59:2). Pss 35:23; 44:23 call on him to awake.

[30]Although the verbs are transitive, an object is lacking in the Latin. R. H. Charles (*APOT* 2.567) supplies "things," B. M. Metzger (in J. H. Charlesworth, ed., *Old Testament Pseudepigrapha* 1.530) supplies "them," referring to the times, and W. Harnisch (*Verhängnis* 285-86) supplies "the souls of the just," from v 35.

[31]For example, J. Dupont ("Semence" 381-83) translates the phrase, "And he gives the impression of being uninterested in what is happening." Mark 4:27c, however, speaks not of the impression that is made on outside observers by the farmer, but of the farmer's own subjective experience. V. Fusco (*Parola* 347-52) argues that the emphasis is not on epistemology but on the farmer's lack of participation. If such were the case, however, Mark could just as well have omitted the phrase; vv 27ab, 28a express the farmer's passivity clearly enough by themselves.

describes that which grows up by itself, apart from any human agricultural activity. In Lev 25:5, 11, it is used of that which grows up in the sabbatical year. The nature of the sabbatical year itself, by the lying fallow of the land, emphasizes that Yahweh is the lord of the land; thus *automatos* describes a growth that is radically and totally God's affair[32] and is, as such, the opposite of human action.[33] Similarly, in 4 Kgdms 19:29 the *automata* are part of a "sign" (*sēmeion*) of God's miraculous deliverance of his people from the Assyrian foe.

Philo makes explicit these OT connotations of *automatos*; in a commentary on Lev 25:11 (*On Flight and Finding* 170-72) he notes that in the sabbatical year the *automaton* only *seems* to be self-grown, "since God sows and by his tending brings it to perfection; it is only self-grown inasmuch as it does not require human attention."[34] Similarly, in other passages[35] Philo uses *automata* to describe the paradisiacal conditions prevailing before the Fall; the word preserves in his works a connotation of "miraculous, worked by God alone."

Thus the "automatic" earth, not the farmer, is the divine actor in the parable, and it is unlikely that Mark intended the farmer to be understood as God.

The man as the Christian disciple. A second possibility, and an obvious one, given the designation of the farmer as an *anthrōpos*, is that he represents some sort of human figure; many interpreters have identified him with the Christian disciple.[36] Arguments drawn from both the history of

---

[32]R. Stuhlmann, "Beobachtungen" 156.

[33]H.-J. Klauck, *Allegorie* 221.

[34]Translation from LCL edition, altered. Unless otherwise noted, all Philo citations and translations are from this edition. On this and other Philo passages containing *automatos*, see R. Stuhlmann, "Beobachtungen" 154-56.

In the passage cited, God is the farmer, a fact which may at first seem to threaten our argument that he cannot be the farmer in Mark 4:26-29. However, in *On Flight* there is no contrast between the farmer and the "automatic" earth, as there is in Mark. In Philo, the farmer (God) is *amalgamated* with the image of automatic growth, rather than *contrasted* to it. Note also that in Philo God as farmer does precisely what the farmer in Mark does *not* do, namely tend the growing plant.

[35]*On the Creation* 40-43, 80-81, 167 (cf. Josephus *Ant.* 1.46, 49); see H.-J. Klauck, *Allegorie* 222.

[36]Gregory the Great, for example (*Hom. in Hiezech.* 2.3.5, CChrSL 142.239) says that he is a Christian who places a good intention in his own

religions and from redaction criticism can be used to support this identification.

In Jewish apocalyptic literature, particularly 4 Ezra and Syriac Apocalypse of Baruch,[37] the point is often made, in reply to the seer's anguished question of when the end will come, that the date of its coming can be neither influenced nor known by human beings. This assertion is all the more interesting for a comparison with Mark 4:26-29 because the coming of the end is sometimes likened to a natural process such as a woman's pregnancy or the growth of a plant. For example, in *2 Apoc. Bar.* 22:5-7; 23:2, the divine reply to Baruch's question, "How long will corruption remain?" (21:19) includes the following passage:

> He who sows the earth—does he not lose everything unless he reaps its harvest in its own time? Or he who plants a vineyard—does the planter expect to receive fruit from it, unless it grows until its appointed time? Or a woman who has conceived—does she not surely kill the child when she bears it untimely? . . . Why, then, are you disturbed about that which you do not know, and why are you restless about that of which you do not possess any knowledge?

In spite of Baruch's privileged position as one of the elect, there is a divinely imposed limitation on his knowledge. All that he and the rest of the elect can do is to wait patiently until the appointed time. *Only God knows* when the end will come (48:3; 54:1); that coming can neither be known nor influenced by human beings.[38] Yet this limitation does not prevent the seer from being identified as one who has received mysteries; immediately after the Syriac Apocalypse of Baruch passage cited at length above, we read, "And further, it is given to you to hear that which will come after these times" (23:6). If the farmer in Mark 4:26-29 is to be identified with the person of faith, then a similar combination of revelation and limitation would apply to him: he has been given the mystery of

---

heart. Gregory's interpretation, however, stresses the man's activity rather than his passivity; one of the devices that Gregory uses to achieve this effect is to ignore the verb "sleep" in v 27, so that he has the man "rising night and day."

[37]Both of the latter are probably late first century documents; see J. H. Charlesworth, *Pseudepigrapha and Modern Research* 111-113.

[38]A similar point is made in 4 Ezra 4:26-43, near the end of which the image of a woman in travail is again used. On these passages see W. Harnisch, *Verhängnis* 283, 286.

the kingdom of God (4:11), yet he does not know exactly how that kingdom manifests itself (4:27), since its emergence is attributable to God alone.[39]

There is also, however, a difference between the form that the ignorance takes in the apocalyptic texts and in Mark 4:27. In the former, it is given to the elect to know *what* will happen, but not *when* it will happen. In Mark 4:27, however, the ignorance concerns not *when* the kingdom comes but *how* it comes.[40] This difference may be due to the kingdom's mysteriousness in Mark; even as the man in the parable waits for the kingdom's full manifestation, it is already present in a hidden way. Thus the question is not "when?", as an exclusively future eschatology would require, but "how?"[41]

The attribution of growth to divine rather than human activity is also found in 1 Cor 3:6-7:

> I planted, Apollos watered, but God gave the growth. So neither he who plants nor he who waters is anything, but only God who gives the growth.

Here the "planting" is the proclamation of the word; in spite of this initial human act, it is God, not the Christian preacher, who is responsible for the success of the preaching.[42] So also in Mark 4:26-29 not only is the image of the plant used to stress that it is God, not the human figure, who is responsible for growth, but according to 4:14 "the seed" (*ton sporon*) is "the word" (*ton logon*).[43] Both 1 Cor 3:6-7 and Mark 4:26-29, therefore, could be interpreted as asserting that the success of the Christian preacher's proclamation depends not on him but on God.

---

[39]If Mark has eliminated the verb "to know" from 4:11 (see the discussion in chapter 3), this redaction would be consonant with a limitation on the disciples' knowledge in 4:27.

[40]Cf. however Mark 13:32-37.

[41]S. Freyne, "Disciples" 7-23: "Mark . . . sees the future kingdom already breaking into the present through the ministry of Jesus and his disciples and so greater attention is given to the present aspect of the struggle than in Daniel ."

[42]Cf. 1 Cor 15:38, which again uses the seed metaphor and emphasizes that it is God who gives a "body" to the seed.

[43]Since Mark has stated that the Parable of the Sower is the key to all parables (4:13), it is reasonable to use an identification made in the interpretation of that parable in explicating 4:26-29, especially when 4:26 uses the definite article with *sporos*; see A. Ambrozic, *Hidden Kingdom* 120-21.

Redactional considerations from the rest of the Gospel of Mark can be used to support the position that the farmer in 4:26-29 is the Christian disciple. In 6:12 the disciples are described as preachers; thus it is not *a priori* unlikely that Mark's readers would identify them with the man in 4:26 who sows the seed.[44] In 13:9-11, Jesus instructs his disciples about fearless testimony. Their responsibility is to bear witness, not to worry about how their witness will be received; that is the work of the Holy Spirit who is speaking through them. This is similar to the picture in 4:26-29 of the man casting the seed in the ground, then passively waiting for the ground to do the work of bringing the seed to fruition.

Perhaps the strongest redactional argument for the identification of the farmer with the disciple, however, is the closeness between the phrase "as he himself does not know" in v 27c and the theme of the disciples' incomprehension throughout the Gospel of Mark. That theme has already been sounded in chapter 4; the reader of *hōs ouk oiden autos* (v 27c) would still remember clearly Jesus' rebuke of the disciples in 4:13, "Do you not know this parable?"[45] Outside of chapter 4, the theme appears in the Gethsemane scene, in conjunction with the verbs "to sleep" and "to rise" (cf. 4:27a) and the motif of the eschatological hour (cf. 4:29a). In 14:37-42 Jesus three times comes and finds the disciples asleep; the verb *katheudein* occurs in vv 37 (2x), 40, and 41. After the second time, Mark records that the disciples "did not know" (*ouk ēdeisan*, v 40) what to answer him, and after the third time, Jesus, having declared that "the hour has come" (v 41), tells the disciples to "arise" (*egeiresthe*, v 42).

Despite these verbal parallels, however, the scene in Gethsemane also points up a difference between the theme of the disciples' incomprehension and the non-knowing of 4:27c. The disciples' incomprehension is blameworthy, and Jesus often rebukes them for it (4:13; 8:17-21, 33; cf. 4:40; 14:37, 41). The non-knowing of 4:27c, on the other hand, is not identified as blameworthy. The farmer in 4:27 is doing what is appropriate

---

[44]However, the disciples are never specifically linked to "the word" (*ho logos*) as a technical term, as Jesus is in 2:2; 8:32.

[45]See H. Baltensweiler, "Das Gleichnis von der selbstwachsenden Saat (Markus 4, 26-29) und die theologische Konzeption des Markusevangeliums," *Oikonomia: Heilsgeschichte als Thema der Theologie: Festschrift für Oscar Cullmann* (ed. F. Christ; Hamburg-Bergstedt: H. Reich, 1967) 69-75 and A. Ambrozic, *Hidden Kingdom* 120-22.

for him to do during the time before the harvest; it is not for him to know how the seed grows.[46]

Furthermore, the sower must also be the reaper,[47] but nothing suggests that such a role is ascribed to the Markan disciples, while there are good reasons for identifying the reaper with God, as we have previously seen, or with Christ, as we shall presently see. It is unlikely that Mark expected his readers to identify the man with the Christian disciple.

The man as Jesus. We have noted so far that there are problems both with the identification of the farmer as God and with the identification of him as the Christian disciple. If he is God, why is he *contrasted* to the productive earth, and why is incomprehension attributed to him? If he is solely a human figure, how can he be the eschatological reaper? Yet we have also noted that features of the farmer link him with both God and humanity. One way to reconcile these conflicting data would be to identify the farmer with Jesus, a figure who, in Mark's Gospel, is akin to both God and humanity, yet in a way distinct from both.[48]

We have seen in our discussion of the Parable of the Sower that Mark's readers would have identified the sower in 4:3 with Jesus; therefore they probably would have thought of the sower in 4:27 as Jesus also. Further evidence for this identification comes from the Markan Jesus' relationship to both *the word* and *the eschatological harvest*. Since for Mark the seed in 4:26 is the word, the most likely candidate for the sower of the seed is Jesus, who has a close connection with the word throughout Mark's

---

[46]This appropriateness emerges not only from the inner logic of the parable, but also from the *religionsgeschichtlich* parallels cited above.

[47]G. Harder, "Das Gleichnis von der selbstwachsenden Saat Mk 4,26-29," *ThViat* 1 (1948-49) 56-57, 60-61.

[48]See, for example, the scribes' objection to Jesus' forgiveness of the paralytic's sins: "Who can forgive sins except God alone?" (2:7). Indirect evidence for this identification comes from the common Markan antithesis "God/human being" (*theos/anthrōpos*; 8:33; 10:9, 27; 11:30-32; cf. 7:7-8; 8:27; 12:17). If, in spite of this antithesis, a *comparison* is made in 4:26 between the kingdom of *God* and the actions of a *man*, this remarkable exception suggests that the man in question may be one who bridges the otherwise unbridgeable gap between God and humanity. Significantly, the only other passage where a man is linked with God in this way is 15:39, where the centurion, seeing Jesus die, exclaims, "Truly this man (*houtos ho anthrōpos*) was the Son of God!" Furthermore, the phrase in 4:26, *hōs anthrōpos* ("as a man"), is repeated in 13:34, where Jesus compares *himself* to a man away on a journey.

Gospel. The reader of 4:26, for example, has already seen him "speaking the word to them (the people)" in 2:2 (cf. 4:2), and the exact same phrase will recur shortly, in 4:33. Furthermore, the initial act of Jesus' ministry is to preach the gospel of the kingdom of God (1:14-15), and "gospel" is almost synonymous with "word" in Mark.[49] Hence 4:26 is parallel to 1:14-15; both describe the initial proclamation of the word which is linked with the initial manifestation of God's kingdom. Thus, reading 4:26 in the light of 1:14-15, the "sower" of the word would be Jesus. The irresistible power of the seed, pictured in 4:27-28, to cause the plant to sprout and unfold, is in line with the OT and Jewish conception of the dynamism of the word, which comes strongly to the fore elsewhere in Mark, e.g. 13:31, where *Jesus' words* are said to outlast the world.

Moreover, Jesus, unlike the Christian disciple, can easily be understood as the reaper of 4:29. Although, as we have seen, in Joel 4:13 God is the reaper at the eschatological judgment, this linkage creates no insuperable problem for an identification of the reaper with Jesus, since in Jewish apocalyptic literature God can exercise judgment through an agent, such as the Messiah or the Son of Man.[50] Judgment through either of these figures would amount to practically the same thing as judgment through God himself; thus Rev 14:15—the only other NT citation of Joel 4:13— gives to the Son of Man the sickle which Joel sees in God's hand.[51]

Moreover, Mark himself, in 8:38, records Jesus' prediction that the Son of Man will come "in his father's glory," i.e. as his designated agent of judgment, and the verse contains two elements that are implicit in 4:26-29: a contrast between the two ages[52] and a reference to Jesus' words.

---

[49]See the parallelism between "gospel" and "my words" in 8:35, 38.

[50]See S. Mowinckel, *He That Cometh* (Nashville/New York: Abingdon, 1954; orig. 1951) 393-99; V. Fusco, *Parola* 356 n. 61. God's delegation of judgment to the Son of Man is explicit in John 5:27, which in turn depends upon Dan 7:13; see R. E. Brown, *The Gospel according to John, I-XII* (AB 29; Garden City: Doubleday, 1966) 220.

[51]V. Fusco, *Parola* 356 . . . C. E. Carlston (*Parables* 206), while strenuously denying that Mark 4:26-29 is an allegory, admits that in 4:29 only the Sower perhaps is Christ. It is unlikely, however, that Mark would allow the figure of the farmer to jump around in the confusing way that Carlston suggests, being merely a human figure in vv 26-28 but Christ in v 29. See G. Harder, "Gleichnis" 56-57.

[52]This contrast is implicit in the disjunctive *de* of v 29, which sets apart the time of the eschatological harvest from the period of growth that precedes it.

Thus in both 4:26-29 *ex hypothese* and 8:38, the present is the age of Jesus' word and the reaction to it, while the future is the age of his coming as God's agent to execute judgment; yet there is continuity between the two ages.

The many parallels between 4:26-29 and chapter 13 are also compelling. In the latter, in a context which, like 4:28-29a, uses an agricultural image for the eschatological measure (13:28-29), the Son of Man is described as "sending out" (*apostelei*, 13:27) the angels to gather the elect; the same verb is used in 4:29 of the farmer "sending out" the sickle. Furthermore, the description in 13:27 of the angels "gathering" the elect suggests a harvest.[53]

A consideration of Matthew's redaction of Mark 4:26-29 further supports the interpretation of the Markan farmer as Jesus, since Matthew seems to have interpreted him in that way. H.-J. Klauck, after pointing out the numerous verbal parallels between Mark 4:26-29 and the Parable of the Weeds in Matt 13:24-30, 36-43, concludes that the latter is a "free paraphrase" of the former.[54] Although this may not be the *whole* story behind the Parable of the Weeds (Matthew may have combined a paraphrase of Mark 4:26-29 with another parable from the tradition),[55] it is still significant for Matthew's reading of Mark that Matt 13:37 interprets the sower as the Son of Man, and that Matt 13:41 declares that at the eschatological harvest (*therismos*) the Son of Man will send out (*apostelei*) his angels. Matthew has thus used the imagery of Mark 13:27 (Son of Man sending out the angels) to interpret Mark 4:26-29, and, while we cannot say that all of Mark's readers did so, Matthew's redaction reveals how at least one first century reader probably interpreted Mark.

It is also significant, however, that in the Parable of the Weeds

---

[53]The word used in 13:27 for gathering, *episynagein*, is synonymous with the uncompounded form *synagein* (BAG 301). The latter is used in the NT for gathering crops as an eschatological metaphor (Matt 3:12; 6:26; 13:30; Luke 3:17; BAG 782[2]).

[54]The parallels include the following: The kingdom of God is compared to a man (*anthrōpō*, Matt 13:24); the motif of sleeping (*en de tō katheudein tous anthrōpous*, v 25); the words for "grain," (*siton*, vv 25, 30) and "sprouted," "grass," "fruit," (*eblastēsen, chortos, karpon*, v 26), "harvest" and "first" (*therismos* 2x , *prōton*, v 30); the farmer at the end "sending out" (*apostelei*) agents for the harvest. Klauck, *Allegorie* 226-27; cf. M. D. Goulder, "Characteristics of the Parables in the Several Gospels," *JTS* 19 (1968) 52-53.

[55]Oral suggestion from R. E. Brown.

Matthew omits the motif of the farmer's incomprehension and attributes sleep, not to the farmer, but to human beings in general.[56] These two elements, as we saw above, cause difficulty for the interpretation of the Markan farmer as God, and they also apparently caused difficulty for Matthew in his interpretation of the farmer as Jesus. Is there any way from a *Markan* perspective to make sense of a sleeping and unknowing Jesus?

Jesus as sleeper. We noted above that in the OT God's apparent absence from his elect people can be pictured through the metaphor of sleeping; the transfer of this metaphor from God to Jesus, like the transfer of the metaphor of reaping, is not an impossibility. Such a transfer begins to seem likely when we investigate the passage which immediately follows the end of the parable collection, 4:35-41. Here Jesus is asleep in the stern of a boat; a great storm arises, and the disciples in terror awaken Jesus, who calms the storm. The wording of v 38 is particularly important for our purposes:

> But he himself was in the stern, on a cushion sleeping (*katheudōn*). And they rouse (*egeirousin*) him and say to him, "Teacher, do you not care that we perish?"

Thus, a few verses after our parable, in which the man sleeps and rises (*katheudē kai egeirētai*), we are confronted with a scene in which Jesus is portrayed as a sleeper and riser (*katheudōn kai egeirousin auton*). The striking similarity of language means that the reader, in whose mind the parable of 4:26-29 would still be fresh, would be likely to consider that the identity of the man in the parable was illuminated by the scene in the boat.[57]

Mark 4:35-41 certainly reflects the Markan community's experience of

---

[56]"While men were sleeping," *en de tǭ katheudein tous anthrōpous,* Matt 13:25.

[57] D. Rhoads and D. Michie (*Mark as Story* 109) link the parable in 4:26-29 with the scene in 4:35-41: "The sower sows the word and has no control over the variety of responses, but 'sleeps and rises,' trusting God to bring growth and a harvest. (Just so, after Jesus finishes 'sowing' the words of this riddle, he sleeps in the boat during the storm!)." When Rhoads and Michie speak of a "variety of responses," they are conflating the Parable of the Sower with our parable. Their comment, however, is important for Mark's overall understanding of the parable chapter.

Christ's apparent absence from them: "Teacher, do you not care if we perish?" That absence is an important Markan motif. The time of the church, according to 2:20, is one in which the bridegroom is taken away from his people, and they fast. Correspondingly, Jesus "fasts" during the time of the church; the Last Supper is the last meal he will take with the disciples until the messianic banquet (14:25). The Last Supper thus represents his leavetaking from the disciples; from now on he will, in some sense, no longer be with them (14:7).[58] Those who assert that Christ has already arrived, therefore, are wrong (13:5-6, 21-22); he is still absent, and will be absent until the sudden intervention described in 13:24-37. He is the "man away from home" who has left his house, and whose return could happen at any time (13:34-35). For the present, however, he is exalted at God's right hand, and inactive himself while *God* is subduing his enemies (12:36).[59]

The theme of Jesus' absence until the parousia, however, is a dialectical one for Mark. If, as asserted above, the Markan community would have seen its own situation reflected in the storm scene of 4:35-41, then Jesus' rising to calm the storm there is also a reality for it. Similarly, in another storm scene (6:45-52), the impossibility of Jesus' coming to his disciples is overcome by a miracle.[60] "Although the absence of Jesus is 'a presiding feature in the Markan gospel,' still 'the gospel (itself) functions in such a way as to extend Jesus into the Markan present.'"[61] Furthermore, if, after the resurrection, following Jesus is still a possibility (8:34; 10:28-30), and Jesus "goes before" his disciples into Galilee (14:28; cf. 16:7); and if

---

[58]On the Last Supper and Jesus' absence from the Markan community, see V. K. Robbins, "Last Meal: Preparation, Betrayal, and Absence," *The Passion in Mark: Studies on Mark 14-16* (ed. W. H. Kelber; Philadelphia: Fortress, 1976) 21-40, especially 35-36.

[59]J. D. Crossan ("Empty Tomb" 135-52) sees Christ's absence from the Markan community as emphasized by the empty tomb narrative, especially by the formulation "he is not here" (16:6).

[60]M. E. Boring (*Sayings of the Risen Jesus: Christian Prophecy in the Synoptic Tradition* [SNTSMS 46; Cambridge/London/New York: Cambridge University, 1982] 202) asserts that Jesus' presence with the Markan church is implied in Mark 6:45-52. Q. Quesnell (*Mind of Mark* passim) thinks that Jesus' presence in the eucharist is implied by the saying in 6:52.

[61]M. E. Boring (*Sayings* 202), bringing together two passages from W. H. Kelber.

he who receives a child in Jesus' name receives Jesus (9:37), then Jesus is present to the Markan community.[62]

Despite these qualifications, Jesus' physical absence from the Markan community is an important theme in the Gospel. While his "sleeping" is already a factor in the period of his ministry, it is a more profound problem in the period after his death and resurrection. Indeed, the sleeping and rising of the man in our parable could not help but awaken for Mark's readers secondary associations, at least, with Jesus' death and resurrection. Early Christian texts such as 1 Thess 5:10 and Eph 5:14 use "sleeping" and "rising" imagery to speak of death and resurrection, and indeed Mark himself uses this imagery in the same way in the story of the healing of the synagogue ruler's daughter (5:39-42; cf. 9:26-27).

Granted that the farmer in 4:26-29 is Christ, then, how will the Markan community have heard the parable? We recall that Mark's hearers are members of a community that is subject to persecution from without and division within. To such a community our text would say that, while the end has not yet arrived, the interim period of suffering and of Christ's apparent absence does not imply a going awry of the divine plan, but is willed by God, inevitably bound up with the nature of the kingdom, and will speedily issue in Christ's coming in glory.[63]

Jesus as the unknowing man. The comment in 4:27c that the man who sows the seed does not know how it grows creates greater difficulty for the interpretation of the man as Jesus than the description of him sleeping. This difficulty is evident in the various devices used by ancient and medieval commentators to soften the impact of 4:27c,[64] as well as in the

---

[62]See the review of E. Manicardi's *Il cammino di Gesù nel Vangelo di Marco* by S. Kealy (*CBQ* 46 [1984] 169-71).

[63]The parable's emphasis on the necessity of this interim period of waiting contrasts interestingly with another agricultural Gospel parable, John 4:35-36. (R. E. Brown [*John* 1.181-82] in his discussion of John 4:35-36, mentions Mark 4:26-29.) In the passage from John, it is implied that the usual interval between sowing and reaping has miraculously disappeared; already the time of reaping has arrived. The differing emphases of Mark 4:26-29 and John 4:35-36 illustrate the greater stress in John on the "already," and the greater stress in Mark on the "not yet."

[64]See for example Pseudo-Jerome's paraphrase of *nescit*, "he does not know," by *facit vel permittit nos nescire*, "he makes or permits us not to know" (cited by K. Weiss, *Voll Zuversicht! Zur Parabel Jesu vom zuversichtlichen Sämann Mk 4, 26-29* [NTAbh 10.1; Münster: Aschendorff, 1922] 41).

similar devices used by some modern commentators.[65] However, the situation would be even more desperate if *God* were chosen as the referent for the man, and indeed a redaction-critical consideration shows that the theme of incomprehension is compatible with Mark's portrayal of Jesus.

In 4:27c-28a the theme of the farmer's incomprehension does not appear by itself, but in *contrast* to the "automatic" (divine) growth of the plant. The latter theme, for the reader of Mark's Gospel up to this point, would resonate with the descriptions he has already read (1:33; 2:2, 13; 3:7-10, 20; 4:1) of crowds pressing around Jesus, even to the point of endangering his life. Of these descriptions, the one at the beginning of the parable chapter represents a sort of climax.[66]

Furthermore, throughout the Gospel people flock to Jesus, even though he tries to remain hidden, and disobey his orders to keep silent about his miracles, so that his fame spreads in a way that is contrary to his own plan (1:44-45; 6:32-33; 7:24, 36; 9:25a). All of these episodes contribute to the reader's impression of the irresistible manifestation of the kingdom of God, even in a way that is contrary to Jesus' intention, and beyond his control.[67] This impression that ultimately it is God, not Jesus in himself, who is responsible for the advent of the kingdom, is strengthened by Markan passages in which Jesus emphasizes his subordination to God;[68] this motif is similar to the subordination of the farmer to the ground in 4:28.[69]

Still other passages in the Gospel more openly imply a limitation of

---

[65]J. Jeremias translates the phrase (*Parables* 151) as "without his taking anxious thought"; K. Weiss (*Zuversicht* 11-14) gives a similar interpretation.

[66]See above, chapter 1.

[67]Cf. 10:18 (God, not Jesus, is the one who deserves the adjective "good"); 10:40 (places on Jesus' right and left are not his to give); and 14:36 ("not my will, but yours be done"). Jesus' submission to God's will is also implied by the statement in 14:49 that the scriptures must be fulfilled, and by the passion predictions.

[68]The farmer's incomprehension of how the seed grows is not exactly parallel to Jesus' inability to control the manifestations of the kingdom. There is, however, an overlap between the two limitations, partly in that both imply subordination to God.

[69]This subordination is seen in the implied contrast between the farmer's "sleeping and rising" and the "God-directed" (*automatē*) growth of the seed.

Jesus' knowledge. Of these, 13:32 is the most obvious: "But of that day or that hour no one knows, not even the angels in heaven, *not even the Son,* but only the Father." C. E. Carlston is partially right when he asserts that 4:27 and 13:32 refer to two different kinds of non-knowing.[70] Mark 4:27 speaks of an ignorance about how the kingdom grows, while 13:32 speaks of an ignorance about when it will reach its consummation. Still, 13:32 at least reveals that, with regard to some matters having to do with the course of God's kingdom, a certain kind of ignorance can be predicated of Jesus in Mark.

There are several other places where Jesus seems not to know how the kingdom manifests itself. In 5:30 he does not know who touched him, and in 6:6, he is amazed at the people's unbelief.[71] In 14:35-36 he acknowledges that the cup/hour is in God's hands, not his. Finally, the cry of dereliction in 15:34 must be considered. Although Jesus' suffering on the cross obviously does not come as a complete surprise to him,[72] the cry in 15:34 implies that the abandonment he experiences there is something that he has not expected.

The phrase "in what manner, he himself does not know," therefore, refers to a kind of incomprehension on the part of Jesus which is reflected throughout the Gospel. Statements about incomprehension on the part of the Markan Jesus, however, must be balanced by others about his insight. Overwhelmingly, in Mark's Gospel, Jesus is one who is granted a special kind of vision by God, from his baptism to his insight into the future to his penetration of human hearts.[73] If "even he does not know"[74] how the kingdom arrives, this is due not so much to any limitation on his part as to the mysteriousness of the kingdom and to his identification with a blinded humanity.[75]

Conclusions. Overall, then, we believe that the portrait of the farmer in 4:26-29 corresponds more closely to Mark's picture of Jesus than it does to his picture of either the disciples or God. Jesus' proclamation of the

---

[70]C. E. Carlston, *Parables* 204-205 n. 17.

[71]D. Rhoads and D. Michie, *Mark as Story* 106.

[72]See the passion predictions in 8:31-33; 9:30-32; 10:32-34.

[73]See his insight into people's thoughts (2:8; 9:33-35) and his status as a visionary and a clairvoyant (1:10-11; 11:1-4; chapter 13; 14:13-16).

[74]On this translation of the *autos* in 4:27, cf. BAG 123 (1h).

[75]Jesus' solidarity with blinded human beings is most starkly visible at the cross, where he takes their place in the darkness of the old age, so that they might see; see above, chapter 4.

word marks the inauguration of God's kingdom, yet in some ways Jesus' role in the Gospel is a passive one, as God himself prospers his preaching, is the power behind his miracles, and directs in a hidden way the events that lead to his crucifixion and resurrection. Both during his ministry and, by implication, in the time of the church, Jesus can be experienced by his disciples as absent or asleep, but when the measure is filled, he will suddenly return to reap the eschatological harvest.

The interpretation of the farmer as Jesus incorporates most of the strengths of the two alternatives for the farmer's identity, while avoiding their weaknesses. Like God, but unlike the disciples, Jesus can be identified as the eschatological reaper; but unlike God it is possible to attribute incomprehension to him. Like human beings, he can be described as "not knowing" and as subordinate to God in causing the growth of the kingdom, but unlike them and like the farmer in the parable his incomprehension is not blameworthy, but rather appropriate for the interim period before the full manifestation of the kingdom. His "not knowing" is the proper stance of one who is confronted by the "mystery of the kingdom of God."

The Periodization of the Kingdom

History-of-religions background. Aside from the identity of the man, the other main exegetical problem posed by Mark 4:26-29 is the significance of the way in which the plant grows.

Some exegetes deny that the description of the growth of the plant in vv 27-29a has any independent significance.[76] Many of these commentators seem motivated by a desire to refute the liberal notion of the immanent development of the kingdom of God. It is important, however, to retain the baby while disposing of the bath water. Ideas of theological immanence are certainly foreign to our parable, since it is God, symbolized by the ground, who causes the seed to grow. Manifestation of the kingdom in discrete stages, however, does not necessarily imply immanence,[77] as is evident from an examination of apocalyptic texts which

---

[76]See J. Jeremias, together with rebuttal by H.-W. Kuhn, cited in n. 10; also G. Harder ("Gleichnis" 61) who says that the only reason for the description of stages of growth is to build up narrative tension.

[77]N. A. Dahl, "The Parables of Growth," *Jesus in the Memory of the Early Church* (Minneapolis: Augsburg, 1976; orig. 1951) 164-65.

combine a strong sense of God's transcendence with the motif of linearity.[78] The salient points observable in such texts are as follows:

1. *Time is divided into "times," which have a semi-independent existence.* Examples of the pluralizing of "time" in apocalyptic are found in 4 Ezra 3:14; 4:36-37; 11:44; 13:58; 14:9-10; *2 Apoc. Bar.* 48:2-3; 54:1.[79] This notion is also found in the QL; see CD 16:2-4, which directs the reader to Jubilees, "the book of the divisions of the times" (*spr mḥlqwt hʿtym*), in which the "exact detail of the times" is taught. This detail is hidden from Israel as a whole in view of their blindness, but revealed to the elect.

The elevation of "time" to a semi-independent existence is already observable in Qoheleth. As K. Galling notes,[80] in that work the "course of time" (*ʿôlām*) "takes on an almost personal character, . . . an independence which can be compared with extra-biblical aeon-conceptions." A good example of the semi-independence of the times vis-à-vis God in apocalyptic literature is 4 Ezra 11:44: "And the Most High has looked upon his times, and behold, they are ended, and his ages are completed!"

2. *These times are directed by God, so that they occur in an orderly progression.* See 4 Ezra 4:36-37:

> For he has weighed the age in the balance and measured the
> times by measure, and numbered the times by number; and he
> will not move nor arouse them until that measure is ful-
> filled.[81]

Along similar lines is *2 Apoc. Bar.* 48:2: "You arrange the course of the periods, and they obey you," and 1QpHab 7:12-13: "For all the seasons of God come to pass at their appointed time as he has decreed concerning them in the mysteries of his wisdom."[82] Again, Qoheleth paves the way for this development.[83]

---

[78]N. A. Dahl, "Growth" 147-48.

[79]On the pluralizing of "time" in apocalyptic, see W. Harnisch, *Verhängnis* 281.

[80]Cited by M. Hengel, *Judaism* 1.121.

[81]See above, n. 30 on translation.

[82]Trans. G. Vermes, *Dead Sea Scrolls* 239.

[83]See M. Hengel (*Judaism* 1.120): "To every happening that God brings about he gave a fixed *kairos* (3:1-8), and in the light of its particular *kairos*, all that happens is good (3:11), for all *kairoi* are included in the unalterable course of God's time."

3. *Because of this orderliness, the progression of the times can be compared to "natural" phenomena.*[84] In *2 Apoc. Bar.* 22:5-6, the coming age will follow the present one as the time of fruits follows sowing and planting. In *4 Ezra* 5:46-49, as a woman does not bear ten children at one time, but each in its own time, so God has laid down for the world a set progression.[85]

Similar emphases are found in *1 Enoch* and the Qumran literature. In *1 Enoch* 2-5, examples of the orderliness of nature (course of the heavens, growth of trees) are first given, followed by this statement:

> All of them belong to him who lives forever. His work pro-
> ceeds and progresses from year to year. And all his work
> prospers and obeys him, and it does not change; but every-
> thing functions in the way which God has ordered it (5:1-2).

In 1QH 12:4-11 the orderliness of the universe is emphasized, using vocabulary ("dominion of darkness," "end," "appointed hour" [*tqwph*], "time" [*ct*], and "season" [*mwcd*]) which elsewhere in the QL (already in 1QH 12:14-18) is used for *eschatological* realities.

4. *Each "time" has its own peculiar character, including its own mixture of hiddenness and revelation.* For the Dead Sea Sect, the law apparently changed with the times. L. H. Schiffman, in his analysis of this change, speaks of "progression or evolution of the law with the stages of history" and of "progressive revelation."[86] Since the law changes with the time, the *maskil* instructs people *according to the time* (1QS 9:20), and the Council of Twelve and the three priests "behave toward everyone *according to the order of the time*" (*btkwn hct*; 1QS 8:3-4; trans. mine). The present age, for the Qumran community, is a penultimate one in which the true meaning of the ancient prophecies has been revealed, but

---

[84] The word "natural" is placed in quotation marks because the concept of nature, as it develops in Greek thought, implies an immanence and independence from God's direct activity that is foreign to the spirit of the OT, Jewish apocalyptic, and our parable; see H. Koester, *"physis,"* TDNT 9 (1974) 251-277. We will retain the word in quotation marks to refer to phenomena such as the growth of plants, recognizing that, in Mark's view, all such phenomena are "worked by God alone."

[85] H.-J. Klauck, *Allegorie* 223.

[86] L. H. Schiffman, *The Halakhah at Qumran* (SJLA 16; Leiden: Brill, 1975) 25-27.

only within the elect community; and in spite of this decisive revelation, "perfection of knowledge" must wait for the time of renewal.[87]

A different extent of knowledge for each time is also implied in *1 Enoch*.[88] While at the close of the seventh week of the Apocalypse of Weeks, wisdom is given to the elect (*1 Enoch* 93:10; 91:11), in the eighth week God's righteous judgment will be revealed *to the whole world* (93:10).[89]

5. *Only the elect know the "course of the times," although even they do not know exactly when the end will come.* While in Qoheleth, the course of God's time (*'ôlām*) is completely concealed from human beings,[90] in *2 Apoc. Bar.* 56:1-2 the interpreting angel tells Baruch that it has been given to him to know the course of the times.[91] This knowledge sets the elect off from the rest of humanity (cf. *2 Apoc. Bar.* 27:15 with 28:1). Yet exactly when the end will come is hidden from all people (*2 Apoc. Bar.* 22:5-7; 23:2; 48:3; 54:1; 4 Ezra 4:26-43).

6. *When the "eschatological measure" is filled, the end will come swiftly.*[92] See 4 Ezra 4:36-37, cited above under §2. Also important is 4 Ezra 4:40-43, where the coming of the end is compared to the experience of a pregnant woman. The coming of the end, as there described, is not dependent on human activity, occurs only after a predetermined time has elapsed, and is swift as a woman's labor when it finally arrives.

Here the image for the eschatological measure is a "natural" process (pregnancy); cf. *2 Apoc. Bar.* 22:5-6, where the image is the growth of a seed "until its appointed time." A similar image is used in *1 Clem* 23:4-5,

---

[87]See my "Mark 4:10-12" 567-69. In addition to the passages cited there, see also 1QS 9:13-14.

[88]On the following passages, see G. W. E. Nicklesburg, "The Epistle of Enoch and the Qumran Literature," *JJS* 33 (1982) 333-348.

[89]Cf. Mark 4:25, contrasted with 4:21-22; 13:26; 14:62. M. Hengel (*Judaism* 1.208), basing his conclusions mostly on *1 Enoch*, distinguishes between two stages in the apocalyptic understanding of wisdom: the "provisional and imperfect" revelation to the elect in the temptations of the last time, and the perfect wisdom of the time of salvation itself.

[90]M. Hengel, *Judaism* 1.120.

[91]See W. Harnisch, *Verhängnis* 262.

[92]On the concept of the eschatological "measure" in the New Testament, see now R. Stuhlmann, *Das eschatologische Mass im Neuen Testament* (FRLANT 132; Göttingen: Vandenhoeck & Ruprecht, 1983).

with the intent of showing that "the future glory cannot come until everything has happened which according to the will of God must precede it."[93]
This passage describes several stages of growth, culminating finally in
ripeness, and concludes that, when that ripeness is attained, "his will shall
be quickly and suddenly accomplished."

The swiftness of the end when the measure is filled is sometimes
expressed through the idea that an acceleration of time will occur in the
last days.[94]

7. *Knowledge of the orderly progression of the times, and the certainty
of their fulfillment, inspire confidence among the elect.* See 2 Apoc. Bar.
20:6, where God comforts Baruch by saying, "I shall command you with
regard to the course of the times, for they will come and will not tarry."
Cf. 1QpHab 7:10-14:

> Its explanation concerns the men of truth who do the Law,
> whose hands do not slacken in the service of truth when the
> final time is delayed; for all the seasons of God come to pass
> at their appointed time as he has decreed concerning them in
> the mysteries of his wisdom" (trans. mine).

In both of these passages, the end has been delayed and there is a temptation to despair, but God's control of the "course of times" is adduced as a
cause for hope.

*   *   *   *   *

The similarities between this outline and Mark 4:26-29 are striking. In
the latter, as in the former, history is divided into discrete stages[95] under
the direction of God,[96] and the image for those stages is an orderly
growth that occurs in the "natural" sphere. Furthermore, our parable too

---

[93]N. A. Dahl, "Growth" 152.

[94]W. Harnisch (*Verhängnis* 271-73) cites as examples 4 Ezra 4:26;
2 Apoc. Bar. 20:1-2; 48:30b-31; 83:1, 6-7; 1 Enoch 80:2; Apoc. Ab. 29:13;
already Isa 5:19; 60:22; Zeph 1:14; Hab 2:3; Sir 36:6-8; Pss. Sol. 17:44-45.

[95]See especially the words "first . . . then . . . then" (*prōton . . . eita
. . . eita*) in 4:28.

[96]See our discussion above of *automatē* in Mark 4:28.

contains the idea that when this growth is finished, but not before, the end will come suddenly.[97]

The periods in the Gospel of Mark. What are the discrete stages envisaged by Mark in the development of the kingdom of God? Although C. H. Dodd may be right when he asserts that, for Jesus himself, the preliminary stages of growth in our parable corresponded to the work of the prophets and of John the Baptist,[98] when we ask about *Mark's* understanding such an interpretation is impossible. The whole process of growth begins with the sowing of the seed by the farmer, which for Mark, as we have seen, is Jesus' proclamation of the word; the growth of the plant follows this initial proclamation.

The last statement, however, points up a difference between Mark and Jewish apocalyptic texts which mention the Messiah or the Son of Man. In the latter, the messianic figure's coming is usually the climax of the periods described, rather than the initiation of a set of periods.[99] Some apocalyptic texts, it is true, postulate linearity even after the coming of the Messiah,[100] but they are a minority, and none of them use the image of growth. The difference between Mark and the apocalyptic texts is

---

[97] N. Dahl (cited in A. Ambrozic, *Hidden Kingdom* 118) draws out the connection between certain apocalyptic texts (4 Ezra 7:74; 4:28-29, 35-40; 2 *Apoc. Bar.* 70:2; James 5:7-8) and Jesus' parables of growth, speaking of the "periodicity of history" in these texts. We prefer to speak of "periodization," which is defined as "division (as of history) into periods," rather than of periodicity, "the quality, state, or fact of being regularly recurrent" (*Webster's New Collegiate Dictionary* [8th ed.; Springfield, Mass.: Merriam, 1981]).

[98] *Parables* 132-33. Dodd recognizes the linearity of the parable, but places Jesus' coming at the end of the line, rather than at the beginning, where it is for Mark.

[99] For example, in 2 *Apoc. Bar.* 39:7 the revelation of the kingdom of the Messiah occurs after the fulfillment of the reign of the evil kingdom, and in Dan 7, the Son of Man comes after the four earthly kingdoms have had their day, and destroys them.

[100] See 4 Ezra 7:26-44; 12:31-34; 2 *Apoc. Bar.* 40:3. W. Harnisch (*Verhängnis* 256-57) asserts that in 4 Ezra 12:31-34 the messianic period is the last phase of the *old* age, a transitional period which is delimited by the final judgment. In 2 *Apoc. Bar.* 40:3 also, the time of the Messiah is not identical with the time of salvation, but rather the last phase of this transitional age (*Verhängnis* 259).

probably due to Mark's realization that, although the future kingdom had already broken into the present in the ministry of Jesus, Jesus' earthly ministry had *not* fully brought about the "kingdom of God come in power," that certain events would have to happen before the kingdom could be manifested publicly.

Moving from the beginning of the parable to its end, we next ask to what the harvest described in v 29 corresponds. In our discussion of the identity of the reaper, we have pointed to the strong ties between 4:29 and the description of the eschaton in chapter 13; also, we have noted that the harvest is a stock OT metaphor for the eschatological judgment, and that Joel 4:13, which is cited in Mark 4:29, uses the metaphor in this way. In Jewish apocalyptic literature roughly contemporary with the New Testament, harvest continues to be a metaphor for the eschaton, and this metaphor is sometimes combined with the metaphor of growth.[101] In the only other NT passage which quotes Joel 4:13, namely Rev 14:15,[102] the harvest is the eschatological judgment.[103] Further evidence for the equivalence of the harvest with the eschaton is provided by Matthew's Parable of the Weeds, which specifically identifies it as such (13:39); we have previously shown that this is Matthew's version of Mark 4:26-29.

It is true that there are two NT passages where harvest is used as a metaphor for Christian mission (Luke 10:2 par Matt 9:37-38; John

---

[101]Besides Joel 4:12-16, other examples of harvest as a metaphor for the last judgment are Isa 17:5-6; 18:5; 27:12; 63:1; Micah 4:12; Matt 3:12; 4 Ezra 4:28-37; 2 Apoc. Bar. 70:2 (Dupont, "Semence" 379). The 4 Ezra and 2 Apoc. Bar. passages cited combine with the metaphor of *harvest* the metaphor of *growth*. Cf. 2 Ap. Bar. 22:5-6, which speaks of growth until the appointed time of harvest, and 1 Clem 23:4, which in its context describes growth in discretes stages until a swift harvest (although the harvest is implied rather than explicit).

[102]This is also the only other NT passage to use the noun *drepanon*, "sickle"; see H.-W. Kuhn, *Sämmlungen* 106 n. 37.

[103]B. B. Scott (*Symbol-Maker* 86-88), while admitting that the Joel citation in Mark 4:29 by itself suggests the Last Judgment, asserts that this suggestion is a "trap" for the reader, whose association of harvest with the Last Judgment is undone by the motifs of the man's ignorance and passivity, and the peaceful sabbatical of the land implied by *automatē*: "The audience fell asleep waiting for the eschatological war." This over-ingenious interpretation, however, goes against the structure of the parable; if the motifs in vv 27-28 were meant to supercede those of v 29, they should follow v 29, not precede it. It is a strange trap that is sprung before the bait is put out!

4:35),[104] but both passages lack the element of the sickle, which in both Old and New Testaments is always associated with the Last Judgment.[105] It is also true that in both *Gos. Thom.* logion 21 and *Ap. Jas.* 12:22-31 the harvest seems to have no relation to any eschatological expectation, but rather refers to an event which can take place right now, but this non-eschatological interpretation is possible only because the two passages lack several of the most characteristic features of Mark 4:26-29, including:

1.   A specific citation of Joel 4:13.
2.   The farmer's non-knowing.
3.   The farmer's passivity until the harvest.

All of these elements make the Markan harvest more eschatological than its gnostic cousins. The citation of Joel 4:13, as we have just seen, introduces a classic OT Last Judgment text, and the motif of the farmer's ignorance excludes an interpretation of the harvest as timeless gnosis. The length of the description of the period of passivity until the harvest suggests that this period is a central concern in the Markan parable. This intermediate period is of crucial concern because, as we have seen, it symbolizes the moment in which the Markan community feels itself to be living, a moment in which Jesus is physically absent and does not intervene to save the community from persecution. But if the present moment is included in this interim period of Christ's passivity, then the harvest lies in the future. The parallels between Mark 4:26-29 and 13:24-31 confirm that this future point is the parousia.

The eschatological "measure" in Mark. The hypothesis that the harvest is the eschaton is further strengthened by a consideration of the way in which the motif of the eschatological "measure" functions in 4:29 and in the rest of Mark.

Mark 4:29a begins with the words *hotan de,* "but when." The *de* here is disjunctive, and the sentence speaks of discontinuity from what has gone before, which is further emphasized by the word *euthys,* "immediately"; whereas the farmer has been inactive while the seed has grown (vv 27-28), now he suddenly springs into action. The discontinuity, and the suddenness of action, are in line with the Jewish apocalyptic concept of the

---

[104]H.-W. Kuhn, *Sämmlungen* 106 n. 37.
[105]V. Fusco, *Parola* 353.

"measure." Although history seems to continue as it always has, all the while the "measure," conceived as a container, is secretly filling up. Suddenly a flashpoint will be reached, and the end will come swiftly.

As N. A. Dahl points out,[106] the concept of the "measure" appears throughout Mark's Gospel, in that a divine necessity (dei) demands that certain things must happen before the end can come. Elijah must first come (9:11-13);[107] the Son of Man must suffer many things (8:31, etc.) and be baptized in suffering (10:38); the disciples will face suffering and persecution (13:9-13), and many will be led astray (13:21-22); judgment will come on the Temple and the Jewish leaders (12:1-12; 13:2); and the Gospel must first be preached to all nations.

Of all the passages in Mark's Gospel, chapter 13 contains the most references to the concept of the eschatological "measure." This concept is designed to answer precisely such questions as the one the disciples ask in 13:4: "When will this be, and what will be the sign when these things are all to be accomplished?" In reply, Jesus uses the concept of the measure in two different ways:[108] to show that the end is not yet, because the measure is not yet full (13:7, 21-22, 24b-27), and to show that, nevertheless, present events are filling up the measure, and that the swift coming of the end is assured once the measure is full (13:8, 10, 14, 24a, 28-29, 30).[109]

Several specific aspects of the notion of the "measure" in chapter 13 link it with 4:26-29. For example, the point that present events are filling

---

[106]N. A. Dahl, "Growth" 154.

[107]Note that 9:11, like 4:28, contains the idea that one event must happen "first" (prōton) before others can occur. Cf. 7:27, where the word prōton again occurs: "Let the children first be fed."

[108]On the ways in which the motif of the measure can function in the NT, see R. Stuhlmann, "Beobachtungen" 159-60.

[109]M. D. Hooker ("Trial and Tribulation in Mark XIII," BJRL 65 [1982] 78-99) asserts that there are actually three themes touching on signs of the end in chapter 13: 1) the end is not yet, because the true sign has not arrived (vv 5-13); 2) when the true sign is given, the end will come immediately (vv 14-20, 24-27); 3) there will be no sign at all (vv 33-37). The first two themes, which are compatible, represent complementary sides of the notion of the eschatological measure, but the third, which does not fit in well with the first two, contradicts the whole concept of the measure; Hooker believes that the third theme goes back to Jesus, while the first two are contributions of the church. However, Hooker's separation of the third theme from the first two is unnecessary if the signs of vv 14-27 are viewed as part of the kairos of the Lord's coming described in vv 32-37.

up the eschatological measure is made at the end of chapter 13 by means of the image of the fig tree (13:28-32), in a passage which, like 4:26-29, not only uses the growth of a plant as a metaphor for the coming of the end, but also speaks of the potency of Jesus' word, a theme which we have seen to be implied in 4:26.[110]

Considering the redactional framework provided by the Gospel as a whole, then, the image of the "measure" in 4:29 is meant to impart both a note of caution and one of encouragement. The caution is that "the end is not yet" (cf. 13:7), despite the eschatological fervor which apparently has some segments of the Markan community in its grip. There will be no mistaking the end; when it arrives, Christ's passivity and apparent absence will suddenly be transformed into swift, dramatic action. The return will not be an event that is visible only to some (13:6, 21); when the Son of Man swings the sickle, all humanity will recognize that the harvest is taking place (13:26).

The encouragement is that this return will come as inevitably as the period of reaping follows that of sowing. The factors that are driving some within the Markan community to the point of despair—persecution from the outside, dissension on the inside—are part and parcel of the manifestation of the kingdom, which until the parousia is a hidden king-dom. Eyes which have been opened see, even in the intensification of sufferings past anything that has been known before, a sign that the kingdom is rolling with irresistible divine power toward its public manifes-tation (13:19). The blade has sprouted, the ear has formed and is filling with grain—can anyone doubt that the harvest is near?[111]

The intermediate stages. Thus the casting of the seed into the ground corresponds to Jesus' proclamation of the kingdom, and the harvest corre-sponds to the parousia. To what, then, if anything, do the intermediate stages of growth correspond? Although Mark does not specifically allego-rize the blade, ear, and full grain, a consideration of the notion of "times" in his Gospel illuminates how he would have understood the intermediate stages in 4:26-29.

---

[110]V. Fusco (*Parola* 363), taking 4:26-29 in its Markan context, writes that the "measure" includes the diffusion of the word (4:14-20) and the expansion of the church (4:30-32). We have arrived at a similar conclusion through an examination of chapter 13; see especially 13:10.

[111]Thus Mark, like other apocalypticists in their delineations of the course of history, sees himself and his community near the end of the course.

Mark 4:28 describes the way in which the kingdom gradually manifests itself, approximating more and more closely, and in discrete periods, its final shape. When grain is in its "shoot" stage, an expert eye is needed to identify it as grain. When it begins to ear, less discernment is needed to identify it, and by the time the crop is ripe practically anyone can see what it is.

Mark's Gospel as a whole, like our parable, and in line with the Jewish apocalyptic notion that the extent of knowledge changes with the "times," presents discrete stages in the manifestation of the kingdom: the period of Jesus' ministry, the period of the church, and the parousia.[112] All three of these stages are part of what me might call "kingdom time,"[113] but nonetheless a distinction between them is important for understanding Mark's apocalyptic.

The period of Jesus' ministry, in Mark's Gospel, is already a time of fulfillment and revelation. The "time has been fulfilled" (1:15), and the disciples have been given the mystery of the kingdom of God (4:11). Indeed, Jesus' custom is to teach even the crowds (see especially 10:1).

---

[112]On the importance of these three stages in early Christian thought, see especially H. Conzelmann's work on the "history of salvation" in Luke, *The Theology of St. Luke* (New York: Harper & Brothers, 1960) passim; cf. more recently the excellent discussion in J. Fitzmyer, *The Gospel According to Luke I-IX* (AB 28; Garden City: Doubleday, 1981) 181-87.

Several of the church fathers (cited by V. Fusco, *Parola* 356 n. 62) saw these three periods adumbrated in Mark 4:26-29. In Mark, however, the time of the church is not as discrete a period as it is in Luke. Mark's Gospel has no second volume, as Luke's does; rather, Mark, like John, writes about the post-Easter period in a story set during Jesus' lifetime. For Mark, the events of Jesus' lifetime are not just events that occurred once-and-for-all, long ago, as in Luke (see J. Fitzmyer, *Luke* 1.186); they *are* that, but they are also more. An eschatological tension ties together Jesus' earthly ministry, his post-Easter empowerment of the Markan community, and his coming in glory at the parousia. Nevertheless, because the crucifixion/resurrection and the parousia are such radically disjunctive events in Mark (9:9; 13:26; 14:62), we can still say that Mark distinguishes the stages of Jesus, church, and parousia, always remembering (as our parable itself implies) that these three "times" are all part of what we might call "kingdom time"; Mark never uses the word *kairos* in the plural.

[113]I am grateful to Barbara Hall of General Theological Seminary for this formulation, which she articulated in a discussion of a portion of this study at the Paul Study Group, Union Theological Seminary, New York, February 21, 1985.

Yet in other ways the period of Jesus' ministry is a penultimate, even an antepenultimate, stage in the manifestation of the kingdom. The kingdom has not fully arrived, but is "at hand" (1:14-15); correspondingly, epistemological clarity is not fully realizable in this period; the closest that a discerning person can be is "not far from the kingdom" (12:34).

In this antepenultimate period, even the disciples, who have been given the mystery of the kingdom, suffer from the blindness that in apocalyptic texts is characteristic of the old age and even afflicts the elect community. They do not yet have faith (4:40; cf. 8:21); indeed, they *cannot* have full faith until after the crucifixion and resurrection of Jesus (14:27-28; cf. 9:9).[114] As we have seen, the story of the healing of the blind man in 8:22-26 is paradigmatic for the disciples, whose imperfect spiritual vision before the resurrection will be made perfect by their second contact with Jesus, after the resurrection.[115]

The crucifixion and resurrection, then, inaugurate the second stage in the manifestation of the kingdom of God, a stage in which many things that were only inchoate during Jesus' ministry come out into the open. At the foot of the cross a human being for the first time discerns Jesus' true identity (15:39),[116] and after the resurrection the disciples will see Jesus in Galilee (16:7) and reveal matters that were hidden during Jesus' ministry (9:9). Now Jesus' proclamation of the good news about God (1:14-15) becomes the church's proclamation of the good news about Jesus (1:1; cf. 8:35; 10:29; 13:10; 14:9).[117]

Although there is discontinuity between the period of Jesus' ministry and that inaugurated by the resurrection, there is also continuity. As the blade adumbrates the ear, so events in Jesus' ministry adumbrate events

---

[114]Faith, *pistis*, is never attributed to the preresurrection disciples in Mark, though Jesus several times recognizes that people who come to him have the *pistis* to be healed (2:5; 5:34; 10:52). Rather, Jesus *exhorts* the disciples to have faith (11:22-24), as he exhorts the crowds (1:15) and individuals who come to him for healing (5:26; 9:23-24). In 9:42 Jesus speaks of "these little ones who believe in me," but here the context makes clear that the reference is to post-resurrection disciples.

[115]See above, chapter 4.

[116]It is significant that this human being is a Gentile, for Jesus' earthly ministry, in Mark's view, was for the most part restricted to Jews. See 7:27, "Let the children first be fed," on which cf. n. 107.

[117]See A. Ambrozic, *Hidden Kingdom* 245 and J. Gnilka, *Evangelium* 1.65-66.

in the time of the church.[118] The redactional composition 8:27-9:1 brings out strongly the similarity between Jesus' destiny and that of faithful Christians.[119] Further, the "handing over" of the disciples in the Markan present (13:9, 11, 12) recapitulates the "handing over" of Jesus during the Passion Narrative.[120] Moreover, the spiritual condition of the Twelve during Jesus' ministry foreshadows that of some in the Markan community.[121] The warning to the Markan community to stay awake, since no one knows the hour of the Son of Man's coming (13:32-36), has its counterpart in the disciples' failure to stay awake in Gethsemane while Jesus, after initially praying that "the hour" may pass from him, finally realizes that "the hour has come" (14:32-42).[122] The "leading astray" of disciples in the time of the church (13:22-23) is foreshadowed by Judas' betrayal of Jesus and Jesus' abandonment by the rest of the Twelve.[123] There is even a parallel between the three-hour intervals implied in 13:35, which will immediately precede the parousia, and those described in the Passion Narrative.[124]

The second period pictured by Mark's Gospel, then, the period of the church, is in continuity with, yet distinct from, the period of Jesus' ministry. It is also distinct from the parousia, in that, although a time of revelation and fulfillment, it also contains an emphatic "not yet." The *kairos*

---

[118]This puts the situation in the terms of 4:28. However, in the Gospel as a whole, since chapter 13 *precedes* the Passion Narrative, the terms are reversed: the present and future, as portrayed in chapter 13, cast their shadow on the past, as portrayed in the Passion Narrative.

[119]A. Ambrozic, *Hidden Kingdom* 245-46.

[120]14:10, 11, 18, 21, 41, 42, 44; 15:1, 10, 15; cf. 3:19; 9:31; 10:33. Cf. N. Perrin and D. C. Duling, *Introduction* 110. Elsewhere (*Introduction* 238) Perrin and Duling note that the ministry of John the Baptist foreshadows those of Jesus and the church; first John preaches and is delivered up (1:7, 14), then Jesus preaches and is delivered up (1:14; 9:31; 10:33), and finally the Christians preach and are delivered up (13:9-13).

[121]A. Ambrozic, *Hidden Kingdom* 246.

[122]The solemn opening of the Passion Narrative (14:1) buttresses the impression that the momentous hour has now come.

[123]Yet there are two "escape clauses" for the disciples in 13:22-23: "if possibe" and "Take heed, I have told you all things beforehand." These correspond to the promises of renewed fellowship in 14:28; 16:7.

[124]14:68, 72; 15:1, 25, 33, 42. Our comments on the relationship between chapter 13 and the Passion Narrative develops ideas found in R. H. Lightfoot, *The Gospel Message of St. Mark* (Oxford at the Clarendon, 1950) 48-59.

has not yet come, and no one knows the hour of its coming (13:33). In the period until its arrival, not *all* will see the truth; some will persecute Jesus' disciples as they persecuted him (8:34-35; 13:9-13), and even within the elect community there will be those who are led astray by false Christs and false prophets (13:22). During this time, Jesus will be exalted to God's right hand, but his enemies will not yet be subdued under his feet (12:36). Because of the continuing presence of evil in the world, the period of the church can even be included as part of "this time" (*ho kairos houtos*), in contrast to the coming age (10:30).[125]

Thus, it will remain for the parousia to mark the culmination of the kingdom of God, the final period in which all hiddenness bursts into manifestation.[126] Then, not just the elect, but all human beings, even his enemies, will see clearly who Jesus is (13:26; 14:62).

Like the parable in 4:26-29, then, Mark's Gospel as a whole outlines a movement from hidden revelation to open revelation. This movement has already been foreshadowed in 4:21-22, which contrasts a period of veiling with one of manifestation. The parable in 4:26-29, however, is more subtle than the sayings in 4:21-22 in its delineation of these stages, for it recognizes periods (blade, ear) which contain a *mixture* of hiddenness and openness.

There are thus three stages of growth in the parable, culminating in a stage that is certainly to be identified with the eschaton, and there are also three "periods" pictured in the Gospel as a whole, again culminating in the eschaton. Also, there is a movement in both parable and Gospel from partial manifestation to more complete manifestation to full manifestation. Furthermore, in a broad way the three periods pictured in the Gospel can be termed "the nearness of the kingdom" (= the time of Jesus; 1:14-15; 11:10; 12:34), "the hidden presence of the kingdom" (= the time of the church; 4:11; 10:14-15, 23-25), and "the kingdom come in power"

---

[125]H. C. Kee (*Community* 141) notes that the expression "this age" in 10:30 refers to Mark's own time.

[126]For J. J. A. Kahmann ("Marc. 1, 14-15 en hun plaats in het geheel van het Marcus-evangelie," *Bidragen* 38 [1977] 84-98), God's kingdom in Mark has two *kairoi*; it is already present in Jesus' earthly life, but will be fully realized at the coming of the kingdom with power. See, however, our observation above (n. 112) that Mark never uses the word *kairos* in the plural, and our depiction of the period of the church as an intermediate stage in the manifestation of the kingdom.

(= the parousia; 9:1, 47).[127] It thus seems likely that Mark would have seen in our parable, which after all concerns the kingdom of God (4:26), a sketch of the three phases in the manifestation of the one kingdom of God.

The Kerygma of Mark 4:26-29 for the Markan Community

We saw above that in apocalyptic literature generally it has been given to the elect, in contradistinction from the rest of humanity, to know the "course of the times." Similarly, it is given to those within the Markan community who hear Mark's message rightly, in contrast to *hoi exō*, to receive in 4:26-29 insight into the stages in the kingdom of God.

That kingdom receives its initiation and its termination from Jesus; without his action there would be no kingdom of God. Yet the real motive power is God himself, whose workings escape the full comprehension even of the one whom he has designated to be his agent. How much more will they sometimes appear mysterious and even scandalous, then, to those who are called to take up their crosses and follow Jesus!

The parable teaches that the hiddenness of God's purpose is neither an accident nor a cause for despair, but an inevitable part of the course of the times. The time before the end *must* be a time of hiddenness, and those who prematurely announce a complete end to hiddenness (13:21) or claim to know when the hiddenness will end (13:32-37) are deceivers.

The parable encourages the Markan community by reminding it that it stands poised between the beginning of the kingdom and its final consummation. The community can see that a great deal of divinely-actuated movement toward the eschaton has already taken place. Already the stage has passed when Jesus' identity had to be a closely-guarded secret; now the Markan community openly proclaims it. The movement can also be seen in the way that the seed that Jesus cast into the ground with his proclamation of the kingdom continues its dynamic growth, though he himself is physically absent. The gospel *is* being preached to all nations, and thus the eschatological measure is being filled. Even the sufferings which the community endures are a sign that the harvest is near. The ear has already taken shape; just a few more grains must be formed, and then the Son of Man will send in the sickle.

The end will come quickly and in a way that will be visible to all, not

---

[127]Cf. however the more detailed discussion in chapter 2 of the kingdom in Mark as a whole.

just to those who have insight into the "mystery of the kingdom of God."
With the eschatological harvest, that mystery will be over; no longer will
the kingdom exist in paradoxical hiddenness and weakness, but in power
and glory. The parable ends on a note of great solemnity which foreshadows for the Markan community the joy that will then be experienced:
"For the harvest has come!"

6

The Parable of the Mustard Seed (Mark 4:30–32)

TRANSLATION

4:30a	And he said, How shall we show the likeness of the kingdom of God,
4:30b	or in what parable shall we put it?
4:31a	(It is) as to a grain of mustard seed,
4:31b	which when it is sown upon the earth,
4:31c	being smaller than all the seeds upon the earth,
4:32a	and when it is sown
4:32b	it grows up and becomes greater than all the shrubs,
4:32c	and puts forth large branches
4:32d	so that under its shade the birds of heaven are able to settle.

LITERARY ANALYSIS

Structure

The Markan Parable of the Mustard Seed consists of the introductory formula *kai elegen* ("and he said") followed by a double question (v 30) and then the parable itself (vv 31-32). Both v 30 and vv 31-32 are replete with full "o" sounds,[1] which thus unify the parable.

---

[1] *Pōs homoiōsōmen . . . thōmen; hōs kokkǭ sinapeōs hos hotan . . . mikroteron on pantōn tōn spermatōn tōn . . . hotan . . . meizon pantōn tōn lachanōn . . . poiei kladous megalous . . . hōste hypo . . . ouranou kataskēnoun.*

The structure of the double question in v 30 is ABCA'C'A'B':

	A	how		
	B		shall we compare	
	C			the k. of God
or				
	A'	in what		
	C'			it
	A'	parable		
	B'		shall we put	

The placement of *autēn* ("it," C') between the parts of the dative "in what parable" (A') is responsible for the departure of the second question from the ABC pattern of the first. The separation of the parts of the dative makes the latter emphatic.

The parable itself (vv 31-32) consists of a complex sentence whose implied subject is the kingdom of God, and whose predominant structural feature is a relative clause, narrated in the present tense, describing how a grain of mustard seed grows up, becomes greater than all shrubs, and puts out great branches. There are four subordinate expressions: a) two temporal clauses beginning with "when it is sown" (v 31b, 32a), b) a participial phrase describing the smallness of the seed (v 31c), and c) a result clause about the settling of the birds under the full-grown bush (v 32d).

The introductory formula *hōs kokkō sinapeōs* ("as to a grain of mustard seed," v 31a) is overloaded; either a simple dative ("we shall compare it *to*") or *hōs* followed by a nominative ("it is as . . .") would be smoother.[2] Vv 31b-32b, which follow, are marked by repetition and contrast, as J. D. Crossan makes clear by diagramming their elements:[3]

A	which when sown
B	upon the earth
C	being smaller than all the seeds
B'	upon the earth
A'	and when sown
D	it grows up and becomes
C'	greater than all the shrubs

---

[2]E. Lohmeyer, *Evangelium* 88.
[3]J. D. Crossan, "Seed Parables" 256.

The repetitions are the two instances of *hotan sparē* (A, A') and the two
instances of *epi tēs gēs* (B, B'); the contrast is between the smallness of
the seed and the greatness of the grown plant (C, C'). Of these elements,
C (v 31c) is especially awkward. After the first instance of *hotan sparē*
the reader expects a description of what happens when the seed is sown,
but instead gets a parenthetical participial phrase about the smallness of
the seed. Furthermore, the gender of the participle should be masculine,
corresponding to *kokkos*, but instead is neuter, corresponding to *spermatōn*, which follows it.[4] Apparently the mustard seed is so insignificant
that it cannot even retain its proper gender!

The parable concludes with an OT citation (v 32cd); Mark's readers may
have been alerted to the allusive character of this description by its
departure from the natural picture (birds do not settle, i.e. nest,[5] on the
ground, under the shade of the mustard plant).[6] The citation mingles
features from three OT passages where a king or his kingdom is symbolized by a great tree that provides shelter to birds and beasts. In Ezek
17:23 we find the restored kingdom of David compared to a tree *under the
shade* of which (*hypo tēn skian autou*) every bird will rest. In Ezek 31:6
Pharaoh is likened to a tree, in the boughs of which all the *birds of heaven*
(*ta peteina tou ouranou*) nested, *under* the *branches* (*kladōn*) of which all
the beasts bred, and in the *shade* (*skia*) of which the whole multitude of
nations lived. Similarly, in Theodotion's translation of Dan 4:9, 18 (12, 21),
Nebuchadnezzar is symbolized by a tree *under* which, and in whose

---

[4]On these incongruities, see E. Lohmeyer, *Evangelium* 88; H. Koester,
"Test Case" 82. Lohmeyer also feels that the different meanings of *epi tēs
gēs* in its two usages ("in the field," "on earth") is an awkwardness, but
this is being overly rationalistic.

[5]On the translation of *kataskēnoun*, see W. Michaelis, "*skēnē*," *TDNT* 7
(1971; orig. 1964) 387-89; the word denotes a prolonged stay or permanent residence, and is the usual LXX translation for *škn*.

[6]L. Cerfaux, "Les paraboles du Royaume dans l'Évangile de Thomas,"
Le Muséon 70 (1957) 312; J. Dupont, "Les Paraboles du seneve et du
levain," *NRT* 89 (1967) 904. R. G. Bratcher (*A Translator's Guide to the
Gospel of Mark* [Helps for Translators; London/New York/Stuttgart:
United Bible Societies, 1981] 51) tries to evade this difficulty by suggesting that "shade" denotes the upper branches of the plant, which provide
shade for birds nesting in the lower branches. The referent of *autou*,
however, is the plant as a whole. In any case, birds do not really nest in
the branches of the mustard plant; see J. C. Trever, "Mustard," *IDB* 3
(1962) 477.

branches, the beasts and the *birds of heaven dwelt* (*kateskēnoun*).[7] No one of these texts, however, is being specifically cited.[8]

In the consideration of composition history that follows, the awkwardnesses and repetitions we have noted will play a role in unraveling the history of the tradition of our parable.

Composition History

The versions of the Parable of the Mustard Seed are presented in Chart 10. The two basic forms are those of Mark and Q (Matt 13:31-32 par. Luke 13:18-19); *Gos. Thom.* logion 20 is not an independent witness to primitive tradition, but a gnosticizing reworking of the Synoptic parable.[9] The differences between the Markan form and the Q form, which is substantially identical with Luke 13:18-19,[10] are as follows:[11] 1) In the introductory double question (v 30) Mark uses first person plural verbs and mentions that Jesus speaks "in a parable," and his phrasing is not as

---

[7]For a compilation of the LXX texts, see R. Pesch, *Markusevangelium* 1.262 n. 12.

[8]R. Pesch, *Markusevangelium* 1.262; J. Gnilka, *Evangelium* 1.187.

[9]See esp. L. Cerfaux, "Paraboles" 311-312, and cf. V. Fusco (*Parola* 377 n. 49) for a list of those who support this position; *contra* C.-H. Hunziger, "*sinapi,*" *TDNT* 7 (1971; orig. 1964) 287-91. In *Thomas,* the parable is introduced by a question from the disciples. Such questions from the disciples are characteristic of the *Gospel of Thomas* (see J. Jeremias, *Parables* 98), and this one was probably suggested by Jesus' rhetorical question in Mark 4:30. The "tilled earth" of the *Thomas* parable is a gnostic touch, symbolizing the soul that has been prepared to receive the truth; see L. Cerfaux, "Paraboles" 318-319, 324; J. D. Crossan, "Seed Parables" 258. Thomas' version of the OT citation at the end of the parable shows the least evidence of OT phraseology, consistent with the general tendency of *Gospel of Thomas* to decrease OT references. Thomas thereby distances his logion from the hope in Ezekiel and Daniel of a "this-worldly" fulfillment of God's blessings; see H. K. McArthur, "Parable of the Mustard Seed," *CBQ* 33 (1971) 203-204, 208. Thomas has replaced Mark's plural "branches" with a singular, perhaps under the influence of Mark 13:28, as Cerfaux suggests. Finally, as we will show below, Mark's phrase about the smallness of the seed is almost certainly his redaction, but Thomas has copied this element.

[10]C. H. Dodd, *Parables* 141-42; H. K. McArthur, "Parable" 200-202.

[11]On these differences, see H. K. McArthur, "Parable" 205; R. Laufen, *Doppelüberlieferung* 176-77.

CHART 10

Mark 4:30-32	Luke 13:18-19	Matt 13:31-32	Gos. Thom. 20
How shall we com- pare the kingdom of God or in what parable shall we put it? As	To what is com- parable the king- dom of God and to what shall I compare it? It is comparable	The kingdom of heaven is com- parable	It [the kingdom of heaven] is like
to a grain of mustard which when sown	to a grain of mustard which taking, a man cast into his garden	to a grain of mustard which taking, a man cast into his field, which is smaller than all seeds	a mustard seed
upon the earth being smaller than all seeds upon the earth and when sown			smaller than all seeds
			but when it falls on tilled earth
goes up and becomes greater than all shrubs	and it grew	yet when it grows it is bigger than the shrubs and becomes a tree	
and puts forth large branches so as to be able under its shade the birds of heaven	and became a tree		it produces a large branch and becomes shelter
to settle	and the birds of heaven settled in its branches	so as to come the birds of heaven and settle in its branches	for the birds of heaven

homogeneous as that of Q.[12] 2) Mark's v 31a ("as to a grain of mustard seed") is rougher than its Q counterpart. 3) In form, Mark's passage is a similitude, while that of Q is a parable proper.[13] Mark's finite verbs are in the present, while those of Q are in the aorist; Mark pictures a common event, whereas Q pictures a one-time occurrence: a man (lacking in Mark) took a grain of mustard seed and cast it into the ground, and it grew up and became a tree. 4) Mark has a specific reference to the smallness of the seed (v 31c). 5) In Mark the seed is sown in the ground, in Q in a garden. 6) Mark and Q use different verbs for growing (*anabainein/auxanein*), and in Mark the seed grows into a shrub, whereas in Q it grows into a tree. 7) Mark's OT citation is hypotactic, and it is closest to Ezek 17:23 (birds *under the shade* of the tree), though it also has elements from Ezek 31:6 and Dan 4:12, 21 ("birds of heaven," *kataskē-noun*); the citation in Q is paratactic, and it is closest to Dan 4:12, 21 Theodotion (the birds *settled* [*kateskēnōsen*] *in the branches* of the tree). 8) Mark's passage contains the word *dynasthai*, "to be able," which is lacking both in Q and in the OT passages.

Some of these differences point in the direction of Markan redaction. The departure of v 30b from v 30a (contrast Q's redundancy) is probably redactional; here as elsewhere in Mark the second part of a double question "brings the question to precision."[14] We have noted the emphasis accruing to the phrase "in what parable" by the separation of its parts; in chapter 3 above we ascribed a similar emphatic separation to Markan redaction. Such is also the case here. There would be no good reason for Q to leave out a reference to Jesus speaking in a parable, but there would be a good reason for Mark to introduce one: to drive home forcefully the point that Jesus taught about the kingdom *in parables* (cf. 4:1-2, 11-12, 33-34; also 3:23; 12:1; 13:28).[15] It looks as though Mark has introduced v 30b.

The word *thōmen* also supports the hypothesis that we have Markan redaction in v 30b; an unusual word to use for parables,[16] it corresponds to the repeated *tethē* in 4:21, which in context speaks of God's word in the

---

[12]See Mark's *homoiōsōmen . . . thōmen* as opposed to Q's *homoia . . . homoiōsō*.

[13]On the distinction between these two forms, see above, chapter 2, n. 90.

[14]F. Neirynck, Duality 55-56.

[15]R. Laufen, *Doppelüberlieferung* 177; A. Casalegno, "La parabola del granello di senape (*Mc.* 4, 30-32)," *RivB* 26 (1978) 145-46.

[16]E. Lohmeyer, *Evangelium* 88.

parables (see above, chapter 4).[17] According to our analysis, *thōmen* replaces *homoia estin,* a construction which takes a dative; we would suggest that Mark introduced *hōs* to go along with *thōmen,* but neglected to change the original dative to a nominative, thus ending up with *hōs kokkǭ sinapeōs.*[18] It is also possible that the first person plural verbs in v 30 are Mark's work, introduced by him to associate Jesus with the disciples who, in Mark's mind, will continue his teaching.[19]

In the parable itself (vv 31-32), it is hard to imagine why Mark would have eliminated the *anthrōpos,* had the parable as it came down to him contained this figure; by so doing he would have created disharmony with the Parable of the Sower (4:3-8) and the Parable of the Seed Growing Secretly (4:26-29), both of which have a human figure.[20] The only function of the *anthrōpos* in Q is to accommodate the Parable of the Mustard Seed to the Parable of the Leaven which follows it (Matt 13:33 par. Luke 13:20-21).[21] By introducing the man, Q has created the oddity that he sows a single seed; in Mark's version, on the other hand, the mention of the single seed is logical, since the kingdom of God is being compared to

---

[17] Thus the redundancy of Q is probably original, despite the general rule of chapter 4, n. 46; cf. R. Laufen, *Doppelüberlieferung* 177; A. Casalegno, "Parabola" 139-41.

[18] Cf. E. Lohmeyer (*Evangelium* 88), in whose reconstruction of two archaic forms of the parable *hōs* goes with *thōmen* and the dative with *homoiōsōmen.*

[19] See 6:30, and cf. 4:34, where the disciples are associated with Jesus vis-à-vis the parables.

Thus, according to our reconstruction, the pre-Markan version of 4:30 was substantially identical with the double question that introduces the Q version. The components of the Markan and pre-Markan versions can be diagrammed thus (KOG = kingdom of God):

Pre-Mark:	To what is comparable (*homoia estin*)	the KOG
Mark:	How shall we compare (*homoiōsōmen*)	the KOG

Pre-Mark:	and to what	shall I compare (*homoiōsō*) it
Mark:	or in what parable	shall we put (*thōmen*) it

[20] In these parables the man is present, although he is not the center of interest; thus Mark would not have eliminated the human figure in the Parable of the Mustard Seed because his main interest was elsewhere. See H.-J. Klauck, *Allegorie* 210; V. Fusco, *Parola* 379 and n. 64.

[21] See the parallel between *hon labōn anthrōpos ebalen* (Luke 13:19 par. Matt 13:31) and *hēn labousa gynē ekrypsen* (Luke 13:21 par. Matt 13:33); R. Laufen, *Doppelüberlieferung* 178-79.

the growth *of a seed*.[22] Thus Mark's *Gleichnis* form, which lacks the figure of the *anthrōpos*, seems to be original, Q's *Parabel* form secondary. Mark's version is probably also more archaic than Q's in that the seed is sown "on the earth" rather than in a garden; in ancient Palestine, as opposed to the larger Hellenistic world, the mustard was not a garden plant.[23]

On the other hand, we have already noted the repetitiveness and the grammatical roughness of vv 31c-32a; moreover, to the first hearers of the parable v 31c would have been superfluous, since the smallness of the mustard seed was proverbial.[24] The awkwardness of v 31c-32a is similar to that of another Markan insertion, 7:19;[25] also, when Mark makes an insertion he tends to repeat the final expression in his source, as he does here with the second *hotan sparē*.[26] It is unlikely that this section crept into the parable before Mark, since its style is Markan;[27] in addition, the highlighting of the seed's smallness fits in with the Markan emphasis on the mysteriousness and hiddenness of the kingdom of God (cf. 4:11-12, 21-22).[28] Vv 31c-32a are therefore probably Markan redaction.[29]

---

[22]R. Laufen, *Doppelüberlieferung* 178-79.

[23]Ibid., 180.

[24]Str-B 1.669; C.-H. Hunziger, "*sinapi*" 288.

[25]A. Ambrozic (*Hidden Kingdom* 125-26) points out that *katharizōn panta ta brōmata* in 7:19 is Mark's insertion and refers to a subject (Jesus) who is only subsequently implied in the verb *elegen*; cf. in 4:31 the neuter participle *on*, which is only subsequently explained by *spermatōn*.

[26]J. D. Crossan ("Seed Parables" 256-57), citing 2:9, 11; 10:47, 48.

[27]*Contra* R. Laufen, *Doppelüberlieferung* 196.

[28]H.-W. Kuhn and J. D. Crossan claim that, if v 31c is redactional, so is the phrase "and becomes greater than all the shrubs" in v 32b, since it contrasts with v 31c; H.-J. Klauck rightly replies that the conclusion does not necessarily follow (*Allegorie* 212). Mark could have created v 31c to conform to v 32b, and v 32b does not destroy the stylistic smoothness of the parable as v 31c does.

Neither is A. Ambrozic (*Hidden Kingdom* 126-27) convincing in his assertion that *anabainei* in v 32b is redactional; *contra* Ambrozic, *anabainein* is not exclusively Markan vocabulary (it is redactional in 4:8 but not in 4:7; see above, chapter 2). Q's *auxanein* is probably a secondary amelioration of the more Semitic *anabainein*; cf. V. Taylor, *Mark* 253; J. D. Crossan, "Seed Parables" 257; R. Laufen, *Doppelüberlieferung* 179-80. Similarly unconvincing is Ambrozic's assertion that *megalous* in v 32c is redactional.

[29]Unnecessary, then, is M. Black's theory (*Aramaic Approach* 123) of a mistranslation from Aramaic; see H.-J. Klauck, *Allegorie* 100 n. 8.

Of the OT citations at the conclusion of the parable, Mark's version seems to be primitive in its greater indefiniteness;[30] Q, on the other hand, appears archaic in its parataxis,[31] which also characterizes the OT texts to which allusion is made. Markan redaction may be present in the word *dynasthai* in v 32d,[32] which appears neither in Q nor in the OT passages, and is used frequently in Mark to emphasize divine capacity and human incapacity.[33]

Thus, as with the Markan/Q overlaps investigated in chapter 4, there seems to be a link between the Markan and Q traditions of the Parable of the Mustard Seed, but there is no literary relationship.[34] Mark's hand can probably be seen in v 30 (the phrase "in what parable," the verb *theinai*, perhaps the first plurals) and in the entirety of vv 31c-32a ("being smaller than all the seeds upon the earth, and when it is sown"), and perhaps also in the word "to be able" in v 32d.[35]

EXEGESIS

The Introduction (4:30)

Our parable is introduced by the double question in v 30. Rabbinic parables also commonly begin with questions,[36] but more is involved than Mark's use of a stereotyped form; for Mark the double question probably emphasizes the difficulty of speaking about the kingdom of God,[37] which is mysterious (cf. 4:11) and not readily apparent (cf. 4:3-8, 14-20).

---

[30]A. Ambrozic, *Hidden Kingdom* 128-30.

[31]R. Laufen, *Doppelüberlieferung* 180-81.

[32]Ibid., 181 and n. 46. Already, A. Jülicher (*Gleichnisreden* 2.576) labeled this word a probable Markan addition.

[33]A. Casalegno, "Parabola" 152-53.

[34]A major weakness in the work of J. A. Lambrecht ("Redaction and Theology" 285-97) is the assumption of such a literary link, so that any departure of Mark from Q is viewed as Markan redaction.

[35]In the following rendering of vv 31-32, the words that we have identified as probable Markan redaction are underlined; the unstressed words represent the reconstructed pre-Markan form: "*As* to a grain of mustard, which, when it is sown upon the earth, *being smaller than all the seeds upon the earth, and when it is sown*, it grows up and becomes greater than all the shrubs, and puts forth large branches, so that under its shade the birds of the air *are able to* settle."

[36]See H. K. McArthur, "Parable" 202.

[37]E. Schweizer, *Good News* 103.

In spite of this difficulty, the kingdom can be expressed in speech if it is expressed *in a parable,* as the redactional v 30b emphasizes; cf. v 11, where the mystery of the kingdom has been given *in parables.* Why are parables so well-adapted to communicate the kingdom's mystery? Mark hints at his answer in v 31a. The kingdom is like a grain of mustard seed;[38] but we already know from v 14 that the seed is the word in the parables, so that *the kingdom is like the parabolic word.* The parables are fitted to communicate the kingdom precisely because they share in the kingdom's nature; hiding a tremendous divine potency beneath an insignificant, everyday appearance, they resemble the kingdom which, as the Parable of the Sower illustrates, is hidden *sub specie contraria.*

We have suggested above that the first person plural verbs in v 30 may include the disciples. This suggestion gains strength from comparison with 9:39-40, where Jesus associates himself with the disciples by means of first person plurals. In 9:39 he contrasts those who perform miracles "in *my* name" with those who "blaspheme *me*"; but in 9:40 the contrast is between those who are "for *us*" and those who are "against *us*."[39] In 4:30, then, the distance between Jesus and the disciples that was implied by a previous double question, 4:13, seems to have been overcome. The explanation of the Parable of the Sower, which provides the disciples with the key to all parables in a description of post-Easter realities (see above, end of chapter 2), has intervened; thus the distance between the double question of v 13 and that of v 30 is the distance between the time of Jesus and that of the church.[40] The first person plurals, then, may be an indication of the way in which, after the resurrection, the disciples take up Jesus'

---

[38]J. Jeremias (*Parables* 101) points out that the meaning of the rabbinic *lĕ* is not "it is like" but "it is the case with . . . as with." Because of Mark's tendency to allegorize, however, and because he may not have known the meaning of *lĕ*, it is likely that he would have taken the introductory formula more literally.

[39]Cf. Jesus' use of first person plural verbs in 1:38; 4:35; 10:33; and see also 9:17-18, where the father of the epileptic boy says alternately that he brought his son "*to you*" (singular) and that he asked "*your disciples*" to exorcise the demon. In 9:29 Jesus implies that the disciples can enter into effective association with him through prayer.

[40]The implications of the three double questions in Mark 4 can be related. V 13 implies that parabolic speech is intrinsically difficult to understand. V 21 implies that, with the crucifixion and resurrection of Jesus, the meaning of the parabolic word has been revealed. V 30 implies that therefore the parabolic word can be comprehended by those who live in the sphere of Jesus' crucifixion and resurrection.

proclamation of the parabolic word,[41] which communicates the kingdom because it is *like* the kingdom in weakness and power.

The Parable Itself (4:31a-32)

A parable of contrast. Like the Parable of the Seed Growing Secretly, which immediately precedes it, the Parable of the Mustard Seed begins with a seed sown in the ground, ends with a grown plant, and stresses the inevitability with which the former becomes the latter.

The differences, however, are also striking. Our parable lacks the previous parable's concentration on the intermediate stages of linear growth; in the Parable of the Mustard Seed all the attention is on the contrast between the smallness of the seed and the size of the grown plant.[42] The former is emphasized both by the fact that the tininess of the mustard seed was proverbial and by Mark's addition of v 31c; the latter is underlined by the words "grows up," "greater," "large," and "all" in v 32.[43]

The mustard is not absolutely the smallest seed, nor is the final plant huge when compared to a real tree,[44] but it *is* huge when compared to the

---

[41]There is already an association of Jesus with the disciples who are chosen "to be with him" (3:14) during his ministry, but this association is imperfect until the resurrection, as the disciples' subsequent misunderstanding and abandonment of Jesus show. See above, chapter 3. Similarly, the account of the disciples' missionary work (which includes teaching) in 6:7-13, 30 is proleptic of post-Easter activity; see E. Schweizer, *Good News* 127-29; E. Laufen, *Doppelüberlieferung* 197-200.

[42]See A. Ambrozic, *Hidden Kingdom* 131; W. Lane, *Mark* 171; *contra* O. Kuss ("Zur Senfkornparabel," *Auslegung und Verkündigung* [Regensburg: Pustet, 1963; orig. 1951] 40-46; idem., "Zum Sinngehalt des Doppelgleichnis vom Senfkorn und Sauerteig," *Auslegung* 85-97 [orig. 1959]) and H.-J. Klauck (*Allegorie* 217), who assert that our parable implies a period of development. Kuss's argument is based more on his reading of passages from *1 Clement* than on the Markan text itself.

[43]R. Pesch, *Markusevangelium* 1.260. Neither the verb "grows up" (*anabainei*) nor "becomes" (*ginetai*) emphasizes the *process* of growth; both only provide a transition to the description of the largeness of the grown plant, which is the main focus of interest in v 32b. A similar comment applies to v 32c in its relation to v 32d (V. Fusco, *Parola* 373; contra J. D. Crossan, "Seed Parables" 257).

[44]J. C. Trever ("Mustard" 476-77) points out that the orchid seed is smaller than the mustard, and that the mustard does not grow to tree size

small seed;[45] thus it is ideally suited to a parable of contrast. This observation disposes of the interpretation advanced by R. W. Funk and followed
by B. B. Scott, which sees the main point of our parable in the comparison
of the kingdom of God, not to a *tree* as in the OT texts cited in 4:32, but
to a plant of modest size; thus Israel's expectations of eschatological
grandeur are deliberately frustrated.[46] On the contrary, our parable
emphasizes the plant's *largeness*, not its smallness;[47] Funk and Scott have
substituted their own contrast (small plant/large tree) for the one the
parable makes (small seed/large plant).

That Mark's main point is the contrast between the small beginning and
the huge ending is confirmed by the repetition of the clause, "when it is
sown" (vv 31b, 32a). Viewed in terms of tradition history, this repetition
results from Mark's insertion of vv 31c-32a, but viewed in terms of the
parable's final shape, it underlines the contrast. Although *when the seed is
sown* it is the smallest of all seeds, yet *when it is sown*, i.e. from the
moment of its sowing, it begins its transformation[48] into the large
plant.[49]

---

because it is an annual plant. The birds are attracted by the shade and the
seed of the plant; see J. Jeremias, *Parables* 148 n. 73, citing G. Dalman
and K.-E. Wilken.

[45]V. Fusco, *Parola* 366. The mature shrub is often eight to twelve feet
tall; V. Taylor, *Mark* 270.

[46]R. W. Funk, "The Looking-glass Tree is for the Birds; Ezekiel 17:22-
24; Mark 4:30-32," *Int* 27 (1973) 3-9; B. B. Scott, *Symbol-Maker* 71-73.

[47]Cf. Q, where the grown plant is in fact called a tree (*dendron*).

[48]Although we speak here of "transformation," we must emphasize
again that in vv 30-32, in contrast to vv 26-29, the process of the seed's
development is not a central concern, but only the beginning and ending
points. This difference can be illustrated by imagining a short film made
of each parable. "The Seed Growing Secretly" would show through time-
lapse photography the gradual unfolding of the various stages in the
plant's growth. "The Mustard Seed" would begin with a lengthy shot
picturing the mustard seed alongside of other, larger seeds. There would
then follow a brief sequence of tremendously fast time-lapse shots of the
growth of the seed, and the film would conclude with a lengthy shot of the
grown mustard plant dwarfing other shrubs.

[49]*Contra* C. E. Carlston (*Parables* 158), who says that *hotan sparē*
makes sense in v 32 but not in v 31, "since the size of the seed is the same
both before and after sowing."

Comparison with 1QH 8:4-14 (cf. 6:14b-17) supports this argument.[50] In the QL passage, the elect community is compared to a plant whose boughs are food for beasts and a trampling-place for passersby and birds;[51] a plant which, though now hidden and not esteemed, will one day be manifested in glory. As F. Mussner notes, the passage uses the same OT image that is utilized in our passage (tree frequented by birds and beasts)[52] to emphasize the contrast between present hiddenness and future manifestation, and it thus increases our confidence in the hypothesis of a similar emphasis in the Parable of the Mustard Seed.[53]

The initial and final stages in the parable. What are the stages of hiddenness and manifestation that we have just mentioned? We have posed a similar question concerning vv 21-25 and vv 26-29, and have concluded that the stage of hiddenness is both the time of Jesus and that of the church, while the stage of manifestation is both the time of the church and the parousia. Should the stages in the Parable of the Mustard Seed be interpreted in a similar "two-level" manner?

Evidence that they should be so interpreted comes from consideration of the initial stage, the sowing of the seed, in v 31. We can apply to our parable the equation between seed and word that is made in v 14, since vv 14-20 unlock "all the parables" in Mark's mind (cf. v 13). The sowing of the seed, therefore, is the proclamation of the word,[54] and our analysis of the first person plurals in v 30 has suggested that this is the word both of Jesus himself and of the early church which continues his proclamation.

This "two-level" interpretation is supported by analysis of the final stage pictured in the parable, which in our view corresponds to the time

---

[50]F. Mussner, "1Q Hodajoth und das Gleichnis vom Senfkorn," *BZ* 4 (1960) 128-30.

[51]Mussner follows H. Bardtke's translation of 1QH 8:9, "And its branches serve all the birds"; similarly A. Dupont-Sommer, *Essene Writings* 226. It is more likely, however, that the translation for the elliptical Hebrew (*wdlytw lkl 'wf knf*) should parallel that of 1QH 8:8; so E. Lohse (*Texte* 143) and G. Vermes (*Dead Sea Scrolls* 176).

[52]If H. Bardtke's translation is adopted (see previous note), the birds and beasts are viewed in a hostile light, contrary to the OT passages; but there is no doubt that those passages are in the background.

[53]1QH 8:4-14 is also related to Mark 4 by the word "mystery" (*rz*) in 8:6, 11 (cf. Mark 4:11) and by the theme of "seeing without recognizing" in 8:13-14 (cf. Mark 4:12).

[54]J. Dupont, "Paraboles" 908.

of the church and to the parousia. Considering first the latter, we recall
that the stage of the fully-developed plant in the Parable of the Seed
Growing Secretly (4:26-29) corresponded to the eschaton (see above,
chapter 5). Mark's readers would be inclined to relate the ending of our
parable to that of the parable that precedes it, and elsewhere in his
Gospel the parousia is identified as the point at which the Son of Man will
be manifested publicly (13:26; 14:62); until then the kingdom will exist in
a state of mysterious hiddenness. Thus Mark's readers would have some
good reasons for linking the end of our parable, the stage of manifestation, with the parousia.

They would also, however, have some excellent reasons for linking the
end of the parable with the stage in the manifestation of the kingdom
inaugurated by Jesus' death and resurrection. In Mark's Gospel, in spite of
the hiddenness of the post-Easter period, it is also true that Easter inaugurates an age of revelation, as we have shown in chapter 4. Furthermore,
if, as we have maintained, the sowing of the seed is the proclamation of
the word, then the end result of the sowing is plausibly related to the end
result of the proclamation, the entry into the church of multitudes
(mostly Gentiles) who have "heard the word and accepted it" (4:8).[55] That
entry is prefigured in the Gospel by scenes in which huge crowds gather to
Jesus, attracted by the awesome power of his word and healings (1:28, 32-
34, 45; 2:2; 3:7-12; 6:34, 53-56; 8:1),[56] and these scenes are linked to our
parable by the correspondence between the flocking of the birds to the
mustard plant and the gathering of the crowd to Jesus.[57]

This interpretation is confirmed by the observation that Mark 4:32
alludes to OT texts in which a tree shading birds and beasts symbolizes a
great king or kingdom that protects subject peoples.[58] These passages

---

[55]Ibid.

[56]See L. E. Keck ("Mark 3:7-12" 353), who demonstrates that in 3:7-12
Mark has expanded the summary he inherited to include the nations immediately around Galilee.

[57]Thus we disagree with A. Ambrozic (Hidden Kingdom 132-34), who
rejects a link between the end of our parable and the Gentile mission on
the ground that "the word of Jesus, now proclaimed by the community, is
still seemingly powerless; its results outwardly are insignificant."
Although the partial frustration of the word is an aspect of the mystery of
the kingdom (see above, chapter 2), it is incorrect to say that for Mark
the word is powerless.

[58]This link is specified in Ezek 31:6 and in Dan 4:21 LXX; see H.-J.
Klauck, Allegorie 215-216.

were apparently the basis for the equation of birds with Gentiles in some later Jewish texts (*1 Enoch* 90:30; *Midr. Psalms* 104:13).[59] Furthermore, the verb found in Mark 4:32, *kataskēnoun* ("to dwell or settle"), is used in Zech 2:11 and in a variant text of *Joseph and Aseneth* 15:6 to speak of the eschatological gathering of Gentiles to the God of Israel.[60] Thus it is probable that Mark's readers would have thought of the multitudes of Gentiles streaming into the kingdom of God in their own time when they heard of the birds settling under the shade of the plant; it is even possible that some of the them would have been reminded by Mark 4:32d of the Jewish conceit that converts were those who had come to dwell "under the wings of the Shekinah."[61]

These conclusions are supported by several Markan passages. In both of

---

[59]T. W. Manson, *Teaching* 133 n. 1. In *1 Enoch* 90:30 the "birds of heaven" are probably repentant Gentiles who have not participated in the oppression of Israel; cf. 90:33, 37. (V. Fusco's retort [*Parola* 370-71] that in *1 Enoch* the birds assemble at *the Temple* does nothing to refute Manson's point.) *Midr. Psalms* 104:13 says specifically that the birds of Psalm 104:13 are "the nations of the world." Fusco points out that in the midrash the birds are *hostile* to Israel, but this observation actually strengthens Manson's point; the equation between birds and Gentiles seems to have been so firmly fixed that an anti-Gentile polemicist could twist it to serve his' purpose. Perhaps the hostile birds of 1QH 8:9 (see above, n. 52) are also Gentiles; and cf. *Num. Rab.* 13:14, where a reference to a bird recalls Isa 10:14: "And my hand found as a nest the riches of the *peoples*" (cited by Manson, *Teaching* 133 n. 1).

[60]J. Jeremias (*Parables* 147) goes too far when, on the basis of *Joseph and Aseneth* 15:6, he speaks of *kataskēnoun* as "an eschatological technical term for the incorporation of Gentiles into the people of God"; but V. Fusco's observation (*Parola* 370-71) that *kataskēnoun* is not the original reading of *Joseph and Aseneth* 15:6 does not make the latter irrelevant for comparison with Mark 4:30-32, since the variant reading must still be explained (as noted by H.-J. Klauck, *Allegorie* 215-216).

[61]On Mark's concern for Gentiles, see L. E. Keck ("Mark 3:7-12" 353), who cites 3:7-12; 7:24-30; 11:17-18; 12:9; 13:10; and 15:38. On the metaphor of the Shekinah's wings, see G. F. Moore, *Judaism* 1.330; cf. M. Philonenko, *Joseph et Aseneth. Introduction, texte critique, traduction et notes* (SPB 13; Leiden: Brill, 1968) 182. Although most of Mark's readers were probably Gentiles (see 7:3-4, where Mark explains Pharasaic cleansing rules to them), it is not inconceivable that some of them would have heard about the wings of the Shekinah, since the metaphor was used in Jewish proselytizing and occurs in the propaganda tract *Joseph and Aseneth*.

the stories of miraculous feeding (6:35-44; 8:1-10), Jesus, through his eschatological power, multiplies the little that the disciples have, and thus sustains the fainting multitude; and both of the multiplications are preceded by Jesus' invocation of a word of blessing. In addition, Mark probably means the second story to be understood as a feeding of Gentiles.[62] Since the feeding stories are linked to our parable by the themes of multiplication, sustainment,[63] the word, and (in the second story) the Gentiles, and since they would suggest to the Markan community their own experience of being sustained by the word of Jesus, they support a "present" interpretation of Mark 4:32.

This interpretation is further supported by the observation that, when we view Mark's Gospel as a whole, the miraculous fertility of the mustard seed contrasts sharply with the sterility of the barren fig tree of 11:12-14. The latter is a symbol for Israel,[64] the people from whom the vineyard, another symbolic planting, has been taken to be bestowed upon the Gentiles (12:9; cf. the birds in 4:32). If, as seems likely, Mark intends the barren fig tree and the blossoming mustard plant to be antitypes, and if both are to be interpreted in light of 12:9, then the fig tree has been replaced by the mustard plant, which thus is a present reality.

12:10-11, which concludes the Parable of the Vineyard, reiterates many of the themes of our parable: that which is despised and insignificant becomes the cornerstone for the great structure, because God is at work in its construction, and he always works in a way that is amazing to human eyes. The new, eschatological temple, which has Jesus for its cornerstone, is a present reality,[65] and thus we have additional evidence that the end of the Parable of the Mustard Seed speaks of something Mark believes is already in existence.

For Mark's hearers, then, the final state of the plant would suggest not only the parousia but also the period of the church.[66] It is not just that the response to the Gentile mission is the beginning of the complete manifestation of the kingdom that will occur at the parousia;[67] that point

---

[62]V. Taylor, Mark 357; R. Pesch, Markusevangelium 1.402-405; J. Gnilka, Evangelium 1.304.

[63]Some of Mark's readers might be familiar with the fact that the mustard plant not only shades the birds but also feeds them with its tasty seeds; see above, n. 44.

[64]E. Schweizer, Good News 230.

[65]Cf. J. Gnilka, Evangelium 2.148.

[66]Cf. E. Schweizer, Good News 105.

[67]Contra R. Laufen, Doppelüberlieferung 186-89.

has been made in the previous parable; Mark is saying something more dialectical here. The period of the church is *already* the time of fulfillment; yet the parousia can with equal justice be identified as the point at which God's promises will be fulfilled.

The antithetical kingdom of God. The implied contrast between the thriving mustard plant and the barren fig tree reminds us of J. Wellhausen's assertion that the kingdom of God is always conceived antithetically to another kingdom (see above, chapter 2, n. 127). Not only here, but throughout the Gospel, a healthy plant, symbolizing the life-giving power of God's new age (4:8, 20, 26-32; 13:28-29), is juxtaposed to an unfruitful plant whose deadness evokes the sterility of the old aeon (4:4-7, 15-19; 11:12-14, 20).

The same antithesis between two kingdoms is present in the three OT passages upon which Mark 4:32 draws. God's planting of the cedar that represents the restored kingdom of David (Ezek 17:22-24) is a counter to the action of the eagle, the king of Babylon, in taking away the top of the cedar (17:3-6).[68] In the other two passages, the kingly might of Yahweh is portrayed destroying the pretensions of human kings, whether of Pharaoh (Ezek 31) or of Nebuchadnezzar (Dan 4). These great, arrogant "trees" *cannot* in the end provide shelter for the birds and beasts; the true king, Yahweh, cuts them down in judgment for usurping his royal prerogative.[69]

Antithesis is also implied in Mark 4:32 by the (possibly redactional) word *dynasthai*, "to be able to"; in Mark's Gospel this word refers to the ability of God to do what human beings are incapable of doing.[70] "With human beings it is impossible, but not with God; for with God all things are possible" (10:26-27); this rule is illustrated with amazing consistency by the Gospel's usages of *dynasthai*. No one can bind the Gerasene demoniac until Jesus appears on the scene (5:3), nor can anyone feed the multitudes in the wilderness until Jesus multiplies the loaves (8:4). God, however, does what is impossible for human power: bleaching the clothes of the transfigured Jesus whiter than any human fuller can (9:3); enabling Jesus to cleanse a leper (1:40) and forgive sins (2:7); making all things possible for those who believe (9:22-23, 28-29), and, most importantly, enabling Jesus to cast out Satan, bind him, and plunder his kingdom (3:23-27). If, then, the birds are *able* to dwell under the shade of the mustard

---

[68] W. Zimmerli, *Ezekiel* (Philadelphia: Fortress, 1979) 1.367.

[69] V. Fusco, *Parola* 368-69.

[70] A. Casalegno, "Parabola" 153.

plant, not only has the human incapacity to enter the kingdom been over-come (cf. 10:25-27), but the kingdom of Satan has been defeated. Mark does not paint the kingdom of God in a monochrome; God's dominion is only truly seen when it stands out against the dark background of an opposing realm.

The Kerygma of Mark 4:30-32 for the Markan Community

As heard by the Markan community, the Parable of the Mustard Seed contrasts the apparent insignificance of the word when it is proclaimed with its magnificent results. The word is both that of Jesus and that of the disciples who continue Jesus' proclamation in the post-Easter period; and the results are both present in the influx of the nations into the church, and still to come in the complete manifestation of God's kingship at the eschaton.

Thus, in thinking about the parable, Mark's readers would be pulled in two directions: toward identifying their situation with the magnificent, full-grown plant, and toward identifying it with the small, hidden stage of the seed. Different members of the community would probably hear our passage in different ways. Those predisposed to view their situation as one of littleness would be reminded by the parable that God's kingdom is pushing toward a magnificent disclosure of itself, and that the kingdom's grandeur is even now a reality for those with eyes to see. On the other hand, those predisposed to view their situation as a grand one would be reminded by the parable that they presently exist in weakness, in apparent insignificance, subject to temptation and persecution, in short under the sign of the cross, and that such existence will characterize the Christian life until the parousia.

As one would expect in a persecuted church, the temptation to despair seems to be a bigger problem for the Markan community than the tempta-tion to self-glorification.[71] The question, "Is there hope for the world?", has taken on a tormenting urgency for many of Mark's hearers. The par-able concedes to them what they know to be true, the misery in their present situation, but it also points them toward the magnificent ending that is already making itself felt in the present.[72] There *is* hope for the world, our parable says, but one can see it only by looking in the unlikeli-

---

[71]See however 8:31-33; 9:33-34; 10:35-37.
[72]Cf. H.-W. Kuhn, *Sammlungen* 103.

est places, where God seems at first to be most notably absent, where God's people are subjected to the most terrible pressures, but where the mysterious power of his kingdom is secretly at work.

Much of Mark's Gospel contains a stern emphasis on the cost of discipleship, the necessity that Jesus' followers take up their crosses and retrace his steps, that they lose their lives for his sake. Without denying this emphasis in the least, the end of our parable provides a welcome counterpoint to it. The picture of the birds settling under the protective shade of the mustard plant implies that discipleship also means finding refuge, being sustained by God; the same theme is struck in Matthew by Jesus' offer, "Come to me, . . . and I will give you rest" (Matt 11:28-29). The outdoor shelter of the mustard plant, however, is only found by those who forsake the delusive, ironbound security of the Strong Man's house (3:27), flying to Jesus with the abandon of birds of the air.

In our parable the huge plant is already contained in the tiny germ;[73] there is thus continuity between the Markan present and "the kingdom come in power" (9:1). The large shrub *is* the mustard seed; yet it is the mustard seed *transformed*. "Continuity, certainly, but given from above, wrapped in the mystery of God, and not excluding a passage through discontinuity and rupture."[74] The rupture is part of the Markan community's daily experience; the continuity is known by it in faith.

The parable implies that the continuity between the initial intrusion of the kingdom of God into the world and its full explosion at the parousia is provided by Jesus' word, the seed that becomes the large plant. That word "will never pass away" (cf. 13:31) because, our parable suggests, it is the very substance out of which the new age is made. As "in the beginning," so now at the end of the ages a cosmos is being called into existence through God's all-powerful word.

In writing his Gospel Mark is not intent merely on producing a literary work that *describes* Jesus' word; rather, his Gospel also *continues* Jesus' own gospel preaching (1:1, 14).[75] Through Mark as through other Christian evangelists, then, Jesus continues to sow the *logos* which destroys and builds, overthrows and plants (Jer 1:10); the word which brings the old

---

[73]J. Dupont, "Paraboles" 907; N. A. Dahl, "Parables" 155-56.

[74]V. Fusco, *Parola* 375-76. Cf. 1 Cor 15:36-38, where the seed image expresses both continuity and discontinuity.

[75]See J. Gnilka (*Evangelium* 1.43), who emphasizes both the objective and the subjective nature of the genitive *Iēsou Christou* in 1:1, and who adds that the phrase "for my sake and the gospel's" in 8:35; 10:29 implies the presence of Jesus in the gospel.

cosmos to an end and creates a new one. Thus if Mark were asked about the purpose of chapter 4 and of his Gospel as a whole, his reply would probably not be a humble one. He writes about Jesus' word in such a way as to *embody* it, and to produce—by God's graceful power—an instrument for the creation of a new world.

7

Conclusions

The Structure of Mark 4:1-34 as a Whole

While we have looked at the structure of each individual pericope, and while we have consistently commented on the ways in which the pericopes interrelate, we have not yet looked at the global structure of Mark 4:1-34. That structure can be analyzed in a number of different ways, depending upon whether the interpreter concentrates on the forms of the individual pericopes, their themes, or whether insiders or outsiders are being discussed. For example, we have already observed the double chiasm in the alternation between attention to insiders and attention to outsiders (above, chapter 4, discussion of the two groups in 4:24-25).

J. Dupont[1] provides a helpful outline of the chapter that is based on the forms of the individual pericopes:

> A Narrative introduction (vv 1-2)
> > B Seed parable (vv 3-9)
> > > C General statement (vv 10-12)
> > > > D Explanation of parable (vv 13-20)
> > > C' General statements (vv 21-25)
> > B' Seed parables (vv 26-32)
> A' Narrative conclusion (vv 33-34)

This analysis has the advantage of placing at the center of the chiasm the interpretation of the Parable of the Sower (D), which in Mark's eyes provides the key to all parables (cf. v 13); thus thematic and literary

---

[1] J. Dupont, ""Transmission" 206 n. 12, citing his own 1974 course, from which V. Fusco (*Parola* 101-104) picked it up.

considerations reinforce each other. Sections ACC'A' of Dupont's outline are those in which we have seen Mark's hand to be most evident; Mark, therefore, has balanced the introduction with the conclusion, and his concealment theory in vv 10-12 with the statements about revelation in vv 21-25. Furthermore, Dupont's outline is compatible with a division of the chapter by the audience addressed; in sections ABB'A' (vv 1-9, 26-32) Jesus teaches everyone, whereas in sections CDC' (vv 10-25) he teaches only the disciples (see above, chapter 4).[2]

We have already observed, however, another division within Mark's parable chapter: vv 3-20 focus upon the hiddenness of the kingdom, but vv 21-32 present a kingdom that is moving from hiddenness to manifestation. The similarity in form between B and B' and between C and C' ties together these two themes of hiddenness and the movement toward revelation. Mark's readers, then, as they read and reread the chapter, would have linked on the one hand the Parable of the Sower and its interpretation, which portray the kingdom's hiddenness, with, on the other hand, the two seed parables in vv 26-32, which stress the ineluctable movement from hiddenness to manifestation. Similarly, the theme of hiddenness in vv 10-12 and that of the movement toward manifestation in vv 21-25 are linked together by the related imagery and vocabulary[3] of the two sections. We may add that the introduction (vv 1-2), which emphasizes Jesus' open preaching to all, forms an inclusion with the conclusion (vv 33-34), which underlines the division between kinds of hearers.

Thus Mark prevents his readers from thinking that hiddenness and division are the final word about the kingdom, but he also prevents his readers from glorying in revelation to such an extent that they forget the hard realities of their present situation, in which division between believers and unbelievers and the hiddenness of the kingdom are basic facts of life. The readers are drawn from contemplation of the kingdom's hiddenness to contemplation of its manifestation, and vice versa.

We are thus reminded that for Mark's readers the primary experience of the chapter will have been a sequential reading of it. In order, therefore, to summarize the results of our study, we give an outline of the way

---

[2]Dupont's analysis is superior to those of J. Lambrecht ("Redaction" 303; *Astonished* 86-87) and B. Standaert (*Évangile* 209), both of whom divide vv 3-32 into three sections, vv 3-20, vv 21-25, and vv 26-32. Such a division obscures the strong similarity between vv 10-12 and vv 21-25.
[3]Giving, division between two groups, hiding, seeing, hearing, *hina*.

Mark seems to have meant his first hearers to interpret the chapter as they moved through it section by section.

A Sequential Reading of Mark 4:1-34

"And again he began to teach them beside the sea, and there gathers to him a very large crowd, so that, getting into a boat, he sits in the sea; and the whole crowd was by the sea on the land. And he was teaching them many things in parables, and he said to them in his teaching: . . ."

Hearing this introductory passage (vv 1-2), the members of Mark's audience probably would read themselves into the description of the great crowd massed on the shore of the sea; they themselves had once been part of the crowd that, although outside the circle of Jesus' disciples, had begun to feel the pull of Jesus' power. Their impression of that power would be heightened by Jesus' need to get into the boat that has previously been readied; his charisma is so great that he attracts his biggest crowd yet, and he must get into the boat lest the crowd crush him (cf. 3:9). The readers' suspense about what Jesus is about to say would be increased by Mark's alternation between descriptions of Jesus and descriptions of the crowd that faces him on the shore. By his repetition of phrases having to do with teaching, Mark indicates that Jesus is about to speak words that will illuminate the present situation of the Markan community, words that will sustain it in the trials it is undergoing; but because Mark's audience has just heard 3:23-30, they will also be aware that Jesus' parabolic teaching issues in judgment for those who reject it.

Mark next has Jesus relate the Parable of the Sower (vv 3-9): "'Listen! Behold, a sower went out to sow. And it came to pass in the sowing that one part fell on the path, and the birds came and devoured it. And another fell on the rocky ground where it did not have much soil, and immediately it sprang up on account of not having depth of soil; and when the sun came up it was scorched, and on account of not having root it withered. And another fell among the thorns, and the thorns came up and choked it, and it did not yield fruit. And others fell into the good soil, and were yielding fruit, coming up and growing, and were bearing thirtyfold and sixtyfold and a hundredfold.' And he said, "He who has ears to hear, let him hear!'"

Mark has Jesus introduce the parable with the word "Listen!", thus underlining the seriousness of what he is about to teach. He provides clues that would lead his readers to link the sower with Jesus himself; yet the center of focus in Mark's narration of the parable is not the sower but the varying fate of the seed. This variation suggests that, in spite of the world's unredeemed appearance and its resistance to God (cf. the bad soils), God's definitive action has occurred; but this action is visible only to the eye of faith (cf. the good soil). Such a message would be of extreme importance for Mark's first hearers, since it acknowledges the violent opposition they themselves are experiencing, yet affirms the reality of redemption. The concluding exhortation to hear, however (v 9), suggests that not all people are equipped with the organ to receive this good news.

The "parable theory" passage (vv 10-12) makes this division in audience explicit: "And when he was alone, those around him with the Twelve asked him the parables. And he said to them, 'To you the mystery of the kingdom of God has been given, but to those outside all things happen in parables in order that looking they may look, but not see; and that hearing they may hear, but not understand; lest they turn and it be forgiven them.'"

Jesus now withdraws with his disciples; Mark's readers follow Jesus to a secluded place, and thus become part of the group that is "around him with the Twelve." They hear as addressed to *themselves*, therefore, the thrilling announcement, "To you has been given the mystery of the kingdom of God"; and Mark implies that the mystery has been given to them in the Parable of the Sower. The frustration pictured in that parable, then, does not represent a thwarting of the divine plan; on the contrary, God's kingdom *must* manifest itself in the world as a mixture of death and life. The opposition that the Markan community is experiencing is thus actually a sign of the kingdom's advent, and its sufferings are a way in which it participates in the kingdom's mystery.

Those sufferings arise out of the persecution the community experiences at the hands of "those outside," who respond to Jesus' parabolic word in a way that reflects their inner division, as is described in vv 11b-12. Because of contextual clues in chapter 3, Mark's readers would be inclined to link the outsiders with the members of Jesus' immediate family, at least temporarily, and, more importantly, with the scribes and Pharisees who are his principal opponents throughout the Gospel. The Christian use of the term *hoi exō* to apply to non-Christians, however, would also lead them to relate the outsiders to those in their own day who stand outside the circle of faith, especially those whose alienation from the gospel is so complete that they oppose it by violence. Mark implies to his readers that by God's will (*hina*) these opponents live in a half-world of distorted perception, where they see just enough of the truth to cause them to hate it. By hating the truth, in turn, they cement their attachment to the sphere opposed to God, a sphere in which repentance and forgiveness cannot occur.

Not only the outsiders, however, but also the disciples demonstrate incomplete perception, as Mark implies at the beginning of the next section (v 13), the interpretation of the Parable of the Sower (vv 13-20). "And he says to them, 'Do you not know this parable? How then will you know all the parables?'" Yet Mark depicts crucial differences between the incomprehension of the disciples and that of the outsiders. The disciples, unlike the outsiders, consider the parable important enough to ask Jesus about it; and they, unlike the outsiders, receive the interpretation.

Mark's readers would recognize in that interpretation a feature of the time in which they themselves are living, namely the mixed results of the apostolic preaching; that preaching is evoking faith among some of its hearers while it incites others to hatred. "'The sower sows the word. And these are those on the path where the word is sown; when they hear, immediately Satan comes and takes away the word sown in them. And these are those sown on the rocky ground, who, when they hear the word, immediately receive it with joy, but do not have root in themselves but are temporary; then when tribulation or persecution on account of the word arises, immediately they are offended. And others are those sown among thorns; these are those who have heard the word, and the cares of this age, and the deceitfulness of wealth, and the desire for other things entering in, choke the word, and it becomes unfruitful. And these others are those sown on good soil—who hear the word and accept it and bear fruit, thirtyfold and sixtyfold and a hundredfold.'" By means of this description, the readers of Mark's Gospel would be led to see in their own time a continuation of the mystery of the kingdom that existed in Jesus' ministry; through their preaching Jesus is continuing to sow the word, and that sowing is meeting with the same varied fate that it met during his lifetime.

Because in the logic of the parable a soil cannot change its God-given nature, Mark's readers would gather from the parable and its interpreta-tion that the partial frustration of their preaching is in accordance with the mystery of God's will. They would also, however, notice that in the interpretation other agents, from Satan to "the cares of this age," are the more immediate causes of the word's ineffectiveness among the outsiders. The depiction of these enemies of the word would convey to the readers the cosmic nature of the battle in which they are engaged; they would also see in it a depiction of what we might term the fulness of psycholog-ical realities. They would derive from the interpretation a sobering pic-ture of God's opposition: universal in its scope, yet able to reach into the intimate chambers of the human heart. At the same time, however, they would gather from the description of the good soil a renewed sense of the grace bestowed upon them in their deliverance from such terrible foes.

Mark implies also that the word's bearing of fruit in the good soil of Christian communities is not to be the limit of its effectiveness. Moving to the next section of chapter 4 with the sayings about the lamp and the measure (vv 21-25), he paints a picture of hiddenness giving way to manifestation: "And he said to them, 'Does the lamp come in order that it may be put under the bushel or under the bed? Does it not come in order that it may be put on the lampstand? For there is nothing hid, except in order that it may be manifested, nor did anything become hidden, but in order that it might come into manifestation. If anyone has ears to hear, let him hear!'

"And he said to them, 'Take heed what you hear! With the measure you measure, it shall be measured to you, and it shall be added to you. For he who has, it shall be given to him; and he who has not, even what he has shall be taken from him.'"

According to this passage, the stalemate pictured in the Parable of the Sower and the parable theory passage, the division between hearers and non-hearers, will not be God's last word about the power of his gospel to find and even to create hearers. God's manifestation is to have the last say, not Satan's concealment; and the pledge of this promise is the manifestation that has *already* occurred. For Mark's community Jesus' identity as the Son of God, which had to be kept secret during his lifetime, is being openly proclaimed; and at the parousia the whole world will see him coming in glory. Indeed, both in Jesus' time and in the time of the Markan community, hiddenness not only gives way to but also *serves the purpose* of manifestation, because God's power is always revealed at the nadir of human capacity.

In vv 21-25, therefore, the Markan community is assured that it stands on the winning side of the battle line, that it is the vanguard of God's new age; and this assurance is coupled with an exhortation to persevere in the difficult task of hearing and remaining faithful to God's word. Mark's hearers are challenged to listen to that word, rather than to the voice of the world that surrounds them, presses against them, and tries to terrify them and career them into apostasy. They are promised that as they cling to the word, their ability to hear God's voice will deepen beyond all measure, even as their enemies sink further and further into insensibility.

After the sayings about the lamp and the measure, Mark adds two more seed parables to his chapter; both continue from vv 21-25 the theme of the movement from hiddenness to manifestation. The first, the Parable of the Seed Growing Secretly (vv 26-29), would probably be read by Mark's audience as a description of Jesus' relationship to the different phases in the manifestation of the kingdom of God. "And he said, 'Thus is the kingdom of God: as if a man should throw seed upon the earth, and should sleep and arise night and day, and the seed should sprout and grow, in what manner, he himself does not know. By itself the earth bears fruit, first a blade, then an ear, then full grain in the ear. But when the fruit is ripe, he immediately sends out the sickle, for the harvest has come.'"

As read by Mark's audience, this parable would tell how Jesus, who corresponds to the farmer, sowed the divine word in his earthly ministry; and how, when the measure of the *kairos* is filled up, he will return to reap the eschatological harvest. In the meantime, however, Jesus "sleeps and rises" as God directs the kingdom through an intermediate stage, the period of the church. The parable emphasizes that the kingdom is radically God's affair; even Jesus himself, who is God's agent in bringing it, does not know the "how" of its manifestation. The parable would thus address the bafflement of Mark's readers about the strange way in which God's kingship is being revealed in their own time; and it also would assure them that the eschatological measure is rapidly being filled up, and their suffering moving to its end.

In the Parable of the Mustard Seed (vv 30-32) Mark goes on to accent the contrast between the kingdom's initial stage of smallness and its final one of greatness. The introductory questions emphasize the difficulty of speaking about the kingdom: "And he said, 'How shall we show the likeness of the kingdom of God, or in what parable shall we put it?'" Because of this difficulty of expressing the kingdom's nature, the kingdom must be expressed *in parables*, which can reveal the kingdom because they are *like* the kingdom in apparent insignficiance and in hidden potency. Through his use of first person plural verbs in these introductory questions, Mark bolsters the impression gained from vv 13-20 that Jesus' disciples (including the members of the Markan community) continue his proclamation of the parabolic word.

The parable itself goes on to imply that this word, both in Jesus' lifetime and in the Markan present, appears to be insignificant and weak; but because its appearance belies the divine power hidden within it, its final effects are beyond reckoning. "'It is like a grain of mustard seed, which, when it is sown upon the earth—being smaller than all the seeds upon the earth—when it is sown, grows up and becomes greater than all the shrubs, and puts forth large branches, so that under its shade the birds of heaven are able to settle.'" Mark's readers would see the effects of the word's proclamation present in the evangelization of masses of Gentiles; and they would look toward a further demonstration of the word's power at the parousia, when God's new age would become visible to all, and the word would be revealed as the very substance of that age.

Vv 21-32 thus have as their overriding theme the movement from
hiddenness to manifestation; yet the end of the parable chapter returns to
the theme of a division of hearers, and thus implies that the gospel is
hidden from some (vv 33-34): "And with many such parables he used to
speak the word to them, as they were able to hear. Without a parable he
would not speak to them; but privately, to his own disciples, he used to
explain all things." In these concluding verses Mark's readers would again
be led to link themselves with the disciples to whom all things are interpreted, since they themselves have "overheard" the explanation of the
Parable of the Sower that is given only to disciples. They would also be
reminded, however, of the existence of another group of hearers who
remain outside the circle of faith, and thus fail to hear with understanding.

The Place of Mark 4:1-34 in the Gospel

The conclusion of the chapter on a note of division certainly reflects
the experience of Mark's readers that some in their own time are responding to the gospel with faith, while others are responding with disbelief and
even with hatred. The conclusion also, however, points Mark's readers to
the rest of his story, especially to the Passion Narrative. To end the
chapter on a note of manifestation would be premature, because in Mark's
view God's definitive revelation of himself will not occur until Jesus has
been crucified and raised (cf. 9:9). In Jesus' crucifixion the division within
humanity will be altered in a fundamental way, as he gives his life as a
ransom "for many" (10:45), and as an erstwhile outsider (the Gentile
centurion) becomes the first human being with a full appreciation of
Jesus' divine status (15:39).

It is difficult to imagine the Gospel of Mark without a parable chapter;
it is impossible to imagine it without a Passion Narrative. The sections
prior to the Passion Narrative, including our chapter, have a subordinate
function, although M. Kähler's famous description of the Gospels as "passion narratives with extended introductions"[4] goes too far; Jesus' ministry
is important for Mark, and not only as a preamble to his death. Nevertheless, the whole Gospel does is fact point toward that event. Already in
2:6-7 the opposition which will lead to Jesus' death is forming, and in 3:6
this opposition begins consciously to plot his assassination. After our

---

[4]M. Kähler, *The So-called Historical Jesus and the Historic Biblical
Christ* (Philadelphia: Fortress, 1964; orig. 1896) 80 n. 11.

chapter, the death of John the Baptist (6:14-29) foreshadows that of Jesus, the disputes of 7:1-13 and 8:11-13 sharpen the controversy between Jesus and his opponents, and the three passion predictions structure the entire section 8:27-10:45.[5] Chapters 11 and 12 function as a prelude to the Passion Narrative proper, bringing the hostility of Jesus' enemies to the breaking point; and, as we have pointed out, the prophecies of chapter 13 are at least partially fulfilled in the chapters that follow.

Yet, while it does not have the centrality of the Passion Narrative, the Markan parable chapter is still vital to an understanding of the Gospel. One reason why this is so is that the chapter contains Mark's most extended treatment of the kingdom of God; the *basileia* is specifically mentioned in 4:11, 26, and 30, and our study has shown that in Mark's mind the Parable of the Sower also pictures the mystery of the kingdom. Since the parable chapter is a key to understanding the kingdom, it is also of great importance for understanding the Gospel as a whole, because the kingdom is a central theme in Mark. References to the kingdom span the whole length of Mark's work (1:15; 3:24; 4:11, 26, 30; 6:23; 9:1, 47; 10:14-15, 23-25; 11:10; 12:34; 13:8; 14:25; 15:43), beginning with 1:15 where the words "kingdom" and "gospel" are programmatically linked.

The mystery of the kingdom that is explored in our chapter is not identical with the secret of Jesus' divine identity, which is the main message of Mark's Gospel (1:1) and the secret that is revealed to a human being only at the climax of the book (15:39).[6] The mystery of the kingdom and the secret of Jesus' identity are however interrelated; the question, "Who is Jesus?" is inseparable from the question, "Why do people not *see* who Jesus is?", which is one way of expressing the mystery of the kingdom.[7]

Furthermore, our chapter has a great importance within the context of the Gospel as a whole because it lays the foundation for a proper understanding of what happens in Jesus' life, death, and resurrection. To be specific, our chapter ensures that the events described in the rest of the book will be interpreted *apocalyptically*. For example, the Parable of the Sower and its interpretation prepare the reader to view Jesus' ministry as the intersection point of two mutually exclusive spheres of power, and to see the inbreaking of God's new age in events—most notably the crucifixion—that outwardly have the appearance of failure. Reading the

---

[5]See N. Perrin and D. C. Duling, *Introduction* 240-41, 248-51.
[6]Cf. J. D. Kingsbury, *Christology* 173-74.
[7]See above, chapter 4, n. 68.

Passion Narrative through the apocalyptic spectacles provided by the Parable of the Sower, then, we see Jesus triumphing over Satan by bringing a hidden kingdom through his death and resurrection. His death is the occasion for the splitting of the Temple veil (15:38); in the midst of a scene of old-age darkness (15:33), new-age light begins to dawn, as can be discerned by those like the centurion who have eyes to see (15:39). The victory Jesus wins, therefore, is cosmic, one that changes forever the universe in which all human beings live.

Also apocalyptic is the way in which the "parable theory" passage in 4:10-12 and the exhortations to hear in 4:9, 23-24a stress the necessity of a type of perception that sees beyond surface appearance to the "shape of things to come." These passages from chapter 4 thus prepare Mark's readers for scenes (especially prominent in the Passion Narrative) in which people will "look and look without seeing," i.e. will unwittingly display the truth of who Jesus is, even as they oppose him. In addition, the sayings in 4:21-25 and the two parables in 4:26-32 point Mark's readers to an apocalyptic turning point where hiddenness will begin to yield to manifestation. Chapter 4, then, helps prepare Mark's readers to see the centurion's confession and the scene at the empty tomb as apocalyptic events; it also contributes to the readers' impression that some of the characters in Mark's story will be the recipients of further unveilings beyond the end of the Gospel.

A third reason why our chapter is essential for an understanding of the whole Gospel is that it is Mark's most sustained meditation on the subject of *God's word*. In discussing 4:14, we have emphasized that in Mark's mind Jesus continues to sow God's word through the Christian evangelists of Mark's day. Mark would undoubtedly consider himself to be one of these evangelists through whom the Sower is sowing the gospel seed; he writes a Gospel which is not only a proclamation *about* Jesus Christ but also the proclamation *of* Jesus Christ (1:1; see above, chapter 6, n. 75). Thus the description of the purpose and fate of the word in chapter 4 may provide us with valuable hints about how Mark understands the purpose, and anticipates the fate, of the Gospel he writes.

If so, then Mark would expect his Gospel to provoke several different reactions among different sets of hearers, just as the word does in the Parable of the Sower; and indeed Mark would see the creation of these differing responses as being among the purposes for which God is using the Gospel. Mark's "book of parables,"[8] like the parables of Jesus, would,

---

[8]See above, chapter 3, section on the wider meaning of "in parables."

by God's grace, impart to some of Mark's hearers the mystery of the kingdom. These hearers, it is true, would perhaps initially be startled by the Gospel's uncompromising call to follow Jesus, its unrelenting portrayal of the fallibility of the disciples, and its abrupt ending; but these very features would also stimulate them to further inquiry, because they would sense that a momentous significance was hidden beneath the puzzling appearance. Teased into inquiry by the mysteries of the Gospel, they would seek illumination about them, and, in reading and rereading the Gospel, they would find that Jesus himself provides explanations that link the Gospel's conundrums with the paradoxes of the readers' own existence in the world.

Others within the community addressed by Mark, however, would respond differently to the Gospel's conundrums. The call to discipleship would frighten them; the description of Jesus' death would repulse them; the ending of the Gospel would bewilder them. Perhaps the umbrage they would take at Mark's message would make them susceptible to prophets who preached a more palatable gospel (13:5-6; 21-22); perhaps they would finally leave a community that was based on such paradoxical notions (4:17); perhaps they would even end up among the informers and lynch mobs (13:9-13), fueled by the hatred that sometimes belongs to former believers who feel that the scales have now fallen from their eyes.

The latter part of our chapter, however (vv 21-32), implies that the ultimate purpose for which God designed the gospel (and by extension Mark's Gospel) is not to bring about a division between believers and unbelievers, but rather to illuminate the whole world. The movement from hiddenness to revelation that took place in the events of Jesus' life, death, and resurrection, a movement which is pictured in Mark's Gospel, was, Mark implies, the *beginning* of a manifestation that continues in Mark's own time, and will continue until the parousia (1:1).[9] In Mark's time, Jesus continues to speak to the world, but now in a new way, through Christian evangelists and teachers such as Mark himself. Through such instruments, the dynamic word that actualizes God's presence is now moving out into the whole world with irresistible force (cf. 14:9); when this movement has reached its uttermost limit, the end will come (13:10; cf. 4:26-29).

---

[9]On the interpretation of *archē* in 1:1 as applying to the whole Gospel see R. Pesch, *Markusevangelium* 1.75-76. One advantage of this interpretation is that it makes an ending at 16:8 reasonable; the *beginning* of the gospel story is over on Easter morning.

The ultimate effectiveness of the gospel is emphasized strongly in vv 21-32. The seed parable of vv 3-9, 14-20, in which frustration of the word was a major theme, now gives way to the seed parables of vv 26-32, in which the ineluctable growth of the seed fills the entire canvas, and there is no hint of resistance to the word. In these latter parables the word is pictured as God's means of manifesting his dominion, of transforming the old age into the new age, of creating a new cosmos. Mark drops some hints as to how the word effects this transformation. Through the gospel Jesus becomes present in situations, such as that now being experienced by the Markan community, in which God's people face a counterattack by the forces of the old age. These forces seek to blind the elect by presenting the specter of a world still securely in Satan's grasp, and to terrify them with the threat of persecution (4:15-19). Into such situations of despair and bewilderment the word enters with a power that transforms death into life. It proclaims that those being crucified are crucified *with Christ* (cf. Gal 2:20); therefore the apocalyptic reversal that occurred at the crucifixion is a reality not only for Jesus but also for those who follow him to the cross (8:34-35). And as it proclaims this reality, the word simultaneously brings it into being for them.

If the reversal that occurs at the cross is truly apocalyptic, however, the words "for them" in the previous sentence may finally be superfluous. Is it true for Mark, as it is for Paul (1 Cor 15:24; Rom 8:19-21) that the apocalyptic hope looks forward not merely to the deliverance of a group of people but also to the renewal of creation? Is the transformation that began at Jesus' crucifixion a reality not only for the church but also for the world? Could it be that in Mark's mind even those who reject the gospel and are judged by it will ultimately share in the new world that it creates? The images used in vv 21-32 do indeed seem to imply that in the end no pocket of resistance to God's victorious word will remain.[10]

Mark himself does not resolve the tension between his portrayal of a dramatic fissure between the unbelieving world and the church, and, on the other hand, his hints about the universal effect of Christ's death. For him this tension is probably yet another aspect of the mystery of the kingdom, a mystery that cannot be explained but only conveyed in para-doxical teachings and parabolic stories, such as those that make up his book of parables. In God's own good time, God will explain all these mys-teries; until that final revelation, God's word, even if imperfectly

---

[10]Cf. J. C. Beker, *Paul the Apostle: The Triumph of God in Life and Thought* (Philadelphia: Fortress, 1980) 194.

understood, remains the most powerful weapon in his arsenal for routing the dominion of Satan. Through the word God continues the transformation of old-age darkness into new-age light that was proleptically begun in Jesus' ministry and decisively inaugurated in his crucifixion. By means of the word God extends his rule ever more deeply into the universe he created, by that same word, as humanity's home.

Mark's Gospel, as a bearer of the word, alienates some of its hearers while it reveals the hidden kingdom to others; the Gospel thereby accomplishes God's double purpose of bringing out into the open, and even intensifying, the darkness of the old age, in order that the light of the new age may break forth. The kingdom of Satan, stirred into hatred by the word, creates "such tribulation as has never been" (13:29); but this tribulation only hastens the plundering of the Strong Man's house, not only because the tribulation is the prelude to the manifestation of God's kingship (13:24-27), but also because it is, in a lefthanded way, its cause. For those with ears to hear, even the hate-filled cries of the crucifiers contain a powerful testimony to God's triumph in Jesus' Christ; in the hour of tribulation, the Holy Spirit speaks (13:11), bringing God's new world into existence. Mark's ultimate word of empowerment to his beleaguered community, then, is that it is not to become discouraged, but rather actually *to be heartened* at times when it seems increasingly difficult to trace God's ways in the world. "For there is nothing that becomes hidden, except *in order that* it may be revealed" (Mark 4:22).

Bibliography

Achtemeier, P. J., "'And he followed him': Miracles and Discipleship in Mark 10:46-52," *Semeia* 11 (1978) 115-45.

_____, "'He Taught Them Many Things': Reflections on Marcan Christology," *CBQ* 42 (1980) 465-481.

_____, *Mark* (Proclamation Commentaries; Philadelphia: Fortress, 1975).

_____, "Mark as Interpreter of the Jesus Traditions," *Int* 32 (1978) 339-352.

_____, "The Origin and Function of the Pre-Markan Miracle Catenae," *JBL* 91 (1972) 198-221.

_____, "Toward the Isolation of Pre-Markan Miracle Catenae," *JBL* 89 (1970) 265-91.

_____, Review of H. C. Kee, *Community of the New Age, Int* 32 (1978) 324-25.

Althaus, P., *The Theology of Martin Luther* (Philadelphia: Fortress, 1966).

Ambrozic, A. M., *The Hidden Kingdom: A Redaction-Critical Study of the References to the Kingdom of God in Mark's Gospel* (CBQMS 2; 1972).

_____, "Mark's Concept of the Parable. Mk 4, 11f. in the Context of the Second Gospel," *CBQ* 29 (1967) 220-27.

_____, "New Teaching with Power (Mk 1:27)," *Word and Spirit; Essays in Honor of David Michael Stangley, S.J. on his 60th Birthday* (ed. J. Plevnik; Willowdale, Ont.: Regis College, 1975) 113-149.

Anderson, B. W., *Understanding the Old Testament* (3d ed.; Englewood Cliffs: Prentice-Hall, 1975).

Bacon, B. W., *The Beginnings of the Gospel Story* (New Haven: Yale University, 1909).

Baird, J. A., "A Pragmatic Approach to Parable Exegesis: Some New Evidence on Mark 4:11.33-34," *JBL* 76 (1957) 201-207.

Baltenweiler, H., "Das Gleichnis von der selbstwachsenden Saat (Markus 4, 26-29) und die theologische Konzeption des Markusevangelisten," *Oikonomia: Heilsgeschichte als Thema der Theologie: Festschrift für Oscar Cullmann* (ed. F. Christ; Hamburg-Bergstedt: H. Reich, 1967) 69-75.

Barth, K., *Church Dogmatics* 4.3.1 (Edinburgh: T. & T. Clark, 1961).

Barth, M., "Autonome statt messianische Ethik?" *Judaica* 37 (1981) 220-33.

Bartnicki, R., "Il carattere messianico delle pericopi di Marco e Matteo sull'ingresso di Gesù in Gerusalemme (*Mc.* 11,1-10; *Mt.* 21,1-9)," *RivB* 25 (1977) 5-27.

Bartsch, H.-W., "Eine bisher übersehene Zitierung der LXX in Mark 4, 30," *TZ* 15 (1959) 126-28.

Bauer, J. B., "Et adicietur vobis credentibus Mk 4:24f.," *ZNW* 71 (1980) 248-51.

Bauer, W., et al., *A Greek-English Lexicon of the New Testament and Other Early Christian Literature* (2d ed.; Chicago/London: University of Chicago, 1979).

Beare, F. W., "Hermas, Shepherd of," *IDB* 2 (1962) 583-84.

Behm, J., "*exō*," *TDNT* 2 (1964; orig. 1935) 575-76.

Beker, J. C., *Paul the Apostle: The Triumph of God in Life and Thought* (Philadelphia: Fortress, 1980).

Bengel, J. A., *Gnomon Novi Testamenti* (Edinburgh: T. & T. Clark, 1859; orig. 1742).

Bernas, C., Review of V. Fusco, *Parola e Regno* in *CBQ* 44 (1982) 146-47.

Bertram, G., "*strephō*," *TDNT* 7 (1971; orig. 1964) 714-29.

Best, E., *Following Jesus: Discipleship in the Gospel of Mark* (JSNT Sup 4; Sheffield: JSOT, 1981).

_____, "Mark's Use of the Twelve," *ZNW* 69 (1978) 11-35.

_____, "The Role of the Disciples in Mark," *NTS* 23 (1977) 377-401.

Beyer, K., *Semitische Syntax im Neuen Testament*, Band I: Satzlehre, Teil 1 (Göttingen: Vandenhoeck & Ruprecht, 1962).

Black, M., *An Aramaic Approach to the Gospels and Acts* (Oxford University, 1946).

Blass, F., et al., *A Greek Grammar of the New Testament and Other Early Christian Literature* (Chicago/London: University of Chicago, 1961).

Blevins, J. L., *The Messianic Secret in Markan Research, 1901-1976* (Washington: University Press of America, 1981).

Boers, H., *Theology out of the Ghetto: A New Testament Exegetical Study concerning Religious Exclusiveness* (Leiden: Brill, 1971).

_____, "The Unity of the Gospel of Mark," *Scriptura* 4 (1981) 1-7.

Boobyer, G. H., "The Redaction of Mark 4, 1-34," *NTS* 8 (1962-63) 59-70.

_____, "The Secrecy Motif in St. Mark's Gospel," *NTS* 6 (1959-60) 225-35.

Boomershine, T. E., *Mark, the Storyteller: A Rhetorical-Critical Investigation of Mark's Passion and Resurrection Narrative* (Ph.D. thesis, Union Theological Seminary, New York, 1974).

Boring, M. E., *Sayings of the Risen Jesus: Christian Prophecy in the Synoptic Tradition* (SNTSMS 46; Cambridge/London/New York: Cambridge University, 1982).

Bornkamm, G., "*mystērion*," *TDNT* 4 (1967; orig. 1942) 802-828.

Boucher, M., *The Mysterious Parable: A Literary Study* (CBQMS 6; 1977).

Bover, J. M., "Nada hay encubierto que no se descubra," *EstBib* 13 (1954) 219-23.

Bowker, J. W., "Mystery and parable: Mark IV.1-20," *JTS* NS 25 (1974) 300-317.

Bratcher, R. G., *A Translator's Guide to the Gospel of Mark* (Helps for Translators; London/New York/Stuttgart: United Bible Societies, 1981).

Braun, H., *Spätjüdisch-häretischer und frühchristlicher Radikalismus. Jesus von Nazareth und die essenische Qumransekte II. Die Synoptiker* (BHT 24; Tübingen, 1957).

Brooten, B. J., "Konnten Frauen im alten Judentum die Scheidung betreiben? Überlegungen zu Mk 10,11-12 und 1 Kor 7,10-11," *EvT* 42 (1982) 65-80.

_____, "Zur Debatte über das Scheidungsrecht der jüdischen Frau," *EvT* 43 (1983) 466-78.

Brown, F., et al., *A Hebrew and English Lexicon of the Old Testament with an Appendix Containing the Biblical Aramaic* (Oxford: Clarendon, 1907).

Brown, R. E., *The Gospel According to John, I-XII* (AB 29; Garden City: Doubleday, 1966).

_____, "Parable and Allegory Reconsidered," *New Testament Essays* (New York: Doubleday, 1968; orig. 1962).

_____, *The Semitic Background of the Term "Mystery" in the New Testament* (FBBS 21; Philadelphia: Fortress, 1968; orig. 1958-59).

_____, and J. P. Meier, *Antioch and Rome: New Testament Cradles of Catholic Christianity* (New York/Ramsey, N.J.: Paulist, 1983).

_____, et al., *Mary in the New Testament: A Collaborative Assessment by Protestant and Roman Catholic Scholars* (United States Lutheran—Roman Catholic Dialogue; Philadelphia/New York: Fortress/Paulist, 1978).

Brown, S., "The Secret of the Kingdom of God (Mark 4:11)," *JBL* 92 (1973) 60-74.

Bultmann, R., *History of the Synoptic Tradition* (ET Oxford: Blackwell, 1968; orig. 1931).

_____, "Die Interpretation von Mk. 4, 3-9 seit Jülicher," *Jesus und Paulus. Festschrift für Werner Georg Kümmel zum 70. Geburtstag* (ed. E. E. Ellis and E. Grässer; Göttingen: Vandenhoeck & Ruprecht, 1975) 30-34.

_____, *Theology of the New Testament* (2 vols. in 1; New York: Scribners, 1951-55).

Burkill, T. A., "The Cryptology of Parables in St. Mark's Gospel," *NovT* 1 (1956) 246-62.

_____, *Mysterious Revelation: An Examination of the Philosophy of St. Mark's Gospel* (Ithaca: Cornell University, 1963).

_____, *New Light on the Earliest Gospel: Several Markan Studies* (Ithaca, New York: Cornell University, 1972).

Butterworth, R. and M. Smith, *A Reading of Mark's Gospel* (Religious Studies Publication 4; London: Roehampton Institute, 1982).

Cadoux, C. J., "The Imperatival Use of *hina* in the New Testament," *JTS* 42 (1941) 165-73.

Calvin, J., *Commentary on a Harmony of the Evangelists, Matthew, Mark, and Luke* (3 vols.; Grand Rapids: Eerdmans, 1949; orig. 1555).

Carlston, C. E., "Parable and Allegory Revisited: An Interpretive Review," *CBQ* 43 (1981) 228-42.

_____, *The Parables of the Triple Tradition* (Philadelphia: Fortress, 1975).

Casalegno, A., "La parabola del granello di senape (*Mc.* 4,30-32)," *RivB* 26 (1978) 139-61.

Cerfaux, L., "La connaissance des Secrets du Royaume d'après Matt XIII.11 et parallèles," *NTS* 2 (1955-56) 238-249.

_____, "Les paraboles du Royaume dans l'Évangile de Thomas," *Le Muséon* 70 (1957) 311-17.

Charles, R. H., ed., *The Apocrypha and Pseudepigrapha of the Old Testament* (2 vols.; Oxford: Clarendon, 1913).

Charlesworth, J. H., ed., *The Old Testament Pseudepigrapha* (2 vols.; Garden City: Doubleday, 1983).

_____, *The Pseudepigrapha and Modern Research with a Supplement* (SBLSCS 7; Chico, Calif.: Scholars, 1981; orig. 1976).

Childs, B. S., *Introduction to the Old Testament as Scripture* (Philadelphia: Fortress, 1979).

Chronis, H. L., "The Torn Veil: Cultus and Christology in Mark 15:37-39," *JBL* 101 (1982) 97-114.

Conybeare, F. C. and St. George Stock, *A Grammar of Septuagint Greek* (Grand Rapids: Zondervan, 1980; orig. 1905).

Conzelmann, H., *The Theology of St. Luke* (New York: Harper & Brothers, 1960).

Couroyer, B. "De la mesure dont vous mesurez il vous sera mesuré," *RB* 77 (1970) 366-70.

Coutts, J., "'Those Outside' (Mark 4, 10-12)," *SE* II (TU 87; 1964) 155-157.

Cramer, J. A., *Catenae in Evangelia s. Matthaei et s. Marci* (Oxford, 1840).

Cranfield, C. E. B., *The Gospel According to Saint Mark* (Cambridge Greek Testament Commentary; Cambridge University, 1974; orig. 1959).

_____, "Message of Hope; Mark 4:21-32," *Int* 9 (1955) 150-64.

_____, "St. Mark 4:1-34," *SJT* 5 (1952) 49-66.

Crossan, J. D., "Empty Tomb and Absent Lord (Mark 16:1-8)," *The Passion in Mark: Studies on Mark 14-16* (ed. W. H. Kelber; Philadelphia: Fortress, 1976) 135-52.

_____, *Four Other Gospels: Shadows on the Contours of Canon* (Minneapolis: Winston, 1985).

_____, *In Parables* (New York: Harper & Row, 1973).

_____, "The Parable of the Wicked Husbandmen," *JBL* 90 (1971) 451-65.

_____, "The Seed Parables of Jesus," *JBL* 92 (1973) 244-66.

Culpepper, R. A., *Anatomy of the Fourth Gospel: A Study in Literary Design* (NT Foundations and Facets; Philadelphia: Fortress, 1983).

Dahl, N. A., "The Parables of Growth," *Jesus in the Memory of the Early Church* (Minneapolis: Augsburg, 1976; orig. 1951) 141-166.

Dalman, G., "Viererlei Acker," *Palästinajahrbuch* 22 (1926) 120-32.

Daube, D., "Public Pronouncement and Private Explanation in the Gospels," *ExTim* 57 (1945-46) 175-177.

Davis, J. L., *The Literary History and Theology of the Parabolic Material in Mark 4 in Relation to the Gospel as a Whole* (Ph.D. thesis, Union Theological Seminary, Richmond, Virginia, 1966).

Derrett, J. D. M., "Allegory and the Wicked Vinedressers," *JTS* 25 (1974) 426-32.

Derrett, J. D. M., *Law in the New Testament* (London/New York: Darton, Longman & Todd/Fernhill, 1971).

Dibelius, M., "Wer Ohren hat zu hören, der höre," *TSK* 83 (1910) 461-471.

Dietzfelbinger, C., "Das Gleichnis von angestreuten Samen," *Der Ruf Jesu und die Antwort der Gemeinde. Exegetische Untersuchungen für Joachim Jeremias zum 70.Geburtstag gewidmet von seinen Schülern* (ed. E. Lohse; Göttingen: Vandenhoeck & Ruprecht, 1970) 80-93.

Diez Macho, A., *Neophyti 1: Targum Palestinense MS de la Bibliotecha Vaticana*, vol. 1, *Genesis* (Madrid/Barcelona: Consejo Superior de Investigaciones Cientificas, 1968).

Dodd, C. H., *The Parables of the Kingdom* (London: Fontana, 1961; orig. 1935).

Doeve, J. W., *Jewish Hermeneutics in the Synoptic Gospels and Acts* (Assen: Van Gorcum, 1953).

Donahue, J. R., "Jesus as the Parable of God in the Gospel of Mark," *Int* 32 (1978) 369-86.

Doudna, J. C., *The Greek of the Gospel of Mark* (JBLMS 12; Philadelphia: Society of Biblical Literature and Exegesis, 1961).

Dozzi, E. E., "Chi sono quelli attorno a lui di Mc 4, 10," *Marianum* 36 (1974) 153-83.

Dupont, J., "Le chapitre des paraboles," *NRT* 89 (1967) 800-820.

_____, "Encore la parabole de la Semence, qui pousse toute seule (Mk. 4, 26-29)," *Jesus und Paulus: Festschrift für Werner Georg Kümmel zum 70. Geburtstag* (ed. E. E. Ellis and E. Grässer; Göttingen: Vandenhoeck & Ruprecht, 1975) 96-102.

_____, "La parabole de la semence qui pousse toute seule (Marc 4, 26-29)," *RSR* 55 (1979) 367-92.

_____, "La Parabole du semeur," *Foi et Vie* 66 (1967) 3-25.

_____, "Les Paraboles du seneve et du levain," *NRT* 89 (1967) 897-913.

_____, "La transmission des paroles de Jésus sur la lampe et la mesure dans Marc 4,21-25 et dans la tradition Q," *Logia. Les Paroles de Jésus—The Sayings of Jesus. Memorial Joseph Coppens* (J. Delobel, ed.; BETL 59; Leuven University: Peeters, 1982) 201-36.

Dupont-Sommer, A., *The Essene Writings from Qumran* (Glouchester, Mass.: Peter Smith, 1973; orig. 1961).

_____, "Note archéologique sur le proverbe evangelique: Mettre la lampe sous le boisseau," *Melanges Syriens offers à Monsieur R. Dussard* 2 (Paris: 1939) 789-94.

Eakin, F. E., "Spiritual Obduracy and Parable Purpose," *The Use of the Old Testament in the New and Other Essays: Studies in Honor of William Franklin Stinespring* (ed. J. M. Efird; Durham, N.C.: Duke University, 1972) 87-109.

Ebeling, H. J., *Das Messiasgeheimnis und die Botschaft des Markusevange-lium* (BZNW 19; Berlin: Töpelmann, 1939).

Eichholz, G., *Gleichnisse der Evangelien. Form, Überlieferung, Auslegung* (Neukirchen, 1971).

Englezakis, B., "Markan Parable: More than Word Modality, a Revelation of Contents," *Deltion Biblikon Meleton* 2 (1974) 349-57.

Enslin, M. S., "A New Apocalyptic," *Religion in Life* 44 (1975) 105-110.

Essame, W. G., "*kai elegen* in Mark iv. 21, 24, 26, 30," *ExpTim* 77 (1966) 121.

Evans, C. A., "The Function of Isa 6:9-10 in Mark and John," *NovT* 24 (1982) 124-38.

_____, "Isaiah 6:9-10 in Rabbinic and Patristic Writings," *VC* 36 (1982) 275-81.

_____, "A Note on the Function of Isaiah, VI, 9-10 in Mark, IV," *RB* 88 (1981) 234-35.

Farmer, W. R., *The Synoptic Problem: A Critical Analysis* (New York: Macmillan, 1964).

Fitzmyer, J. A., *To Advance the Gospel: New Testament Studies* (New York: Crossroad, 1981).

_____, *The Gospel According to Luke I-IX* (AB 28; Garden City: Doubleday, 1981).

_____, "The Oxyrhynchus Logoi of Jesus and the Coptic Gospel According to Thomas," *Essays on the Semitic Background of the New Testament* (Sources for Biblical Study 5; Missoula: Scholars' Press, 1974; orig. 1959) 355-433.

Flusser, D., *Die rabbinischen Gleichnisse und der Gleichniserzähler Jesus. Teil 1: Das Wesen der Gleichnisse* (Judaica et Christiana 4; Bern: Lang, 1981).

Freyne, S., "The Disciples in Mark and the *maskilim* in Daniel. A Compari-son," *JSNT* 16 (1982) 7-23.

Fuller, R. H., *The Formation of the Resurrection Narratives* (New York: Macmillan, 1971).

Funk, R. W., "The Looking-glass Tree Is for the Birds; Ezekiel 17:22-24; Mark 4:30-32," *Int* 27 (1973) 3-9.

Fusco, V., "L'áccord mineur Mt 13,11a/Lk 8,10a contre Mc 4,11a," *Logia. Les Paroles de Jésus—The Sayings of Jesus. Memorial Joseph Coppens* (J. Delobel, ed.; BETL 59; Leuven University: Peeters, 1982) 355-61.

_____, "L'économie de la Révélation dans l'evangile de Marc," *NRT* 104 (1982) 532-54.

_____, *Parola e regno: La sezione delle parabole (Mc. 4, 1-34) nella prospettiva marciana* (Aloisiana 13; Brescia: Morcelliana, 1980).

Galling, K., "Die Beleuchtungsgeräte im israelitisch-jüdischen Kulturgebiet," *ZDPV* 46 (1923) 1-50.

Gealy, F. D., "The Composition of Mark IV," *ExpTim* 48 (1936) 40-43.

Geischer, H.-J., "Verschwenderische Güte. Versuch über Markus 4, 3-9," *EvT* 38 (1978) 418-27.

Gerhardsson, B., "The Parable of the Sower and its Interpretation," *NTS* 14 (1967-68) 165-193.

Giesen, H., "Mk 9,1—ein Wort Jesu über die nahe Parusie?" *TTZ* 92 (1983) 134-48.

Gillabert, E., et al., *Évangile selon Thomas. Présentation, Traduction et Commentaires* (Marsanne: Métanoïa, 1979).

Gnilka, J., *Das Evangelium nach Markus* (2 vols.; EKKNT 2; Zürich: Benziger/Neukirchener, 1978).

_____, *Die Verstockung Israels: Isaias 6, 9-10 in der Theologie der Synoptiker* (SANT 3; München: Kösel, 1961).

Goulder, M. D., "Characteristics of the Parables in the Several Gospels," *JTS* 19 (1968) 51-69.

Graham, H. H., "The Gospel According to St. Mark: Mystery and Ambiguity," *ATR* supplement 7 (1976) 43-55.

Grant, R. M., *The Apostolic Fathers: A New Translation and Commentary* (5 vols.; New York/Toronto/London: Nelson, 1964-67).

Grundmann, W., *Das Evangelium nach Markus* (2d ed.; THKNT 2; Berlin, 1959).

Guillaumont, A., et al., *The Gospel According to Thomas: Coptic Text Established and Translated* (San Francisco: Harper & Row, 1959).

Haacker, K., "Erwägungen zu Mc. IV 11," *NovT* 14 (1972) 219-225.

Haenchen, E., *Der Weg Jesu. Eine Erklärung des Markus-Evangeliums und der kanonischen Parallelen* (2d ed.; Berlin: De Gruyter, 1968).

Hahn , F., "Das Gleichnis von der ausgestreuten Saat und seine Deutung (Mk iv.3-8, 14-20)," *Text and Interpretation: Studies in the New Testament Presented to Matthew Black* (eds. E. Best and R. McL. Wilson; New York/London: Cambridge University, 1979) 133-42.

_____, "Die Rede von der Parusie des Menschensohnes Markus 13," *Jesus und der Menschensohn* (ed. R. Pesch and R. Schnackenburg; Freiburg: Herder, 1975).

_____, "Die Worte vom Lichte Lk 11, 33-36," *Orientierung an Jesus. Zur Theologie der Synoptiker. Für J. Schmid* (ed. P. Hoffmann; Freiburg: Herder, 1973) 107-38.

Hanson, P. D., *The Dawn of Apocalyptic: The Historical and Sociological Roots of Jewish Apocalyptic Eschatology* (rev. ed.; Philadelphia: Fortress, 1979).

Harder, G., "Das Gleichnis von der selbstwachsenden Saat Mk 4,26-29," *ThViat* 1 (1948-49) 51-70.

Harnisch, W., *Verhängnis und Verheissung der Geschichte. Untersuchungen zum Zeit- und Geschichtsverständnis im 4. Buch Esra und in der syr. Baruchapokalypse* (FRLANT 97; Göttingen, 1969).

Harvey, A. E., "The Use of Mystery Language in the Bible," *JTS* NS 31 (1980) 320-36.

Hauck, F., "*parabolē,*" *TDNT* 5 (1967; orig. 1954) 744-761.

Haufe, G., "Erwägungen zum Ursprung der sogennanten Parabel theorie Markus 4, 11-12," *EvT* 32 (1972) 413-21.

Hedrick, C. W., "Kingdom Sayings and Parables of Jesus in *The Apocryphon of James:* Tradition and Redaction," *NTS* 29 (1983) 1-24.

Hengel, M., *Judaism and Hellenism: Studies in their Encounter in Palestine during the Early Hellenistic Period* (2 vols. in 1; Philadelphia: Fortress, 1974).

Hennecke, E. and W. Schneemelcher, *New Testament Apocrypha* (2 vols.; Philadelphia: Westminster, 1964).

Hermaniuk, M., *La Parabole Evangélique: Enquête exégétique et critique* (Catholic University of Louvain Dissertation Series II, vol. 38; Bruges: Desclee de Brouwer, 1947).

Hesse, F., *Das Vertockungsproblem im Alten Testament. Eine frommig-keitsgeschichtliche Untersuchung* (BZAW 74; Berlin: Töpelmann, 1955).

Hillers, D. R., *Covenant: The History of a Biblical Idea* (Baltimore/London: Johns Hopkins University, 1969).

Holzmeister, U., "Vom angeblichen Verstockungszweck der Parabeln des Herrn," *Bib* 15 (1934) 321-64.

Hooker, M. D., "Trial and Tribulation in Mark XIII," *BJRL* 65 (1982) 78-99.

Hubaut, M., "Le 'mystère' révéle dans les paraboles (Mc 4, 11-12)," *RTL* 5 (1974) 454-461.

Humphrey, H. M., *A Bibliography for the Gospel of Mark, 1954-1980* (Studies in the Bible and Early Christianity 1; New York/Toronto: Edwin Mellin, 1981).

Hunzinger, C. H., "Aussersynoptisches Traditionsgut im Thomas-Ev.," *TLZ* 85 (1960) 843-46.

_____, "*sinapi*," *TDNT* 7 (1971; orig. 1964) 287-91.

Igarashi, P. H., "The Mystery of the Kingdom (Mark 4, 10-12)," *JBR* 24 (1956) 83-89.

Jeremias, J., *The Parables of Jesus* (2d rev. ed.; New York: Scribners, 1972; orig. 1954).

_____, "*polloi*," *TDNT* 6 (1968; orig. 1959) 536-45.

_____, "Die Lampe unter dem Scheffel," *ZNW* 39 (1940) 237-40.

_____, "Palästinakundliches zum Gleichnis vom Sämann (Mark IV:3-8)," *NTS* 13 (1966) 48-53.

Johnson, E. S., "Mark viii. 22-26: The Blind Man from Bethsaida," *NTS* 25 (1979) 370-83.

Juel, D., *Messiah and Temple: The Trial of Jesus in the Gospel of Mark* (SBLDS 31; Missoula, Montana: Scholars, 1977).

Jülicher, A., *Die Gleichnisreden Jesu* (2d ed.; 2 vols. in 1; Tübingen: Mohr, 1910; orig. 1888).

Kähler, M. *The So-called Historical Jesus and the Historic Biblical Christ* (Philadelphia: Fortress, 1964; orig. 1896).

Kahmann, J. J. A., "Marc. 1,14-15 en hun plaats in het geheel van het Marcus-evangelie," *Bidragen* 38 (1977) 84-98.

Kallas, J., *Jesus and the Power of Satan* (Philadelphia: Westminster, 1968).

Käsemann, E., *New Testament Questions of Today* (Philadelphia: Fortress, 1969).

Kautzsch, E., *Gesenius' Hebrew Grammar* (2d Eng. ed.; Oxford: Clarendon, 1910).

Kealy, S. P., *Mark's Gospel: A History of its Interpretation from the Beginning Until 1979* (New York: Paulist, 1982).

_____, Review of E. Manicardi, *Il cammino di Gesù nel Vangelo di Marco*, *CBQ* 46 (1984) 169-71.

Kearns, R., *Vorfragen zur Christologie III. Religionsgeschichtliche und Traditionsgeschichtliche Studie zur Vorgeschichte eines christologischen Hoheitstitels* (Tübingen: Mohr-Siebeck, 1982).

Keck, L. E., "Mark 3:7-12 and Mark's Christology," *JBL* 84 (1965) 341-58.

Kee, H. C., *Community of the New Age: Studies in Mark's Gospel* (Philadelphia: Westminster, 1977).

_____, "Mark's Gospel in Recent Research," *Int* 32 (1978) 353-68.

Kelber, W. H., *The Kingdom in Mark: A New Place and a New Time* (Philadelphia: Fortress, 1974).

_____, *Mark's Story of Jesus* (Philadelphia: Fortress, 1979).

_____, *The Oral and Written Gospel: The Hermeneutics of Speaking and Writing in the Synoptic Tradition, Mark, Paul, and Q* (Philadelphia: Fortress, 1983).

Kermode, F., *The Genesis of Secrecy* (Cambridge, Mass./London: Harvard University, 1979).

Kilpatrick, G. D., "*idou* and *ide* in the Gospels," *JTS* 18 (1967) 425-26.

Kingsbury, J. D., *The Christology of Mark's Gospel* (Philadelphia: Fortress, 1983).

_____, *Jesus Christ in Matthew, Mark, and Luke* (Proclamation Commentaries; Philadelphia: Fortress, 1981).

Kirkland, J. R., "The Earliest Understanding of Jesus' Use of Parables: Mark IV 10-12 in Context," *NovT* 19 (1977) 1-21.

Kissinger, W. S., *The Parables of Jesus* (Metuchen, N.J./London: Scarecrow, 1979).

Klauck, H.-J., *Allegorie und Allegorese in synoptischen Gleichnistexten* (NTAbh 13; 1978).

Koester, H., "History and Development of Mark's Gospel (From Mark to Secret Mark to 'Canonical' Mark)," *Colloquy on New Testament Studies: A Time for Reappraisal and Fresh Approaches* (ed. B. Corley; Macon, Georgia: Mercer University, 1983).

_____, *Introduction to the New Testament* (2 vols.; Hermeneia Foundations and Facets; Philadelphia: Fortress, 1982).

_____, "*physis*," *TDNT* 9 (1973) 251-77.

_____, *Synoptische Überlieferung be den Apostolischen Vatern* (TU 65; Berlin: Akademie, 1957).

_____, "A Test Case of Synoptic Source Theory (Mk 4:1-34 and Parallels)," SBL Gospels Seminar, SBL Convention, Atlanta, 31 October 1971.

_____, "Three Thomas Parables," *The New Testament and Gnosis: Essays in honour of Robert McLachlan Wilson* (eds. A. H. B. Logan and A. J. M. Wedderburn; Edinburgh: T. and T. Clark, 1983) 195-203.

Kugel, J. L., *The Idea of Biblical Poetry: Parallelism and its History* (New Haven/London: Yale University, 1981).

Kuhn, H.-W., *Ältere Sammlungen im Markusevangelium* (SUNT 8; Göttingen: Vandenhoeck & Ruprecht, 1971).

Kümmel, W. G., *Introduction to the New Testament* (rev. ed. Nashville: Abingdon, 1973).

_____, *The New Testament: The History of the Investigation of its Problems* (Nashville/New York: Abingdon, 1972).

_____, "Noch einmal: Das Gleichnis von der selbstwachsenden Saat. Bemerkungen zur neuesten Diskussion um die Auslegung der Gleichnisse Jesu," *Orientierung an Jesus; zur theologie der Synoptiker; für Josef Schmid* (ed. P. Hoffmann, N. Brox, W. Pesch; Freiburg: Herder, 1973) 220-37.

Kuss, O., "Zur Senfkornparabel," *Auslegung und Verkündigung* (Regensburg: Pustet, 1963; orig. 1951) 78-84.

Kuss, O., "Zum Sinngehalt des Doppelgleichnis vom Senfkorn und Sauerteig," *Auslegung und Verkündigung* (Regensburg: Pustet, 1963; orig. 1959) 85-97.

Lafon, G., "Qui est dedans? Qui est dehors? Une lecture de Marc 3,31-35," *Christus* (Paris) 21 (1974) 41-47.

Lagrange, M. J., "Le but des paraboles d'après l'evangile selon saint Marc," *RB* 7 (1910) 5-35.

_____, *Évangile selon Saint Marc* (Etudes Bibliques; 2d ed. Paris: Lecaffre, 1920; orig. 1910).

Lambrecht, J., *Once More Astonished: The Parables of Jesus* (New York: Crossroad, 1981.

_____, "Redaction and Theology in MK., IV," *L'Évangile selon Marc. Tradition et redaction* (ed. M. Sabbe; BETL 34, 1974).

Lampe, P., "Die markinische Deutung des Gleichnisses von Sämann Markus 4, 10-12," *ZNW* 65 (1974) 140-150.

Lane, W., *The Gospel of Mark* (NICNT; Grand Rapids: Eerdmans, 1974).

Lang, F. G., "Kompositionsanalyse des Markusevangeliums," *ZTK* 74 (1977) 1-24.

Laufen, R., *Die Doppelüberlieferung der Logienquelle und des Markus-evangeliums* (BBB 54; Bonn: Königstein, 1980).

Lee, G. M., "New Testament Gleanings," *Bib* 51 (1970) 235-40.

Lemcio, E. E., "External Evidence for the Structure and Function of Mark iv. 1-20, vii. 14-23 and viii. 14-21," *JTS* 29 (1978) 323-38.

Leon-Dufour, X., *Études d'Evangile* (Paris: Editions du Seuil, 1965).

Liddell, H. G. and R. Scott, *A Greek-English Lexicon with a Supplement* (Oxford: Clarendon, 1968).

Lightfoot, J. B., *The Apostolic Fathers: Clement, Ignatius, Polycarp* (5 vols.; Grand Rapids: Baker, 1981; orig. 1889-90).

_____, *The Gospel Message of St. Mark* (Oxford University, 1950).

Lindars, B., "Jotham's Fable—A New Form-Critical Analysis," *JTS* NS 24 (1973) 355-366.

_____, *New Testament Apologetic: The Doctrinal Significance of the Old Testament Quotations* (Philadelphia: Westminster, 1961).

Lindemann, A., "Die Osterbotschaft des Markus. Zur theologischen Inter-pretation von Mark. 16.1-8," *NTS* 26 (1980) 298-317.

Lindeskog, G., "Logia-Studien," *ST* 4 (1950) 129-184.

Link, W., "Die Geheimnisse des Himmelreiches. Eine Erklärung von Matth. 13.10-13," *EvT* 2 (1935) 115-27.

Linnemann, E., *Parables of Jesus: Introduction and Exposition* (London: S.P.C.K., 1966; orig. 1961).

Lohmeyer, E., *Das Evangelium des Markus* (11th ed.; Göttingen: Vandenhoeck & Ruprecht, 1951; orig. 1937).

_____, "Vom Sinn der Gleichnisse Jesu," *ZST* 15 (1938) 319-46.

Lohse, E., *Die Texte aus Qumran. Hebräisch und Deutsch* (München: Kösel, 1964).

Loisy, A., *Les Evangiles Synoptiques* (Ceffonds, 1907-1908).

Luck, U., "Das Gleichnis von Sämann und die Verkündigung Jesu," *Wort und Dienst* 11 (1971) 73-92.

Luz, U., "Das Geheimnismotiv und die markinische Christologie," *ZNW* 56 (1965) 9-30.

Maier, G., *Mensch und freier Wille. Nach dem jüdischen Religionspartien zwischen Ben Sira und Paulus* (WUNT 12; Tübingen: Mohr/Siebeck, 1971).

Maloney, E. C., *Semitic Interference in Marcan Syntax* (SBLDS 51; Chico, Calif.: Scholars, 1981).

Manson, T. W., *The Teaching of Jesus* (2d ed.; Cambridge University, 1935; orig. 1931).

Manson, W., "The Purpose of the Parables: A Re-examination of St. Mark iv. 10-12," *ExpTim* 68 (1956-57) 132-35.

Marcheselli, C. C., "Le parabole del Vangelo di Marco (4,1-34)," *RevistB* 29 (1981) 405-15.

Marcus, J., "Mark 4:10-12 and Marcan Epistemology," *JBL* 103 (1984) 557-74.

Martin, R. P., *Mark, Evangelist and Theologian* (Contemporary Evangelical Perspectives; Grand Rapids: Zondervan, 1973).

Martyn, J. L., "Epistemology at the Turn of the Ages: 2 Corinthians 5:16," *Christian History and Interpretation: Studies Presented to John Knox* (eds. W. R. Farmer et al.; Cambridge: University Press, 1967) 269-87.

_____, "From Paul to Flannery O'Connor with the Power of Grace," *Katallagete* 6 (1981) 10-17.

_____, *History and Theology in the Fourth Gospel* (2d ed.; Nashville: Abingdon, 1979).

Marxsen, W., *Mark the Evangelist* (Nashville: Abingdon, 1969).

_____, "Redaktionsgeschichtliche Erklärung der sogennanten Parabeltheorie des Markus," *ZTK* 52 (1955) 255-271.

Masson, C., *Les paraboles de Marc IV* (Cahiers Théologiques de l'Actualité Protestante 11; Paris: Neuchâtel/Delachaux & Niestle, 1945).

McArthur, H. K., "Parable of the Mustard Seed," *CBQ* 33 (1971) 198-210.

McNamara, M., *The New Testament and the Palestinian Targum to the Pentateuch* (AnBib 27; Rome: Pontifical Biblical Institute, 1966).

Matera, F. J., *The Kingship of Jesus: Composition and Theology in Mark 15* (SBLDS 66; Chico: Scholars, 1982).

Meagher, J. C., *Clumsy Construction in Mark's Gospel: A Critique of Form- and Redaktionsgeschichte* (Toronto Studies in Theology 3; New York/Toronto: Mellen, 1979).

Metzger, B. M., *A Textual Commentary on the Greek New Testament* (London/New York: United Bible Societies, 1971).

Meye, R. P., *Jesus and the Twelve: Discipleship and Revelation in Mark's Gospel* (Grand Rapids: Eerdmans, 1968).

_____, "Mark 4, 10: 'Those about Him with the Twelve,'" *SE* II (TU 87; 1964) 211-218.

Michaelis, W., "*horaō*," *TDNT* 5 (1967; orig. 1954) 315-67.

_____, "*skēnē*," *TDNT* 7 (1971; orig. 1964) 368-94.

Michiels, R., *De parabels van het zaad. Diachrone leesmethode en evangelische parabels* (Cahiers voor levensverdieping 28; Averbode: Werkgroep voor levensverdieping, Abdij Averbode, 1980).

Minette de Tillesse, G., *Le Secret Messianique dans l'Evangile de Marc* (LD 47; Paris: Editions du Cerf, 1968).

Moldenke, H. N. and A. L., *Plants of the Bible* (Waltham, Mass.: Chronica Botanica, 1952).

Molland, E., "Zur Auslegung von Mc 4,33: *kathōs ēdynanto akouein*," *SO* 8 (1929) 83-91.

Moore, C. A., "Mk 4,12: More Like the Irony of Micaiah than Isaiah," *Light unto My Paths: Old Testament Studies in Honor of Jacob M. Myers* (Gettysburg Theological Studies 4; Philadelphia: Temple University, 1974) 335-44.

Moore, G. F., *Judaism in the First Centuries of the Christian Era* (2 vols.; New York: Schocken, 1971; orig. 1927-30).

Moule, C. F. D., "Mark 4:1-20 Yet Once More," *Neotestamentica et Semitica: Studies in Honour of Matthew Black* (Edinburgh, 1969) 95-113).

Moulton, J. H., *A Grammar of New Testament Greek* (4 vols.; Edinburgh: T. & T. Clark, 1908-65).

Mowinckel, S., *He That Cometh* (Nashville/New York: Abingdon, 1954; orig. 1951).

Müller, H.-P., "Der Begriff 'Rätsel' im AT," *VT* 20 (1970) 465-89.

Munro, W., "Women Disciples in Mark?" *CBQ* 44 (1982) 225-41.

Mussner, F., "Gleichnisauslegung und Heilsgeschichte, dargetan am Gleichnis von der selbstwachsenden Saat (Mk 4, 26-29)," *TTZ* 64 (1955) 257-66.

_____, "1Q Hodajoth und das Gleichnis vom Senfkorn (Mk. 4, 30-32 par.)," *BZ* 4 (1960) 128-30.

Nardoni, E., "A Redactional Interpretation of Mark 9:1," *CBQ* 43 (1981) 365-84.

Neirynck, F. *Duality in Mark: Contributions to the Study of the Markan Redaction* (BETL 31; Leuven University, 1972).

_____, *Evangelica. Gospel Studies* (BETL 60; Leuven: Peeters/Leuven University, 1982).

_____, "L'Évangile de Marc. À propos d'un nouveau commentaire," *ETL* 53 (1977) 153-81.

Neuhäusler, E., "Mit welchem Masstab misst Gott die Menschen? Deutung zweier Jesussprüche," *BLe* 11 (1970) 104-113.

Neusner, J., *The Tosefta Translated from the Hebrew* (6 vols.; New York: Ktav, 1979).

Nickelsburg, G. W. E., "The Epistle of Enoch and the Qumran Literature," *JJS* 33 (1982) 333-48.

Niedner, F. A., "Markan Baptismal Theology: Renaming the Markan Secret," *CurTM* 9 (1982) 93-106.

Nineham, D., *The Gospel of Mark* (Pelican New Testament Commentaries; London: Penguin, 1969).

O'Mahony, G., "Mark's Gospel and the Parable of the Sower," *Bible Today* 98 (1978) 1764-68.

Otto, R., *The Kingdom of God and the Son of Man: A Study in the History of Religion* (Boston: Starr King, 1943; orig. 1934).

Oxford Society of Historical Theology, *The New Testament in the Apostolic Fathers* (Oxford at the Clarendon, 1905).

Parente, P., "Un contributo alla riconstruzione dell'apocalittica cristiana originaria al lume degli scritti esseni. Isaia 6. 9-10 in Marco 4. 12," *Rivista Storica Italiana* 74 (1962) 673-96.

Patten, P., "The Form and Function of Parables in Select Apocalyptic Literature and their Significance for Parables in the Gospel of Mark," *NTS* 29 (1983) 246-258.

Paulsen, H., "MK XVI 1-8," *NovT* 22 (1980) 138-75.

Payne, P. B., "The Order of Sowing and Plouging in the Parable of the Sower," *NTS* 25 (1978) 123-29.

Peck, H. T., *Harper's Dictionary of Classical Literature and Antiquities* (New York: Cooper Square, 1965).

Pedersen, S., "Is Mark 4, 1-34 a Parable Chapter?" *SE* VI (= TU 112; 1973) 408-416.

Peisker, C. H., "Konsekutives *hina* im Markus 4:12," *ZNW* 59 (1968) 126-27.

Perrin, N., and D. C. Duling, *The New Testament: An Introduction* (2d ed.; New York: Harcourt Brace Jovanovich, 1982).

_____, *Rediscovering the Teaching of Jesus* (New York/Hagerstown/San Francisco/London: Harper & Row, 1976; orig. 1967).

Pesch, R. *Das Markusevangelium* (2 vols.; HTKNT 2; Freiburg/Basel/Wien: Herder, 1976).

_____, *Naherwartungen: Tradition und Redaktion in Mk 13* (Düsseldorf: Patmos, 1968).

Petersen, N. R., "The Composition of Mark 4:-8:26," *HTR* 73 (1982) 185-217.

_____, *Literary Criticism for New Testament Critics* (Guides to Biblical Scholarship; Philadelphia: Fortress, 1978).

_____, "'Point of View' in Mark's Narrative," *Semeia* 12 (1978) 97-121.

_____, "When is the End Not the End?" *Int* 34 (1980) 151-66.

Philonenko, M., *Joseph et Aséneth. Introduction, texte critique, traduction et notes* (SPB 13; Leiden: Brill, 1968).

Piper, O. A., "The Mystery of the Kingdom of God," *Int* 1 (1947) 183-200.

Pryke, E. J., "*IDE* and *IDOU*," *NTS* 14 (1968) 418-24.

_____, *Redactional Style in the Marcan Gospel: A Study of Syntax and Vocabulary as guides to Redaction in Mark* (Cambridge/London/ New York/Melbourne: Cambridge University, 1978).

Pryor, J. W., "Markan Parable Theology: An Inquiry into Mark's Principles of Redaction," *ExpTim* 83 (1971-72) 242-45.

Quesnell, Q., *The Mind of Mark: Interpretation and Method through the Exegesis of Mark 6:52* (AnBib 38; Rome: Pontifical Biblical Institute, 1969).

Rademacher, L., *Neutestamentliche Grammatik. Das Griechisch des Neuen Testaments im Zusammenhang mit der Volksspruche* (HNT 1,1; Tübingen: Mohr/Siebeck, 1911).

Räisänen, H., *Das "Messiasgeheimnis" im Markusevangelium* (Schriften der Finnischen Exegetischen Gesellschaft 26; Helsinki, 1976).

_____, *Die Parabeltheorie im Markusevangelium* (Schriften der Finnischen Exegetischen Gesellschaft 26; Helsinki, 1973).

Reploh, K. G., *Markus, Lehrer der Gemeinde* (SBM 9; Stuttgart, 1969).

Rhoads, D., and D. Michie, *Mark as Story: An Introduction to the Narrative of a Gospel* (Philadelphia: Fortress, 1982).

Riddle, D. W., "Mark 4:1-34: The Evolution of a Gospel Source," *JBL* 56 (1937) 77-90.

Rigaux, B., "Révélation des mystères et perfection a Qumran et dans le Nouveau Testament," *NTS* 4 (1957-58) 237-62.

Rinaldi, G., "Nota: *Nounechōs*," *Bibbia e Oriente* 20 (1978) 26.

Robbins, V. K., *Jesus the Teacher: A Socio-Rhetorical Interpretation of Mark* (Philadelphia: Fortress, 1984).

_____, "Last Meal: Preparation, Betrayal, and Absence," *The Passion in Mark: Studies on Mark 14-16* (ed. W. H. Kelber; Philadelphia: Fortress, 1976) 21-40.

_____, "Summons and Outline in Mark," *NovT* 23 (1981) 97-114.

Robinson, D. W. B., "The Use of Parabole in the Synoptic Gospels," *Evangelical Quarterly* (1949) 94-99.

Robinson, J. A. T., "The Parable of the Wicked Husbandmen," *NTS* 21 (1974-75) 443-61.

Robinson, J. M., *The Nag Hammadi Library in English* (San Francisco: Harper & Row, 1977).

_____, *The Problem of History in Mark and Other Marcan Studies* (Philadelphia: Fortress, 1982).

_____ and H. Koester, *Trajectories through Early Christianity* (Philadelphia: Fortress, 1971).

Romaniuk, K., "Exegèse du Noveau Testament et ponctuation," *NovT* 23 (1981) 195-209.

Rowland, C., *The Open Heaven: A Study of Apocalyptic in Judaism and Early Christianity* (New York: Crossroad, 1982).

Rüger, H. P., "Mit welchem Mass ihr messt, wird euch gemessen werden," *ZNW* 60 (1969) 174-82.

Russell, D. S., *The Method and Message of Jewish Apocalyptic* (Philadelphia: Westminster, 1964).

Schelkle, K. H., "Der Zweck der Gleichnisreden (Mk 4,10-12)," *Neues Testament und Kirche. Für Rudolf Schnackenburg* (ed. J. Gnilka; Basel/Wien/Freiburg: Herder, 1974) 71-75.

Schiffman, L. H., *The Halakhah at Qumran* (SJLA 16; Leiden: Brill, 1975).

Schlosser, J., *Le règne de Dieu dans les dits de Jesus* (2 vols.; EBib; Paris: Gabalda, 1980).

Schmid, J., *Das Evangelium nach Markus* (RNT 2; Regensburg: Friedrich Pustet, 1963; orig. 1958).

Schmidt, K. L., *Der Rahmen der Geschichte Jesu. Literarkritische Untersuchungen zur ältesten Jesusüberlieferung* (Berlin: Trowitzsch, 1919).

Schmithals, W., *Das Evangelium nach Markus* (2 vols.; Ökumenischer Taschenbuchkommentar zum Neuen Testament 2; Gütersloh/Würzburg: Mohn/Echter, 1979).

Schnackenburg, R., *God's Rule and Kingdom* (Freiburg/Montreal: Herder/Palm, 1963).

_____, *The Gospel According to St. Mark* (2 vols.; New York: Crossroad, 1981; orig. 1966).

Schneider, C., "*katapetasma*," *TDNT* 3 (1965) 629-30.

_____, "*kathēmai*," *TDNT* 3 (1965) 440-44.

Schneider, G., "Das Bildwort von der Lampe," *ZNW* 61 (1970) 183-209.

Schniewind, J., *Das Evangelium nach Markus* (NTD 1; Göttingen: Vandenhoeck & Ruprecht, 1933).

Schottroff, L., "Die Gegenwart in der Apokalyptik der synoptischen Evangelien," *Apocalypticism in the Mediterranean World and the Near East. Proceedings of the International Colloquium on Apocalypticism, Uppsala, August 12-17, 1979* (D. Hellholm, ed.; Tübingen: Mohr/Siebeck, 1983) 707-728.

Schreiber, J., *Theologie des Vertrauens* (Hamburg: Furche, 1967).

Schürmann, H., *Das Lukasevangelium* (HTKNT 3/1; Freiburg: Herder, 1969).

Schweitzer, A., *The Quest of the Historical Jesus: A Critical Study of its Progress from Reimarus to Wrede* (New York: Macmillan, 1968; orig. 1906).

Schweizer, E., "Anmerkungen zur Theologie des Markus," *Neotestamentica: Deutsche und englische Aufsätze 1951-1963* (Zürich/Stuttgart: Zwingli, 1963) 93-104.

_____, "Zur Frage des Messiasgeheimnis bei Markus," *ZNW* 56 (1965) 1-8.

_____, *The Good News According to Mark* (Atlanta: John Knox, 1970; orig. 1967).

_____, "Mark's Contribution to the Quest of the Historical Jesus," *NTS* 10 (1964) 421-432.

_____, "The Portrayal of the Life of Faith in the Gospel of Mark," *Int* 32 (1978) 387-99.

_____, "Scheidungsrecht der jüdishcen Frau? Weibliche Jünger Jesu?" *EvT* 42 (1982) 294-300.

_____, "Du texte à predication; Mark 4:1-20," *ETR* 43 (1968) 256-64.

_____, "Die theologische Leistung des Markus," *Beiträge zur Theologie des Neuen Testaments: Neutestamentliche Aufsätze (1955-1970)* (Zürich: Zwingli, 1970) 21-42.

Scott, B. B., *Jesus, Symbol-Maker for the Kingdom* (Philadelphia: Fortress, 1981).

_____, Review of J. Lambrecht, *Once More Astonished: The Parables of Jesus* in *JBL* 102 (1983) 493-95.

Sellin, E., and Fohrer, G., *Introduction to the Old Testament* (Nashville: Abingdon, 1968).

Sellin, G., "Textlinguistische und semiotische Erwägungen zu Mk. 4.1-34," *NTS* 29 (1983) 508-30.

Siegman, E. F., "Teaching in Parables (Mk 4,10-12; Lk 8, 9-10; Mt 13,10-15)," *CBQ* 23 (1961) 161-81.

Sjöberg, E., *Der Verborgene Menschensohn in den Evangelien* (Lund: Gleerup, 1955).

Smith, M., *Clement of Alexandria and a Secret Gospel of Mark* (Cambridge, Mass.: Harvard University, 1973).

_____, "Comments on Taylor's Commentary on Mark," *HTR* 48 (1955) 21-64.

_____, *Tannaitic Parallels to the Gospels* (Philadelphia: Society of Biblical Literature, 1951).

Smyth, H. W., *Greek Grammar* (Cambridge, Mass.: Harvard University, 1956; orig. 1920).

Soiron, T., "Der Zweck der Parabellehre Jesu im Lichte der synoptischen Überlieferung," *TGl* 9 (1917) 385-94.

Stagg, F., "The Abused Aorist," *JBL* 92 (1973) 222-31.

Standaert, B., *L'Évangile selon Marc. Composition et genre litteraire* (Brugge: Zevenkerken, 1978).

Stauffer, E., "*hina*," *TDNT* 3 (1965) 323-33.

Stone, M. E., "Coherence and Inconsistency in the Apocalypses; The Case of 'The End' in 4 Ezra," *JBL* 102 (1983) 229-43.

Strack, H. L. and P. Billerbeck, *Kommentar zum Neuen Testament aus Talmud und Midrasch* (6 vols.; München: Beck, 1922-65).

Streeter, B. H., *The Four Gospels: A Study of Origins* (London: Macmillan, 1924).

Stuhlmann, R., "Beoabachtungen und Überlegungen zu Markus 4:26-29," *NTS* 19 (1973) 153-62.

_____, *Das eschatologische Mass im Neuen Testament* (FRLANT 132; Göttingen: Vandenhoeck & Ruprecht, 1983).

Suhl, A., *Die Funktion der alttestamentlichen Zitate und Anspielungen im Markusevangelium* (Gütersloh: Mohn, 1965).

Tagawa, K., *Miracles et Evangile. La Pensee Personnelle de l'Evangeliste Marc* (Etudes d'Historie et de Philosophie Religieuses; Paris: Presses Universitaires, 1966).

Taylor, V., *The Gospel According to St. Mark* (London/New York: Macmillan/St. Martin's, 1959; orig. 1952).

Thomas Aquinas, *Catena Aurea: Commentary on the Four Gospels Collected out of the Works of the Fathers* (4 vols.; Oxford: Parker, 1842).

Tolbert, M. A., *Perspectives on the Parables: An Approach to Multiple Interpretations* (Philadelphia: Fortress, 1979).

Trever, J. C., "Mustard," *IDB* 3 (1962) 476-77.

Trocme, E., *The Formation of the Gospel According to Mark* (Philadelphia: Westminster, 1975; orig. 1963).

_____, "Why Parables? A Study Of Mark IV," *BJRL* 59 (1977) 458-71.

Tyson, J. B., "The Blindness of the Disciples in Mark," *JBL* 80 (1961) 261-68.

Vermes, G., *The Dead Scrolls in English* (2d ed.; Middlesex: Penguin, 1975; orig. 1962).

Volz, P., *Die Eschatologie der jüdischen Gemeinde im neutestamentlichen Zeitalter* (2d ed.; Tübingen, 1934).

von Rad, G., *Old Testament Theology* (2 vols.; New York/Evanston/San Francisco/London: Harper & Row, 1965).

Wanke, J., *"Bezugs- und Kommentarworte" in den synoptischen Evangelien. Beobachtungen zur Interpretationsgeschichte der Herrenworte in der vorevangelischen Überlieferung* (Erfurter Theologsiche Studien 44; Leipzig: St. Benno, 1981).

Webster's New Collegiate Dictionary (8th ed.; Springfield, Mass.: Merriam, 1981).

Weder, H., "Perspektive der Frauen?" *EvT* 43 (1983) 175-78.

Weeden, T. J., *Mark: Traditions in Conflict* (Philadelphia: Fortress, 1971).

Weiss, J., *Jesus' Proclamation of the Kingdom of God* (Philadelphia: Fortress, 1971; orig. 1892).

Weiss, K., "Mk. 4.26 bis 29—dennoch die Parabel vom zuversichtlichen Sämann!" *BZ* 18 (1929) 45-68.

_____, *Voll Zuversicht! Zur Parabel Jesu vom zuversichtlichen Samann Mk 4, 26-29* (NTAbh 10.1; Munster: Aschendorff, 1922).

Wendling, A., *Die Entstehung des Markus-Evangelium. Philologische Untersuchungen* (Tübingen: Mohr, 1908).

Wenham, D., "The Interpretation of the Parable of the Sower," *NTS* 20 (1974) 299-319.

_____, "The Synoptic Problem Revisited: Some New Suggestions about the Composition of Mark 4,1-34," *TynBul* 23 (1972) 3-38.

White, K. D., "The Parable of the Sower," *JTS* NS 15 (1964) 300-307.

Wilder, A., "Parable of the Sower: Naivete and Method in Interpretation," *Semeia* 2 (1978) 134-51.

_____, Review of B. B. Scott, *Jesus, Symbol-Maker for the Kingdom* in *JBL* 102 (1983) 497-500.

Wiles, M. F., "Early Exegesis of the Parables," *SJT* 11 (1968) 287-301.

Wilkens, W., "Die Redaktion des Gleichniskapitels Mark. 4 durch Matt.," *TZ* 20 (1964) 305-27.

Windisch, H., "Die Verstockungsidee in Mc 4,12 und das kausale *hina* der späteren Koine," *ZNW* 26 (1927) 203-209.

Wolfson, H. A., *Philo: Foundations of Religious Philosophy in Judaism, Christianity, and Islam* (2 vols.; Cambridge, Mass.: Harvard University, 1947).

Wrede, W., *The Messianic Secret* (Cambridge: James Clark, 1971; orig. 1901).

Wretlind, D. O., "Jesus' Philosophy of Ministry: A Study of a Figure of Speech in Mark 1:38," *Journal of the Evangelical Theological Society* 20 (1977) 321-23.

Zerwick, M., *Untersuchungen zum Markus-Stil* (Scripta pontificii instituti biblici; Rome: Biblical Institute, 1937).

Ziegler, K., and W. Sontheimer, *Der kleine Pauly Lexikon der Antike* (5 vols.; Stuttgart: Druckenmüller, 1964-75).

Zimmerli, W., *Ezekiel* (2 vols.; Hermeneia; Philadelphia: Fortress, 1979-83).

Zimmermann, H., *Neutestamentliche Methodenlehre. Darstellung der historisch-kritischen Methode* (3d ed.; Stuttgart: Kath. Bibelwerk, 1970).

Zohary, M., "Flora," *IDB* 2.285-86.

Indexes

PASSAGES

CPSIA information can be obtained at www.ICGtesting.com
Printed in the USA
LVOW040626150512

281704LV00001B/23/A